THE ARCHAEOLOGY OF CANTERBURY

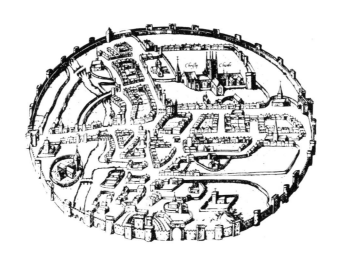

In Memoriam
James Ernest Hobbs

THE ARCHAEOLOGY OF CANTERBURY

(General Editors: A. P. Detsicas, B.A., M.A., F.S.A., and T. W. T. Tatton-Brown, B.A.)

VOLUME I

EXCAVATIONS
AT
CANTERBURY CASTLE

By

P. Bennett, B.A., S.S. Frere, C.B.E., M.A., Litt.D., D.Litt., F.B.A., F.S.A., and S. Stow, B.A.

WITH CONTRIBUTIONS BY

J. Anstee, M. M. Archibald, M.A., F.S.A., F.M.A., P. Arthur, B.A., L. Biek,
J. Bird, B.A., B. Dickinson, B.A., I.P. Garrard, P. H. Garrard, M.B., B.S.,
B. R. Hartley, M.A., F.S.A., K. F. Hartley, B.A., F.S.A., J. Hillam, B.A., A. King, B.A.,
J. Liversidge, M.Litt., F.S.A., D. F. Mackreth, B.A., F.S.A., N. C. Macpherson-Grant,
A. Mainman, B.A., T. P. O'Connor, B.A., R. Powers, B.A., M. Redknap, B.A.,
R. Reece, B.Sc., Ph.D., F.S.A., D. F. Renn, B.A., Ph.D., F.S.A., V. Rigby, B.A.,
T. W. T. Tatton-Brown, B.A., V. Tatton-Brown, B.A., D.Phil., F.S.A., J. Watson,
G. Webster, M.A., Ph.D., F.S.A., A.M.A., M. G. Wilson, M.A., F.S.A.,
and C. J. Young, M.A., D.Phil., F.S.A.

Published for the
Canterbury Archaeological Trust
by the
Kent Archaeological Society
Maidstone
1982

Produced by Alan Sutton Publishing Limited,
17a Brunswick Road, Gloucester.
Printed in Great Britain by
Page Bros (Norwich) Ltd.

Published with the aid of a grant from the Department of the Environment

CONTENTS

LIST OF FIGURES

LIST OF PLATES

BIBLIOGRAPHY

Atkinson 1914

Atkinson, D., 'A Hoard of samian Ware from Pompeii', *J. Roman Stud.*, 4 (1914), 27–54.

Bailey 1963

Bailey, D.M., *Greek and Roman Pottery Lamps*, Brit. Mus., London (1963).

Baillie 1973

Baillie, M.G.L., 'A recently developed Tree-Ring Chronology', *Tree-Ring Bulletin*, 33 (1973), 15–28.

Baillie and Pilcher 1973

Baillie, M.G.L., and Pilcher, J.R., 'A simple Cross-dating Program for Tree-Ring Research', *Tree Ring Bulletin*, 33 (1973), 7–14.

Bird 1977

Bird, J., 'African Red Slip Ware in Roman Britain' in J. Dore & K. Greene (eds.) *Roman Pottery Studies in Britain and Beyond, Brit. Archaeol. Rep. Supp. Ser.*, no. 30, Oxford (1977), 269–77.

Bird and Fulford 1975

Bird, J., and Fulford, M.G., 'Imported Pottery from Germany in late Roman Britain', *Britannia*, vi (1975) 171 & 180.

Bird and Marsh 1978

Bird, J., and Marsh, G., *Southwark Excavations 1972-4*, Southwark and Lambeth Archaeological Excavation Committee, (1978) 527–9.

Blurton 1977

Blurton, T.R., 'Excavations at Angel Court, Walbrook, 1974', *Trans. London., Middlesex Archaeol. Soc.*, 28 (1977), 14–100.

Brailsford 1962

Brailsford, J.W., *Hod Hill, Volume I, Antiquities from Hod Hill in the Durden Collection*, London (1962).

Bushe-Fox 1913

Bushe-Fox, J.P., *Excavations on the Site of the Roman Town at Wroxeter, Shropshire, in 1912, Repts. Res. Comm. Soc. Antiqs. London*, i, Oxford (1913)

Bushe-Fox 1932

Bushe-Fox, J.P., *Third Report on the Excavations of the Roman Fort at Richborough, Kent, Repts. Res. Comm. Soc. Antiqs. London*, x, Oxford (1932).

Bushe-Fox 1949

Bushe-Fox, J.P., *Fourth Report on the Excavations of the Roman Fort at Richborough, Kent, Repts. Res. Comm. Soc. Antiqs. London*, xvi, Oxford (1949).

Casteel 1977

Casteel, R.W., 'Characterisation of faunal Assemblages and the minimum Number of Individuals determined from paired Elements: continuing Problems in Archaeology', *J. Archaeol. Sci.*, 4 (1977), 125–34.

Chaplin 1971

Chaplin, R.E., *The Study of Bones from Archaeological Sites*, London (1971).

Chenet 1941

Chenet, G., *La céramique gallo-romaine d'Argonne du VIème Siècle et la Terre sigillée décorée à la Molette*, Mâcon (1941).

Clifford 1961

Clifford, E.M., *Bagendon: A Belgic Oppidum, A Record of the Excavations of 1954–56*, Cambridge (1961).

Cotton and Gathercole 1961

Cotton, M.A., and Gathercole, P.W., *Excavations at Clausentum, Southampton, 1951-54*, Cambridge (1961).

Cunliffe 1968   Cunliffe, B.W., (ed.) *Fifth Report of the Excavations at the Roman Fort at Richborough, Kent, Repts. Res. Comm. Soc. Antiq. London*, xxiii, Oxford (1968).

Cunliffe 1971   Cunliffe, B.W., *Excavations at Fishbourne 1961–1969*, ii, *Repts. Res. Comm. Soc. Antiq. London*, xxviii, Oxford (1971).

Cunliffe 1975   Cunliffe, B.W., *Excavations at Portchester Castle 1961–1972*, i, Roman. *Repts. Res. Comm. Soc. Antiq. London*, xxxii, Oxford (1975).

Curle 1911   Curle, J., *A Roman Frontier Post and its People, The Fort of Newstead in the Parish of Melrose*, Glasgow (1911).

Déchelette 1904   Déchelette, J., *Les Vases céramique ornés de la Gaule romaine*, Paris (1904).

Detsicas 1977   Detsicas, A., 'First Century Pottery Manufacture at Eccles, Kent' in J. Dore & K. Greene (eds.), *Roman Pottery Studies in Britain and Beyond, Brit. Archaeol. Rep. Supp. Ser.*, no. 30, Oxford (1977), 19–36.

Dore and Greene 1977   Dore, J., and Greene, K. (eds.), *Roman Pottery Studies in Britain and Beyond, Brit. Archaeol. Rep. Supp. Ser.*, no. 30, Oxford (1977).

Down and Rule 1971   Down, A., and Rule, M., *Chichester Excavations*, i, Chichester (1971).

Down 1978   Down, A., *Chichester Excavations*, iii, Chichester (1978).

Fleck-Abbey and King 1975   Fleck-Abbey, A., and King, A.C., In T.W.T. Tatton-Brown, 'Excavations at the Custom House site, City of London,' Part 2, *Trans. London Middlesex Archaeol. Soc.*, 26 (1975), 103–70.

Fölzer 1913   Fölzer, E., *Die Bilderschüsseln der ostgallischen Manufakturen*, Bonn (1913).

Frere 1972   Frere, S.S., *Excavations at Verulamium*, i, *Repts. Res. Comm. Soc. Antiq. London*, xxviii, Oxford (1972).

Fulford 1975   Fulford, M.G., 'The Pottery' in B.W. Cunliffe, *Excavations at Porchester Castle 1961-1972*, i, Roman, *Repts. Res. Comm. Soc. Antiq. London*, xxxii, Oxford (1975).

Fulford 1977   Fulford, M.G., 'Pottery and Britain's Foreign Trade in the Later Roman Period' in D.P. Peacock (ed.), *Pottery and Early Commerce*, London (1977).

Fulford and Young 1978   Fulford, M.G., and Young, C.J., 'A Discussion of the later Roman Fine Wares' in A. Down, *Chichester Excavations*, iii, Chichester (1978), 256–7.

Gillam 1970   Gillam, J.P., *Types of Roman Coarse Pottery Vessels in Northern Britain*, 3rd edition, Newcastle upon Tyne, (1970).

Gose 1975   Gose, E., *Gefässtypen der römischen Keramik im Rheinland, Beihefte der Bonner Jahrbucher*, i, (Kevelaer, 1950), Cologne (1975).

Gould 1967   Gould, J., 'Excavations at Wall, Staffordshire, 1964–6, on the Site of the Roman Forts', *Transactions of the Lichfield and South Staffordshire Archaeological and Historical Society*, viii (1967).

Grant 1975   Grant, A., in B.W. Cunliffe, *Excavations at Portchester Castle 1961–72*, i, Roman, *Repts. Res. Comm. Soc. Antiq. London*, xxxii, Oxford (1975), 378–408.

Greene 1972   Greene, K.T., *Guide to pre-Flavian Fine Wares c. A.D. 40–70*, privately printed. Cardiff, (1972).

Greene 1978   Greene, K.T., 'Imported Fine Wares in Britain to A.D. 250: A Guide to Identification', in P. Arthur and G. Marsh, *Early Fine Wares in Roman Britain, Brit. Archaeol. Rep. Sup. Ser.*, no. 57, Oxford (1978).

Grimes 1930   Grimes, W.F., 'The Works-Depot of Legion XX at Castle Lyons (Holt), Denbighshire', *Y Cwmmrodor*, 31 (1930).

Hammond 1971	Hammond, J., *Hammond's Farm Animals*, London (1971).
Hartley 1960	Hartley, B.R., *Notes on the Roman Pottery Industry in the Nene Valley*, (1960).
Hartley 1977	Hartley, K.F., 'Two major Potteries producing Mortaria in the first Century A.D.' in J. Dore and K. Greene (eds.), *Roman Pottery Studies in Britain and Beyond*, Brit. Archaeol. Rep. Supp. Ser., no. 30, Oxford (1977).
Hartley 1978	Hartley, K.F., 'The Roman Mortaria' in A. Down, *Chichester Excavations*, iii, Chichester (1978), 245–254.
Hawkes and Hull 1947	Hawkes, C.F.C., and Hull, M.R., *Camulodunum, Repts. Res. Comm. Soc. Antiq. London*, xiv, London (1947).
Hayes 1972	Hayes, J.W., *Late Roman Pottery*, Brit. School Rome. Supp. Pub. London (1972).
Hermet 1934	Hermet, F., *La Graufesenque (Condatomago)*, Paris (1934)
Hodges 1981	Hodges, R., *The Archaeology of Sussex Pottery*, D.J. Freke (ed.), Inst. of London Monograph, (1979).
Hollstein 1965	Hodges, R., 'Potters, Pottery and Marketing, A.D. 700–1000' in *The Archaeology of Sussex Pottery*, D.J. Freke (ed.), *Sussex Archaeol. Coll* , 118 (1981), 95–103.
Hollstein 1974	Hollstein, E., 'Eine römische Deichel aus Dillingen, Kreis Saarlouis', *Bericht der Staatlichen Denkmalpflege im Saarland*, 21, (1974), 101–4.
Holwerda 1941	Holwerda, J.H., *De Belgische Waar in Nijmegen*, (1941).
Hull 1963	Hull, M.R., The Roman Potters' Kilns of Colchester, *Repts. Res. Comm. Soc. Antiq. London*, xxi, Oxford (1963).
Isings 1957	Isings, C., *Roman Glass from Dated Finds*, Gröningen (1957).
Jenkins 1950	Jenkins, F., 'Canterbury Excavations in Burgate Street, 1946–8', *Archaeologia Cantiana*, lxiii (1950) 82–118.
Jourdan 1977	Jourdan, L., 'L'Élevage en Mediterranée occidentale', *Institut de Recherches méditerranéennes* (ed.), (1977) Paris, 95–112.
Kenyon 1948	Kenyon, K.M., *Excavations at the Jewry Wall Site, Leicester 1936–39, Repts. Res. Comm. Soc. Antiq. London*, xv, Oxford (1948).
King 1978	King, A.C., 'A Comparative Survey of Bone Assemblages from Roman Sites in Britain', *Bull. Inst. Archaeol.*, 15 (1978), 207–32.
Kirkman 1940	Kirkman, J.S., 'Canterbury Kiln Site: The Pottery', *Archaeologia Cantiana*, liii (1940), 118–36.
Knorr 1919	Knorr, R., *Töpfer und Fabriken verzierter Terra-sigillata des ersten Jahrhunderts*, Stuttgart (1919).
Knorr 1952	Knorr, R., *Terra-sigillata-gefässe des ersten Jahrhunderts mit Töpfernamen*, Stuttgart, (1952).
Lobbedy 1969	Lobbedy, U., 'Red Painted Pottery in Western Europe', J.G. Hurst (ed.), *Medieval Archaeology*, 13 (1969) 121–9.
Marsh 1978	Marsh, G.D., Unpublished B.A. thesis, University College Cardiff, (1978).
Morgan and Schofield 1978	Morgan, R.A., and Schofield, J., 'Tree-rings and the Archaeology of the Thames Waterfront in the City of London', in 'Dendrochronology of Europe' ed. J.M. Fletcher, *Brit. Archaeol. Rep.*, Supp. ser. no. 51, Oxford (1978).
Orton 1977	Orton, C., 'Roman Pottery (excluding samian)', in T.R. Blurton, 'Excavations at

Angel Court, Walbrook, 1974', *Trans. London Middlesex Archaeol. Soc.*, 28 (1977), 14–100.

Oswald 1936–1937   Oswald, P., *Index of Figure-types on Terra Sigillata (Samian Ware)*, Liverpool (1936-1937).

Oswald and Pryce 1920   Oswald, F., and Pryce, T.D., *An Introduction to the Study of Terra Sigillata*, London (1920).

Payne 1973   Payne, S., 'Kill-off Patterns in Sheep and Goats: the Mandibles from Asvan Kale', *J. Anatolian Studs.* 23 (1973), 281–303.

Peacock 1977   Peacock, D.P., *Pottery and Early Commerce: Characterisation and Trade in Roman and Later Ceramics*, London (1977).

Peacock 1977   Peacock, D.P., 'Pompeiian Red Ware' in D.P. Peacock (ed.), *Pottery and Early Commerce: Characterisation and Trade in Roman and Later Ceramics*, London (1977).

Richmond 1968   Richmond, I., *Hod Hill, Volume II, Excavations carried out between 1951 and 1958 for the Trustees of the British Museum*, London (1968).

Ricken and Fischer 1963   Ricken, H., and Fischer, C., *Die Bilderschüsseln der römischen Töpfer von Rheinzabern. Textband*, Bonn (1963).

Rigby 1973   Rigby, V., 'Potters' Stamps on *terra nigra* and *terra rubra* found in Britain', in A.P. Detsicas (ed.), *Current Research in Romano-British Coarse Pottery*, Counc. Brit. Archaeol. Res. Rep., no. 10, London (1973), 7–24.

Ryder 1964   Ryder, M.L., 'The History of Sheep Breeds in Britain', *Agric. Hist. Rev.*, 12 (1964), 1–12 and 65–82.

Stanfield and Simpson 1958   Stanfield, J.A., and Simpson, G., *Central Gaulish Potters*, London (1958).

Terrisse 1968   Terrisse, J.R., *Les Céramiques sigillées gallo-romaines des Martres-de-Veyre (Puy-de-Dôme), Gallia*, Supp. no. 19, Paris (1968).

Unversagt 1916   Unversagt, W., *Die Keramik des Kastells Alzei*, Frankfurt (1916).

Vanderhoeven 1958   Vanderhoeven, M., 'Verres romains tardifs et mérovingiens du Musée Curtius', *Journées Internationales du Verre*, Saison liégeoise (1958).

Webster 1940   Webster, G., 'A Roman Pottery Kiln at Canterbury', *Archaeologia Cantiana*, liii (1940), 109–16.

Wheeler and Wheeler 1936   Wheeler, R.E.M., and Wheeler, T.V., *Verulamium, a Belgic and two Roman Cities*, Repts. Res. Comm. Soc. Antiq. London, xi, Oxford (1936).

White 1970   White, K.D., *Roman Farming*, London (1970).

Wilson 1978   Wilson, R., in M. Parrington, *The Excavation of an Iron Age Settlement, Bronze Age Ring Ditches and Roman Features at Ashville Trading Estate, Abingdon, 1974–6*, London (1978).

Young 1977   Young, C.J., *The Roman Pottery Industry of the Oxford Region*, Brit. Archaeol. Rep., no. 43, Oxford (1977).

PREFACE

This is the first of a series of full reports of large excavations undertaken by the Canterbury Archaeological Trust since 1975. The reports are being published for the Trust by the Kent Archaeological Society with substantial grants from the Department of the Environment.

This volume also contains a full report on the excavations carried out in the area in the 1950s by Professor S.S. Frere, for the old Canterbury Excavation Committee, and it is hoped that subsequent volumes will also combine the excavation reports of the Trust and the Excavation Committee.

We are very grateful to Professor Frere, for reading the text of this report and suggesting many improvements, and to Professor G. McVittie, who has also read parts of this report.

Finally, we should like to dedicate this volume to the memory of James Hobbs who, until his tragic death in 1979, was the chairman of the Management Committee of the Canterbury Archaeological Trust; without his enthusiasm and help, this report may never have been completed, and it is sad that he did not live to see it in print.

ALEC DETSICAS

TIM TATTON-BROWN

PART I

EXCAVATIONS AT CANTERBURY CASTLE

GENERAL INTRODUCTION AND ACKNOWLEDGEMENTS

The excavations carried out by the Trust between 1975 and 1977 in the Canterbury Castle area were the latest in a long series of excavations in the area. In 1939 Dr. Graham Webster recorded the foundations of a later gateway on the south-east side of the Keep.[1] Then in 1953 and 1955 came Professor S.S. Frere's excavation between the Keep and the city wall and within the Keep (Full report below p. 60). Next in 1961, Dr. Frank Jenkins was able to examine the foundations of the eastern side of the Roman Worthgate in a service trench.[2] This gate had been demolished in 1791 to allow Castle Street to continue directly across the Castle courtyard and join up with Wincheap outside the city walls; he also observed Roman remains during work in the 1950s to enlarge the gasworks north-westwards towards St. Mildred's church. Finally in 1971, Miss Louise Millard (then curator of the Royal Museum, Canterbury), excavated the foundations of the original entrance (or forebuilding) to the Keep, with the help of the Canterbury Archaeological Society.[3] These foundations have now been marked out in the ground with loose flints.

Our work started in November 1975 when a small trench was cut across the foundations of nos. 1 and 2 Gas Lane in advance of building work by Canterbury City Council. Early in 1976, when the building of a multi-storey car park between Rosemary Lane, Church Lane and Castle Street on the old gasworks site was imminent, the Trust successfully negotiated with the City Council to be allowed to excavate the site. The City Council also contributed towards the cost of the excavation as well as agreeing to pay for demolition work on the gasworks foundations, which took place under the Trust's supervision. Later, funds were also provided by the Department of the Environment (Ancient Monuments Inspectorate), and the Manpower Services Commission (Job Creation Scheme).

The site was found to be extremely polluted in its lower levels, and on top of this the huge concrete foundations had destroyed many of the archaeological levels. However, in places some stratigraphical levels, pits and ditches had survived and these were excavated although under great difficulty. In 1977 and 1978, the Trust carried out a study of the upstanding remains of the Norman Castle Keep and detailed drawings were made of all the elevations. All known drawings and engravings of the Keep made before the upper parts of the walls were demolished in 1817 were examined in an attempt to reconstruct, as far as possible, the upper parts of the Keep on the drawings (see below p. 77).

1. *Arch. Cant.*, liii (1940), 143-6. Granite sets now mark the site.
2. *ibid.*, lxxxiii (1968), 273-5.
3. *ibid.*, lxxxvii (1972), 205-8.

Since the late eighteenth century when the outer bailey walls of the Castle were demolished, and more so since 1826 when the gas and water works first moved into the area, the medieval topography of the Castle area has been gradually destroyed.[4] Virtually no trace now survives of the Castle ditches or any of the Castle buildings except the Keep. However, until the late nineteenth century the whole Castle area remained an extra-parochial area in the County of Kent (and not within the County Borough of Canterbury), and the County Sessions House of 1730 still remains in the southern corner of the area, though since 1808, when the Sessions House moved to Longport, this large building has been a private house.

The initial excavations in Gas Lane in November 1975 were supervised by Mrs. Pan Garrard, but otherwise all the work has been directed by Paul Bennett whose excavation report follows. The success of these excavations has been entirely due to his tremendous energy and drive. Conditions were always difficult (due both to flooding and pollution) and many archaeologists would have given up half way through. Paul Bennett also drew all the main plans and sections. He was assisted in the early part of the excavation by S.D. Hughes and later by Simon Pratt. Among the excavators who participated, special mention should be made of Ian Anderson and Mr. and Mrs. Wesley McLaughlin, who worked on the site as volunteers nearly every weekend. We were also greatly assisted by a team of 'Job Creation' diggers and the machine drivers of Messrs. B. Gray Ltd. Some on-site photography and all film-processing was carried out by Messrs. Fiske-Moore Studios Ltd. at a nominal sum, and all the pottery-processing was carried out by Nigel MacPherson-Grant. Mrs. Pan Garrard sorted and conserved all the finds (assisted by Marion Green) and pottery and small-find drawings are by Messrs. L. Sartin, M. Duncan, D. Lees, J. Joy and Miss G. Hulse. All publication plans and sections and all the drawings of the Castle are by Mr. J. Bowen. The report was typed and re-typed several times by Mrs. B.J. Kemp and Mrs. R.M. Bennett.

TIM TATTON-BROWN

4. See 'The Story of Canterbury Castle' etc. by Dorothy Gardiner (1951).

EXCAVATIONS IN THE ROSEMARY LANE CAR PARK

PAUL BENNETT

I. INTRODUCTION

Excavations in advance of proposed redevelopment by Canterbury City Council were undertaken by the Canterbury Archaeological Trust from Summer 1976 to Autumn 1977. The area threatened, formerly Canterbury Gasworks, included the north-west quarter of the outer Bailey of Canterbury Castle. Our purpose was to excavate as much of the enclosure as possible, together with the earlier and medieval levels.

Three areas were cleared of substantial gasworks foundations and rubble: (I) an area in the extreme north-west corner of the outer bailey, (II) an area to the north of this outside the Castle enclosure, and (III) an area to the east of the first, wholly inside the Castle bailey, which proved, however, to be too polluted to excavate (Fig. 3). An additional small trench was cut prior to the construction of a new building to the south of Gas Lane, in the Autumn of 1975.

The construction of the gasworks in the 1820's together with the later extensions, some built as recently as 1953, extensively damaged and polluted the archaeological levels. Only in Area II did we find intact stratigraphy, elsewhere only deeply cut features survived. These archaeological features became sumps for tar and other noxious by-products of the manufacture of coal gas, which had soaked into the ground.

II. SUMMARY OF RESULTS (Area I, II and Gas Lane)

Despite severe disturbance and extensive pollution, an extremely valuable archaeological sequence was examined. The first occupation of the site was found to date to the mid-first century. A ditch of two phases and of possible military design was cut, aligned roughly north-east/south-west. First located in Area I, it was also found in Area II; a total length of approximately 55 m. (180 ft. 6 in.) was indicated, 32.6 m. (107 ft.) of which was excavated. The ditch-fills contained large quantities of early Roman coarse wares together with stamped and decorated samian dating from A.D. 50 - 70. A number of human bones sealed by the ditch-fills included an adult male skeleton with a sword-cut on the skull, a male skull complete with lower jaw but without the rest of the body, and the articulated skeleton of a horse lacking head and neck. The evidence indicates two distinct phases of occupation and final abandonment in c. A.D. 70. In Area II, a sequence of Roman street-metallings, dating from the later first century and aligned north-east/south-west, was laid over what may have been the previously demolished rampart of this defensive sequence.

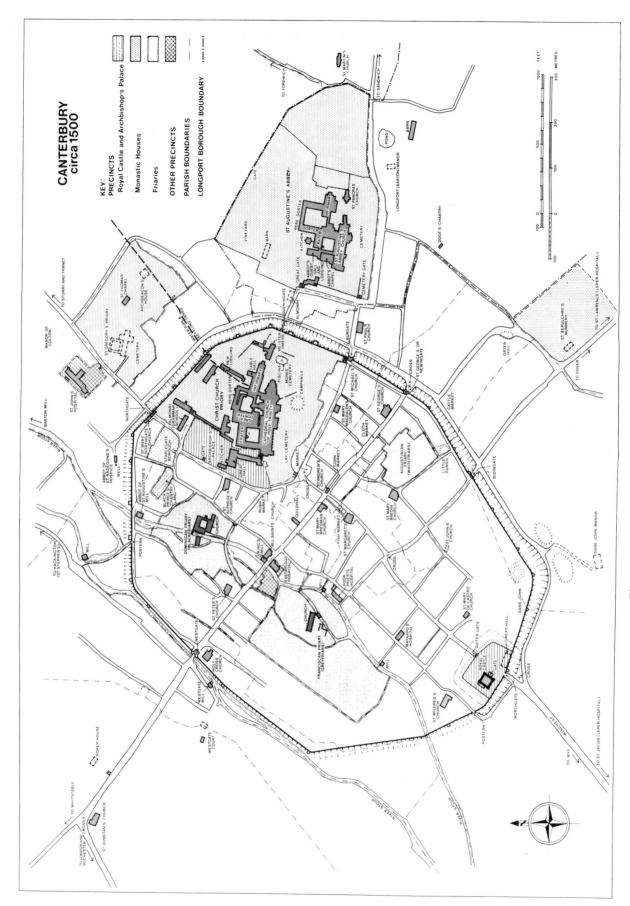

Fig. 1.   Map of medieval Canterbury (c. 1500).

Pits of the late-first to the late-third or fourth centuries were excavated. Two cremation burials of the late-first to the early-second century were uncovered to the east of the street in Area II. These were interred in open ground at a time when the area to the west of the street may have been under the plough.

The elements of one or more timber buildings of post-hole construction of the mid-second century or later, with a sequence of clay or rubble floors and a timber-lined well, were found flanking the street to the east. A remarkable double inhumation with two swords, belt-and-scabbard-fittings was located; it may have been covered by the floors. However, modern disturbances removed the conclusive stratigraphical evidence for this, so the circumstances and date of this obviously hurried and possibly secretive burial remain uncertain. The swords and fittings can be dated stylistically to the second or early-third century. Pottery and coins from the latest floors suggest that the building was abandoned in the third or fourth century. The foundations of a more substantial Roman building were located in the small trench south of Gas Lane. No intact stratified levels were associated with these foundations. Pottery and coins of the first to the fourth centuries were found in the destruction levels together with early medieval pottery.

No early or middle Saxon pottery was recovered from the post-Roman levels. In Area II, where fragments of intact stratigraphy were excavated (Figs. 18 and 20) only a uniform deposit of what may have been plough-soil sealed and disturbed the latest Roman levels. Sherds of eleventh- to thirteenth-century pottery in some quantity were recovered from the lowest levels of the post-Roman deposits in Area II. A number of late Saxon pits cutting the post-Roman levels was excavated, including two wicker-lined wells with barrel shafts; these possibly were related to the 43 or so houses that Domesday Book implies were demolished to make way for the Royal Castle between 1066 and 1086.

No trace of Norman occupation was found, save for the massive Castle ditch, 2.8 m. (9 ft.) deep and 8.9 m. (29 ft.) wide. The clearance of the area prior to the construction of the Castle is suggested by a very mixed layer (3* — Fig. 11) found in the small trench cut in 1975 south of Gas Lane, (Fig. 11). This layer contained early medieval pottery mixed with pottery of the first to the fourth centuries, together with much Roman building-débris including painted plaster, lumps of tessellated flooring; and late Roman coins. This deposit may indicate that the final destruction to its foundations of the Roman structure took place at the same time as the cutting of the Castle ditch and the levelling of the area outside the Castle defences. Sealing this layer was a deposit of plough-soil, indicating that the area outside the Castle was probably used for agricultural purposes for a considerable period after the Castle was built. No trace of the bailey wall was found within the excavated area. Such foundations as there must have been were probably removed when the gasworks were constructed. The approximate alignment of the bailey wall and ditch can still be seen as a 'break in slope' of the ground-surface behind the oast house to the south of Gas Lane (see Fig. 2). The junction between the bailey wall and the Roman City wall can also still be recognised by a change in wall construction (Fig. 2), where the coursed mortared whole flints at the back of the Roman wall are interrupted by the closely set nineteenth-century knapped flints of the repair following the demolition of the bailey wall.

---

* Throughout this excavation report a number in brackets is a layer number.

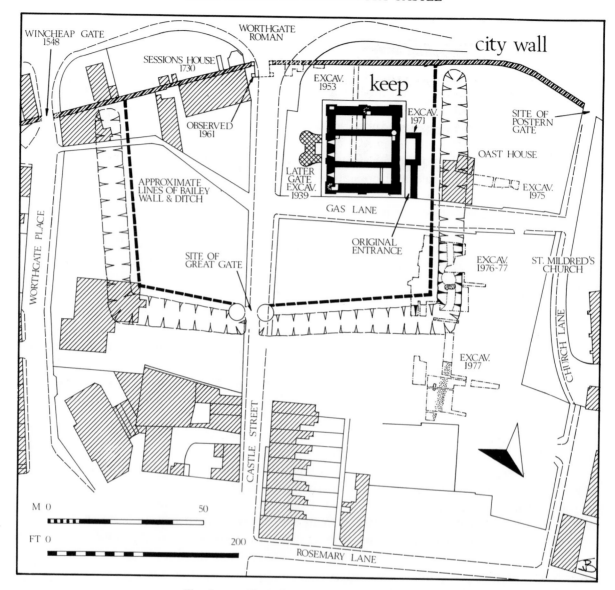

Fig. 2.   Plan of Canterbury Castle, 1 : 500.

A curious mortared flint wall blocking the Castle ditch was examined, this being situated quite close to the north-west corner of the defensive enclosure. This seems unlikely to have been for a postern bridge, but may have been constructed, quite late in the sequence, to regulate the level of water which must have collected in the ditch. A thick deposit of black-brown soil together with a number of pits sealed and cut the archaeological levels in Area II and the small trench to the south of Gas Lane. This deposit and the pits were probably associated with agricultural activity that began soon after Canterbury Castle was constructed. Documentary evidence from 1591/2 indicates that the areas to the east and north of the Castle bailey were hop-fields at that time.

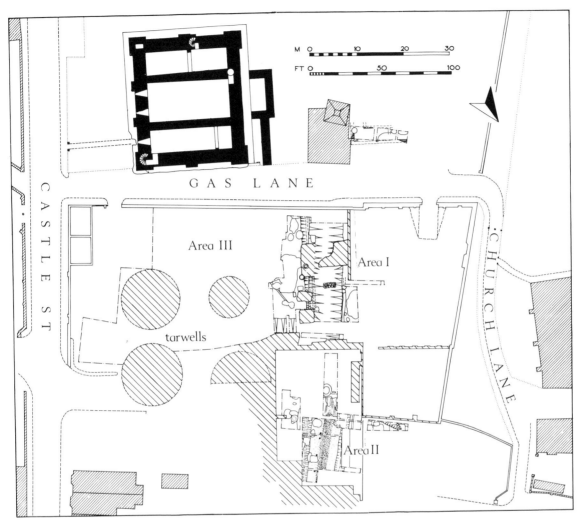

Fig. 3.   General Site Plan of all excavated Features.

A number of eighteenth- and nineteenth-century pits were emptied. These must relate to the period when Area II was open gardens behind houses before the gasworks extension was built. (See W. and H. Doige, *Map of Canterbury*, 1752, and the 1873 1 : 2,500 Ordnance Survey Map.)

III. THE EARLIEST ROMAN LEVELS

In Area II two early Roman ditches were cut longitudinally by the Norman Castle ditch (Fig. 15). They were removed completely by the north-west corner of the Castle ditch and elsewhere by deep gasworks foundations (Fig. 3). The digging of the Castle ditch, and the reduction of the archaeological deposits during gasworks construction to below the pre-Roman natural ground-level, meant that no definite features could be associated with the ditches. In Area II,

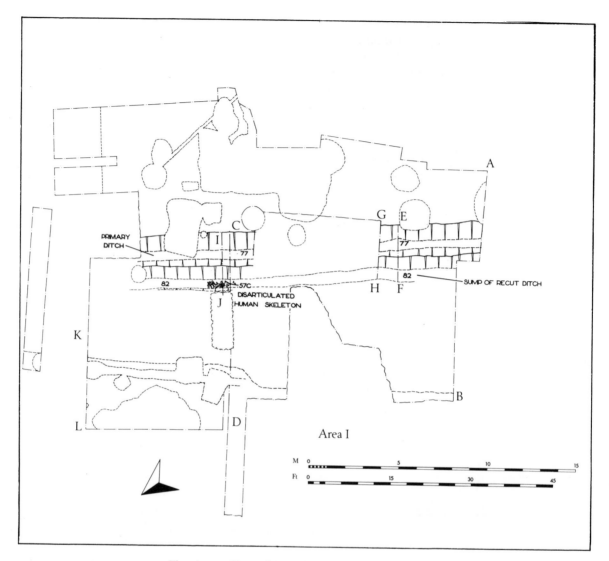

Fig. 4.   Plan of Area I — early Roman Levels.

however, despite much disturbance of the levels, small areas of intact stratigraphy suggested a demolished bank of brick-earth to the west of the ditches.

The Bank (Fig. 5 — Plan)

A compact layer of pebble and flint (206 : Fig. 22), 3 - 5 cm. (1 - 2 in.) thick and compressed into hard natural brick-earth, was thought to be the possible remains of a rampart base. This layer was sealed by a 0.30 m. (1 ft.) deposit of redeposited brick-earth (205 : Fig. 22), containing lumps of light grey-white sandy silt, possibly decomposed turves, which may have been the remains of a slighted rampart. This deposit thickened at the southern end of the ditches forming a slight bank, (most evident in Fig. 22). A single post-hole (290 : Fig. 21), cut the front of this bank to a depth of 0.50 m. (1 ft. 6 in.). The post had probably been withdrawn, the void being filled with grey silt and redeposited brick-earth. The stratigraphy suggests that the bank and the post-holes were probably contemporary. Thorough investigation elsewhere did not reveal any other post-holes in a similar situation. There was no evidence to suggest a two-phase bank. The pebble base (206), the bank (205) and the post-hole (290) were sealed by street-metalling (204 : Figs. 20 - 24), and a possible abandonment level (203 : Figs. 18 and 20 - 24). To the west of the street was a road-ditch (207 : Figs. 20 to 24) which probably removed the back of the rampart. No datable finds were recovered from the bank. It must be noted here that the evidence for the rampart was extremely slight; the extreme nature of the disturbance and pollution did not allow conclusive evidence to survive. The interpretation of the observed remains as a defensive bank and ditch is, therefore, to some extent, conjectural.

The Ditches (Area I, Fig. 4 — Plan; Area II, Fig. 5 — Plan)

In Area I the primary ditch was cut into the natural brick-earth to an average depth of 1.30 m. (4 ft. 6 in.). The probable outer slope was cut at an angle of 50 degrees. The sump had a flat bottom, on average 0.50 m. (1 ft. 8 in.) wide. A thin band of dark grey 'rapid' silt (60A and 78 : Fig. 16), 5 cm. (2 in.) thick, lined the outer scarp and sump. This was sealed by redeposited brick-earth, possibly from the bank. This deposit (52, 60 and 77 : Figs. 15 and 16) yielded only one sherd; it was of Flavian or pre-Flavian date. In Area II only the lowest levels of the inner scarp of the ditch and sump survived recutting. The sump, on average 0.35 m. (1 ft.) wide, was filled with discoloured grey-green sticky brick-earth contaminated with tar residue (263 and 272 : Figs. 18 and 20 - 24). This deposit contained the articulated remains of a horse lacking head and neck (Fig. 5), and a small number of Belgic and early Roman sherds. The ditch here was cut on average 1.20 m. (4 ft.) into the natural brick-earth with the inner slope set at an angle of 50 degrees. Some of the upper ditch-fills consisted of possible rampart material, but no pottery was recovered. In Area I the redeposited brick-earth (52, 60 and 77) was sealed by a layer of dark silty loam flecked with charcoal and mixed with tip-lines of clay and oyster shell (62A, 75 and 76 : Fig. 16). This yielded a silver inlaid brooch (Fig. 88, no. 7), five fragments of an adult skull and pottery, (dated by the fine wares), of the pre- to early-Flavian period. The layer was partly sealed by a lens of clean yellow-buff brick-earth, 3 - 5 cm. (1 - 2 in.) thick, possibly indicating abandonment of weathering.

The Recut Ditch

In Area I the primary ditch was recut to form a larger V-shaped ditch, dug 1.80 m. (6 ft.) into the natural brick-earth. The outer slope was set at an angle of 40 degrees and the sump, due west of the primary sump, was 0.60 m. (2 ft.) wide. A thin band of grey 'rapid' silt, 3 - 5 cm. (1 - 2 in.) thick, was noted on the side and in the sump of the ditch (81 : Fig 16). No datable finds were recovered from the 'rapid' silt which was sealed by a thick layer of redeposited brick-earth (33, 57B, 57C and 82 : Figs. 15 and 16), very similar to that in the primary ditch, and possibly rampart material. An incomplete, partly articulated human skeleton was sealed by this deposit (Fig. 4 — Plan, and Figs. 15 and 16). A possible sword-cut was found on the skull above the right eye. The deposit yielded Belgic-type coarse wares and fine wares dating to the mid-first century and was sealed by successive dumpings of occupation material, consisting of tips of burnt soil mixed with dark brown loamy silt, charcoal lenses and bands of oyster shell (57D, 57A/D, 62, 72, 74, 79, 80 : Fig. 16 and 267). This occupation material yielded a fragment of human skull, two bronze brooches (one of 'AVCISSA', Fig. 88. nos. 2 and 5 type), other small finds and pottery (dated by the fine wares) of *c.* A.D. 60 - 70. The occupation material was sealed by a layer (73 : Fig. 16) of yellow-buff brick-earth, 3 - 5 cm. (1 - 2 in.) thick, possibly indicating abandonment or weathering; it contained only one coarse ware sherd. The uppermost ditch-fill consisted of layers of dark brown loamy silt with tip-lines of pebble, crushed mortar, painted plaster, charcoal, daub and oyster shells. The nature of these layers (57, 57A, 70, 71 : Figs. 16; and 7, 8, 13, 14, 30), suggested a gradual filling over a considerable time. In the ditch was a mass of tiles and *tesserae*, and a number of possible pre-Roman 'bricks' or *briquetage*, as well as several small finds. The pottery dates from the late-first to the third or fourth century. During machine clearance of gasworks foundations the southern end of the ditch-sequence was disturbed (1 and 10 : Fig. 15). The bulk of the finds from these levels has been dated (by the fine wares) to *c.* A.D. 50 - 70. A small quantity of second- to fourth-century pottery was also present. These levels also produced the upper half of the left femur of a male aged about 25 years, and a coin of Claudius I (A.D. 43 - 45). In Area II the primary ditch was also recut. This second ditch, of similar size to the earlier, was much smaller than the recut ditch in Area I. The sump, 0.30 m. (2 ft.) wide, was cut to the east of the primary sump. No trace of silting was detected. The backfill (263A and 263B, 268 : Figs. 18 and 20 - 23), consisted entirely of redeposited brick-earth, possibly rampart material. Lumps of white-buff sandy silt were noticed in the general matrix; these may have been decomposed turves (Fig. 18). The deposit contained pottery dating to *c.* A.D. 50 - 70. A human skull, possibly that of a male aged approximately 25 years, was sealed by this deposit (Fig. 5 — Plan). The lower levels of this material were sealed by a thin lens of charcoal and pebble, possibly a brief abandonment deposit, similar to (73) in Area I. A light buff redeposited brick-earth with possible decomposed turves sealed this lens (268), which was only noticed in section after excavation was complete and may relate to the secondary levelling of the remaining rampart mass, prior to the laying of the primary street-metalling (203).

Conclusions

The size and shape of the primary ditches, taken together with the tentative evidence for a bank to the west of the ditches, suggest a possible military occupation of two distinct phases of the site. The nature of the ditch-fills, with a little sign of silting, followed by a uniform fill of perhaps demolished rampart-material and sealed by occupation-débris, supports this interpretation. The lack of silting in both ditches and the fact that the ditch was recut suggests that both phases of occupation lasted for some time with perhaps a short abandonment between them. The large quantities of early Roman coarse ware and imported fine wares (*terra nigra* and samian), particularly the stamped samian, date the beginning of the sequence to the pre-Flavian period, probably before A.D. 65. Three coins, two of which were associated with the later features, also suggest a pre-Flavian date. In Area I a worn coin of Claudius I (A.D. 41 -

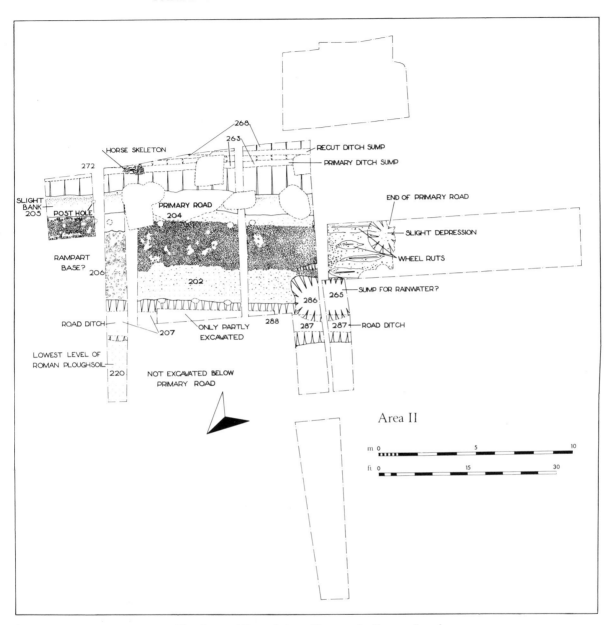

Fig. 5.   Plan of Area II — early Roman Levels.

54) was recovered from the later filling of the ditches (I). In Area II a coin of Caligula (A.D. 37 — 41) was found in the lowest deposit of the road-ditch sump (286 - Fig. 24), associated with the primary street. Another very worn coin of Claudius was recovered from the second phase street-metalling (211 - Fig. 22). The three *fibulae* recovered from the ditch-fills in Area II seem to indicate a mid-first century date and may be of military origin. Two other, *Camulodunum* type brooches (Fig. 88, nos. 1 and 3) were recovered from pits (56 - Fig. 12, Plan and 277 - Fig. 6, Plan) in Areas I and II. The human bones found in the ditch-fills and the scatter of human bones found in the early Roman levels may even suggest a military

engagement fought during the life of these defences. A skull and a semi-articulated human skeleton found in the sump of the recut ditch in Area II could perhaps indicate that executions had taken place.

The ditches in Areas I and II were aligned roughly north-east/south-west, but do not form a straight line, the ditch-sequence in Area II being set slightly to the east of that in Area I. In Area I the sump of the second ditch was cut to the west of the first ditch sump; whereas in Area II the second ditch sump was set to the east of the first ditch sump. The recut ditch in Area I, despite the reduction of the archaeological levels during gasworks construction, was also substantially larger than that in Area II, with an estimated total width of 5 m. (16 ft. 6 in.) in Area I, as opposed to 4 m. (13 ft.) in Area II. These inconsistencies may indicate that the ditches in Area I and II were cut independently, though at the same time and for the same purpose (see Fig. 3). A possibility is that a gate may have interrupted the ditches somewhere between the two areas.

If the bank is correctly recognised on the west side of the ditches, the defensive enclosure will have been situated on the gently sloping ground leading down to the river. No evidence for associated internal structures, streets or features was found to reinforce this hypothesis. These may have been removed by later Roman activity on the site, or possibly the fort was held too briefly to leave substantial structural traces. The accumulation of domestic débris in the upper fill of both the primary and secondary ditches in Area I, from which most of the dating evidence was derived, suggests an evacuation of the area followed by a re-occupation and the existence of nearby structures associated with both phases. The alignment of the minor primary Roman street, set on a north-east/south-west axis (discussed below p. 31), and the similarly aligned major Roman street found during excavations on 77-79 Castle Street, Canterbury in 1976, may well bear a direct relationship to the alignment of the ditch sequence, particularly that in Area II. During the 1978-79 excavations in the back-garden area of 77-79 Castle Street, a small Roman street was found in the earliest occupation levels. This street may well be a continuation of that found in Area II. It is tentatively suggested that the early street-grid, of at least this part of Canterbury, may have been based on the alignment of these early ditches.

In Area II, the remains were of a possible bank sealed by the minor Roman street. In Area I the ditch, after being only partly filled with demolished rampart-material and occupation débris, remained open for a considerable period. The remaining 'hollow' of the former ditch was then gradually filled by silting and then later by dumping, which included building débris. Some of this material may have also derived from later road-silting, though the primary metalling came to a sudden end in Area II, (p. 31). The pottery contained in these later deposits ranges from the late-first century to A.D. 170 or even later. It remains very likely, however, that the military occupation of the site ended in c. A.D. 70.*

---

* Professor S.S. Frere has suggested that a fort may have been established here as early as A.D. 43, as there must have been a fort of that date somewhere at the important Stour crossing. This first base may have been evacuated in A.D. 60 and almost immediately re-occupied, possibly as a result of the Boudican revolt. The final evacuation may have taken place in A.D. 71, in preparation for the concentration of troops for the Flavian campaigns against the Brigantes. An alternative interpretation is that the fort was established as a result of the Boudican revolt and that it was abandoned during the revolt, indicating perhaps that troops were called to join the Governor (or Cogidubnus) and later sent back, with the final abandonment of the base being in connection with movements of troops either in the Civil War of A.D. 69 - 70 or in preparation for the Flavian campaigns under Cerialis.

IV. THE EARLY ROADS AND ASSOCIATED LEVELS (Fig. 5 — Plan)

In Area I the redeposited brick-earth (206) tentatively interpreted as a levelled rampart, was sealed by a narrow, evenly-laid and rammed pebble spread (204 : Figs. 20 - 24, and 178, 181 and 247), which was thought to be an early minor Roman street-metalling, aligned roughly north-east/south-west, and barely 2.20 m. (7 ft. 3 in.) wide. To the east, traces of a small low bank separating the street from the remaining hollow of the filled ditches, may have been the remains of a destroyed rampart. To the west a road-ditch was located (207 : Figs. 22 - 24), separating the street from a disturbed and very polluted dark clayey deposit (220 : Fig. 22), which probably represented plough-soil of early Roman date. To the west of the street a thin layer of fine grey silt (197, 202 : Fig. 22 and 288 : Fig. 23), containing charcoal, burnt soil and daub extended into the sump of the road-ditch, where it was mixed with a thick deposit of dirty grey brick-earth (207 : Figs. 22 and 23).

Fifteen metres (49 ft.) of well-preserved street were uncovered. No signs of excessive wear or patching were detected, but at the southern end of the main trench the metalling was patchy. The cutting to the south of the main trench revealed only a scatter of pebbles embedded in the hard brick-earth, and more pebbles were set in small, shallow gullies and narrow grooves cutting the brick-earth. These intrusions, continuing the line of the road for a further 3 m. (c. 10 ft.), were thought to be wheel-ruts. The ruts were at this point interrupted by nineteenth- and twentieth-century disturbances. The primary metalling probably terminated here, giving way to a rough track leading out of the city perhaps. On the west side, the road-ditch was enlarged and deepened (Fig. 24), possibly indicating that it ended here, for the enlargement may have served as a sump for the collection of rain water. The uniform, silty nature of the deposits (285, 286 and 287), and the erosion of the eastern side of the ditch (which caused the subsidence of the edge of the street), may support this interpretation. Light grey-buff silt striations in the lowest levels here may have been caused by rain-washing or weathering. A human jaw and an *as* of Caligula (286) were found in this matrix, together with pottery of Belgic and early Roman type. A single sherd of fine ware (286) and the coarse wares indicated that the street was in use immediately after the ditches had been filled in (i.e. c. A.D. 60 - 70). Attempts were made to locate this track and the later sequence of street-metalling in Area I, but the reduction of the levels had effectively removed all traces of metalling. A narrow ditch (44), 0.40 m. (1 ft. 4 in.) wide, was found aligned north-east/south-west and filled with dark loamy silt and pebbles to a depth of 0.45 m. (1 ft. 6 in.), (Fig. 8, Plan and Fig. 17). This may have been a drain for a later street; if so, it seems likely that the streets generally followed the alignment of the earlier ditches. The presence of tip-lines of pebble in the uppermost fill of the Area I ditch (57, etc.), may indicate the proximity of a street. The surviving hollow over the ditches may perhaps have been used as a road-gutter. The primary street, (204, 178, 181 and 247), was sealed by a deposit 3 - 5 cm. (1 - 2 in.) thick, of compacted light brown brick-earth (203 : Figs. 18, 20 - 24; 180, 245 and 246). Thin bands of white-buff silt within the matrix of this deposit, possibly formed by rain action, indicated that the street may have been abandoned for a short time or that it was infrequently used. A few sherds of coarse ware were recovered from this deposit (Fig. 73 : nos. 218 - 220). This possible abandonment layer also sealed the road-ditch (201 : Figs. 22 and 23; 265, 275 : Fig. 24), and the remaining hollow of the military ditches (Figs. 18, 20, 21 and 24). This layer was sealed by a new street (211 : Figs. 20 - 22 and 238 : Figs. 22 - 24), which was also aligned north-east/south-west and

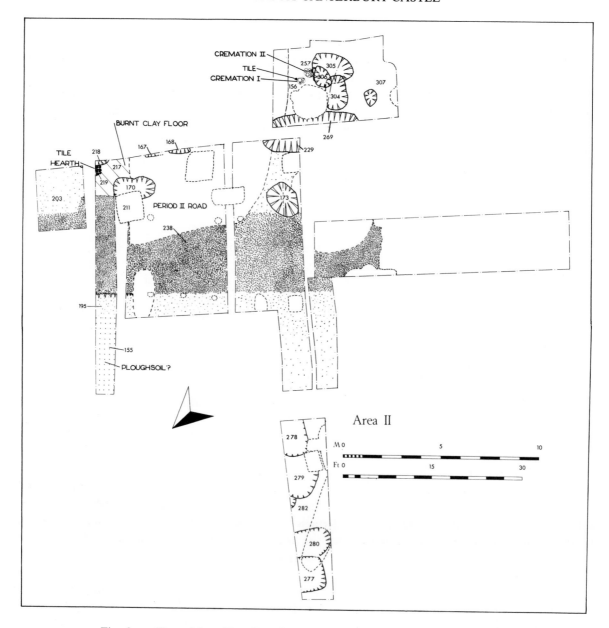

Fig. 6.   Plan of Area II — Late-first and early-second Century A.D. Levels.

was 4 m. (*c.* 13 ft.) wide. The metalling, of small to medium pebbles, 2 - 3 cm. thick, continued into the southern extension to the main trench and was cut by nineteenth- to twentieth-century disturbances. In the north-west corner of the main trench was a shallow road-ditch (195 : Fig. 22) to the west of the street. This petered out after 2 m. (6 ft.), but showed signs of at least one recutting (179 : Fig. 22). No finds came from either ditch. Elsewhere the surviving hollow of the earlier ditches seems to have been used as a gutter. Occupation-material (274, 303 : Fig. 24; 277 : Fig. 23 and 177, 196, 200, 221, 226, 227, 264), partly sealed the street and extended into the road-ditch. This occupation detritus contained a wide range of pottery, dating from the Flavian to the Trajanic periods (Figs. 73 and 74 : nos. 221 - 251). A small number of late second-century sherds was also recovered from this deposit (196 and 200), and may indicate a later date. In the north-east corner of the main trench (Fig. 6, Plan; Fig. 22), and along the southern edge of the north-east trench extension, the street extended for a further 0.80 m. (c. 2 ft. 6 in.) to the east. The street (211 and 238), had an overall width of 4.80 m. (15 ft. 9in.) at this point, and a worn and bent coin of Claudius I was recovered from its surface. A thin layer (217 : Fig. 22 and Fig. 18), of burnt clay 2 cm. thick abutting the street, was possibly a floor, and a pad of burnt tiles (219 : Fig. 22) set in it may have been a hearth. Only a small area survived the cutting of a large nineteenth-century pit (123 : Fig. 18). No post-holes were found, but the widening of the street at this point may suggest a doorway.

V. THE CREMATIONS (Fig. 25; Fig. 6 — Plan; Fig. 7 — Plan)

To the east of these streets in the south-east extension to the main trench, two cremation burials of the late-first or early-second century were found.

Group I (156)

A small shallow pit (157) cut the pre-Roman ground-surface and was filled with light grey silty brick-earth. Its furnishings consisted of the following:
A. Glass vessel.
B. Coarse-ware pot containing the cremation(s).
C. Samian dish (Dr. 36).
D. Coarse-ware flask.
E. Samian platter (Dr. 15/17) with bird bones on it.
The cremation urn contained a minimum of one adult, probably a male and aged from 20 - 40 years. A few fragments of animal bone were found in the fill of the grave, and the samian dish contained the remains of a small bird. Just to the north, four tile fragments stacked one upon the other may possibly have been the base of a grave-marker.

Group II (257)

To the south of Group I a second cremation burial was uncovered. This was also deposited in a small pit (257A), cut into the pre-Roman ground-surface. The grey silty brick-earth fill contained loose coarse-ware sherds dating to the first or second century together with a few animal bones.
The grave contained the following six vessels:
F. Coarse-ware pot containing the cremations.
G. Coarse-ware flagon.
H. Coarse-ware carinated bowl.
I. Bowl imitating samian Dr. 35.
J. Samian dish (Dr. 36).
K. Coarse-ware pot.

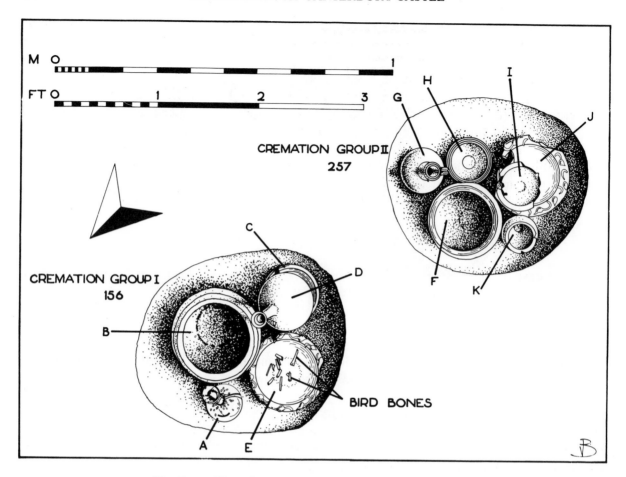

Fig. 7.   Plan of two late-first Century Cremation Groups.

The cremation urn contained a minimum of two individuals; a child 4 - 5 years of age and an adult. No grave-marker was found. The cremation burials were probably interred at about the same time. Vague reports of further cremations seen during gasworks construction in the 1950s indicate that this area may have been a Roman cremation cemetery in the first and second centuries. The early sequence of street-metallings may even have been laid to give access to this cemetery.

In 1953 two cremation vessels were shown to Professor S.S. Frere as having been found at the tannery in St. Mildred's during construction-work. (Fig. 7a)

Left   Rather coarse grey-brown ware, burnished rim and neck, furrowed. First century, post-Conquest Belgic type, perhaps Flavian.

Right   Leathery-brown burnished ware, Belgic type, probably post-Conquest.

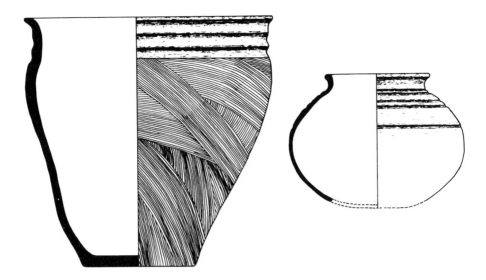

Fig. 7a.   Two Cremation Vessels from St. Mildred's Tannery (¼).

VI. POSSIBLE AGRICULTURAL ACTIVITY TO THE WEST OF THE STREETS

In the north-west extension to the main trench in Area II, a layer (220 : Fig. 22), possibly representing Roman plough-soil, was found to have cut the western edge of the road-ditch. This layer of glutinous grey clayey soil, heavily contaminated with tar residue, yielded pottery dating from the early to mid-second century (Fig. 74 : nos. 254-257). The disturbance of the old ground-surface, perhaps by agricultural activity, may have started during the life of the second-phase street or slightly later. The stratigraphy suggests not only continuity of this activity to the west of the street, but also that it was of long duration. If the disturbances can indeed be attributed to ploughing, then the partly filled road-ditches may also have served as a field boundary. Similar disturbance was not found to the east of the street: the old ground-surface had not been disturbed. This may suggest that to the east of the street-sequence we are dealing with a Roman field. The early plough-soil (220) was mixed with and sealed by similar deposits (155 and 106 : Fig. 22), which cut and finally sealed the second-phase road-ditch (195 : Fig. 22). The later deposits (103, 105 and 106 : Fig. 22) yielded pottery dating from the first to the mid-third or fourth centuries. (Fig. 74 : nos. 252-253, 258-261, 263-267, 269; and 106 : nos. 262 and 268). Two further street-metallings, laid over the second-period street, may have been associated with this agricultural activity, as were perhaps the badly disturbed remains of possible structures to the east of the street. Street III (257, 243 and 237 : Figs. 20, 21, 22, 24; and 257, 243) 4m (c. 13 ft.) wide, sealed Street II, and was associated to the west with a light brown loamy silt deposit (176, 273 : Figs. 22 and 24). The make-up of Street III contained one large and three small fragments of a 'Hertfordshire pudding-stone' quern, and pottery dating from the late-first to the mid- or late-second century. Street IV (236 : Figs. 22 to 24), 3.5 m. (c.

11 ft. 8 in.) wide, was laid soon after Street III, possibly to increase the camber. To the west of Street IV, a light brown sandy loam (176, 226 : Fig. 22; 224 : Fig. 23.), was mixed with, or disturbed by plough-soil layer (106 : Fig. 22); indicating that the agricultural activity was certainly under way for some time before this street was laid. A thin street-metalling, consisting of at least two surfacings (301 and 302 : Fig. 24), approximately 2 m. (6 ft. 6 in.) wide and aligned east-west, was located in the south-west corner of the main trench. The metalling sealed the latest levels filling the early road-ditch (273 and 303), and was possibly associated with Street IV (236). This may well have been a service road leading into the field. Pottery recovered from this metalling dated to the second century.

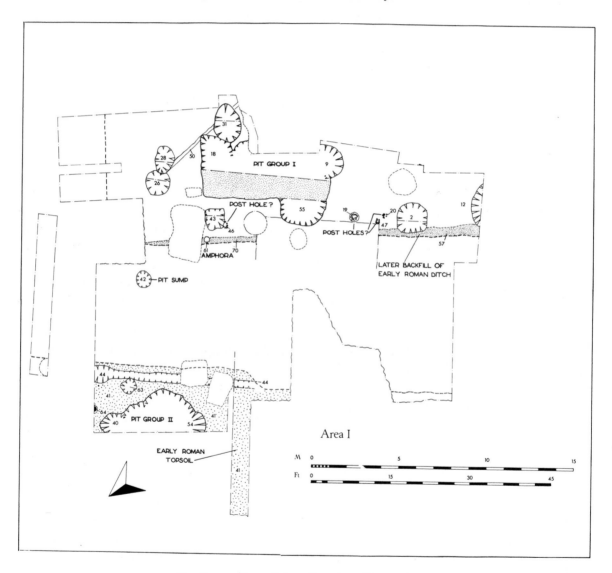

Fig. 8.   Plan of Area I — later Roman levels.

A number of post-holes aligned north-east/south-west, flanking the west side of the streets, may indicate that a fence had superseded the early road/field-ditch. These posts (107, 107A, 107B, 107C and 276 : Fig. 9 — Plan), were on average 10-12 cm. (4-5 in.) in diameter and cut through the edge of the street into the underlying brick-earth. Post-hole (276) was cut from the surface of the service road and set in a post-pit. The post was chocked with large flints and two quern fragments set in redeposited brick-earth; it was possibly either a corner-post or a gate-post.

In the north-west extension a shallow U-shaped ditch was excavated (262 : Fig. 9 — Plan). It was aligned roughly east—west and may have marked the southern boundary of the field. The ditch contained pottery dating from the mid-second to the third century or later. The upper levels in the north-west extension to the main trench (256 : Fig. 27), to the north of the ditch, were very similar to the upper levels to the west of the street sequence and may therefore also be plough-soil. Pottery recovered from these levels dates from the Antonine period to the third or fourth century. A similar level was excavated to the south of the service road (301 and 302), in the second south-west extension to the main trench (235 and 239 : Fig. 9 — Plan). This deposit contained first- and second-century pottery.

VII. THE LATE-FIRST AND EARLY-SECOND-CENTURY LEVELS

To the east of the second-period street in Area II (Fig. 6 — Plan), a deposit of light brown silty soil, 15 cm. (6 in.) thick, (230 : Figs. 18, 21 and 22; 231 : Figs. 18 and 20; and 194) sealed the clay floor (217) and the streets (211 and 237). This deposit contained pottery ranging from the pre-Flavian period to the early second century. Street IV (236 : Figs. 22-24) sealed this deposit, and was itself sealed by Street V (166 : Figs. 22-24). A thin lens of dark silt (216 : Figs. 18 and 20-22) extending eastwards from Street V sealed the rest of the layer (230, 231 and 194). This thin lens contained only coarse pottery which is perhaps early second-century in date.

Four rubbish pits were cut from this horizon and were eventually sealed by levels associated with the construction of a timber building or buildings. A rubbish pit (218 and 233 : Figs. 18, 21 and 22) was cut into the earlier levels, but lay only partially within the excavated area. This pit yielded pottery dating from the pre-Flavian period to the early second century (Figs. 74 and 75 : nos. 270-275). A second rubbish pit (154 and 170 : Fig. 28), situated in the north-east corner of the main trench, was cut by the well (101) and sealed by the floors of the building (213 and 215). It contained pottery dated to the late first century. The third rubbish pit (173 : Fig. 28), was situated in the main trench and was sealed by the remains of a clay floor (118). It contained the right tibia of a very young child and pottery mainly dating to the mid-second century, though a number of sherds found in the fill may indicate a slightly later date. The fourth and largest rubbish pit (229, 242, 249 : Figs. 18 and 24; 269, 270 : Figs. 19 and 25) was sealed by a sequence of clay floors and cut by a nineteenth-century disturbance. This pit contained a number of bones of a very young child (242) and late first- to early second-century pottery, including a whole pot (Figs. 75-78 : nos. 290-342). A number of other rubbish pits, not so clearly defined, also produced pottery of a first- or early second-century date, and may have been associated with this occupation. Rubbish pits (167 and 169 : Fig. 18) lay only partially within the excavated area of the main trench and contained late-first to early-second

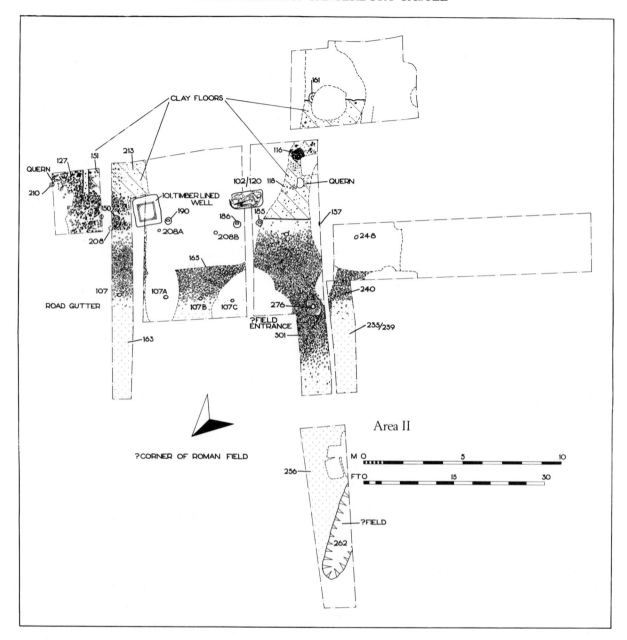

Fig. 9.   Plan of Area II — later Roman Levels.

century pottery. A rubbish pit (168 : Fig. 18), which was also only partly within the excavated area, yielded only a few sherds of coarse ware and a single fine-ware sherd dated c. A.D. 50-56. Two rubbish pits (304 and 305 : Fig. 6 — Plan; and Fig. 28.) situated in the south-east extension to the main trench, were excavated. Pit (305) was cut by pit (304) and contained pottery dating to the pre-Flavian or early-Flavian period. Pit (304) yielded a number of infant bones and pottery, including a whole coarse-ware vessel, dating to the first century. Four rubbish pits were located in the extreme south-west extension to the main trench (Figs. 6 and 27). The pits, only partly within the excavated area, were cut and sealed by layer (262), a light-brown sandy silt (possible Roman plough-soil), which contained pottery dating from the mid-second to the early-third century or later. Pit (277) cut the western edge of pit (280) and contained pottery dating to the pre- or early-Flavian period. Pit (279) was cut by pit (278) and contained pottery dating to the early- or mid-second century. Pit (280) cut pit (277) and contained pottery dating to the early-second century. Pit (282) was cut by pit (279) and yielded only a few sherds of a possible pre-Flavian date. Pit (218), layer (216) and part of Street V were sealed by a 25 cm. (10 in.) deposit of discoloured brick-earth and yellow sandy silt (209, 209A, and 209B : Figs. 18 and 20-22), which yielded pottery dating to the late-first or early-second century (Fig. 75 : nos. 276-289). This layer may have been deliberately deposited to level the area prior to the construction of a timber building and the laying of Street VI (165 : Figs. 22-24). The datable finds from this deposit and from the stratified pits indicate that the building may have been constructed in the early- to mid-second century.

VIII. THE TIMBER BUILDING (Fig. 9 — Plan)

In Area II elements of a timber building or buildings were located in the north-east and south-east corners of the main trench, and in the north-east and south-east extensions. In both areas the building-levels were badly disturbed by post-Roman activity. Any possible stratigraphical link between the northern and southern building-levels was removed by a large modern disturbance (123 : Fig. 18). Only in the north-east corner of the main trench and in the north-east extension was a reasonably intact sequence of levels excavated. It was therefore found to be impossible to formulate a convincing overall plan for the building(s).

In the north-east corner of the main trench, a thin layer of yellow clay, 3-5 cm. (1-2 in.) thick, probably a floor (128, 215 : Figs. 18, 21 and 22), sealed the earlier deposits (209, 209A and 209B). This floor, which yielded pottery of the early- or mid-second century (Fig. 78 : 128, nos. 343-348), carried through into the north-east extension where it abutted against a 25-cm. (10-in.) pad of compacted orange clay set with small flints and tile fragments (Fig. 18). This was possibly a pad for a sleeper-beam and an internal wall. To the north of this, another clay floor (172 : Figs. 18 and 20), containing sherds dating to the early- or mid-second century (Fig. 78 : nos. 349-352), sealed the floor. A row of six post-holes (150, 190, 186, 185, 137 and 210), aligned on a north-east/south-west axis (parallel to the street), was excavated. These were cut on average 40 cm. (c. 1⅓ ft.) deep, and had a diameter of 35 cm. (c. 1 ft.). The post-holes were all packed with grey redeposited brick-earth and small flints. The arrangement of the flints within the post-holes indicates that the posts (possibly split posts) may have rotted *in situ*, and were on average 20 cm. (8 in.) in diameter. Soon after these posts had been sunk a new street (Street VII), (164 : Figs. 22-24), was laid. A number of sherds dating from the later second century was recovered from the street matrix. The clay floor (215) was sealed by a uniform deposit of grey-brown silty brick-earth (214 : Figs. 18, 21 and 22), possibly laid to counteract the subsidence of an underlying pit (218, 233, 151, 213 : Figs. 18, 21 and 22), sealed this deposit. In the north-east extension a similar sequence was observed. Here, a deposit of discoloured brick-earth (171 : Figs. 18 and 20; 158), containing a range of pottery dating from the pre-Flavian period to the early- or mid-second century (Fig. 78 : 158, nos. 353-57), sealed the primary floor. The presence of four sherds of Oxfordshire ware in this deposit may push this date into the third century or later. This deposit was in turn sealed by a new floor (127 : Figs. 18 and 20) composed of flints, broken tile and *amphora* sherds set in clay. The floor contained a mixture of sherds dating from the pre-Flavian period to the mid-third or fourth century (Fig. 78-9 : nos. 358-367).

The internal wall continued in use throughout, with the new floor and dumping levels accumulating on either side. A thin pebble-and-tile metalling, bisecting the partition wall, and overlying floors (128 and 172) indicates a doorway between the two rooms, (see Fig. 21). To the north of the partition wall the floor was sealed by a deposit of dirty brick-earth (125, 136 : Fig. 18). To the south of the wall a similar deposit of brick-earth (122, 162, 212 : Figs. 18, 21 and 22; 232), sealed the floor. These deposits contained mostly derived pottery dating to the early second century (Figs. 80–81 : 122 : nos. 388, 404-409). They were sealed, on either side of the partition wall, by a final clay and pebble floor (110 : Figs. 18, 21 and 22). Post-Roman activity, possibly ploughing (140 : Figs. 18 and 20), severely disturbed the floor in the north-east extension. Elsewhere the floor was sealed and partly disturbed by a deposit of dark brown loam (III, 130 : Figs. 18 and 31). These post-Roman deposits contained a wide range of coarse and fine wares dating from the pre-Flavian to the mid-third century or later, with Saxo-Norman and early medieval material.

IX. THE TIMBER WELL (101 : Fig. 26)

Associated with the primary and secondary floors (213 and 215), and sealed by the later sequence of deposits (162 and 110), was a timber-lined well. The well-shaft had been cut 3 m. (10 ft.) through the natural brick-earth and into the water-bearing gravel-terrace. One and a half courses of oak planking were found preserved at the bottom of the well. The plank lining had dovetailed corners and 'ladder'-rungs inserted in the north-east and south-west corners. Rope-marks were observed on the northern side of the well. The lowest level (101S) was very badly polluted with liquid tar and contained pottery, including a whole pot, dating to the late-second century (Figs. 79-80 : nos. 373 to 379). These levels also contained a number of small finds including a steelyard-weight or plumb-bob (Fig. 93, no. 76) and some fragments of wood mouldings (See below p. 185 and Fig. 97). The uppermost levels (101M, N, G, O and R) constituted an homogeneous dump of dark brown loam mixed with pebble packing that originally surrounded the well structure. These layers contained pottery dating to the late-second or possibly early-to mid-third century. A portion of the original packing was preserved to the east of the well, (101I - K). This comprised deposits of gravel mixed with bands of silt and brick-earth. A number of late second-century sherds were recovered from this deposit (Fig. 79 : Nos. 368-72), traces of the decayed well-timbers were observed in the upper levels of the backfill (101P - R). The backfilling of the well probably took place when the second-phase floor (213) was sealed by layer (162). The datable finds recovered from the well-fill indicate that the well was backfilled in the late second-century (Figs. 80-1 : nos. 380-7, 410-3), a date that is similar to the proposed dendrochronological date for the construction of the well. The final floor (110) sealed layer (162) and the backfilling of the well. After the well was backfilled, and during later occupation, subsidence took place, necessitating the deposition of more material (101B and C). These deposits contained small finds and pottery dating to the late-second to mid-third century.

Fragmentary remains of possible clay floors and associated features were found in the south-eastern corner of the main trench and in part of the south-eastern extension (Fig. 9, Plan). Here, the building levels were badly disturbed by a modern pit (123 : Fig. 18) and by a nineteenth-century pit (266 : Fig. 24). Three phases of possible clay floors were excavated; most of the areas covered by these floors overlay an earlier rubbish pit (229, 242, 249, 269 and 270). The gradual settling of the pit-fill probably necessitated the relaying of the floors. The earliest floor (228 : Figs. 18, 19, 24 and 25), contained pottery dating to the early- or mid-second century. This floor was sealed by a 2-5 cm. (1-2 in.) layer of dirty redeposited brick-earth (188 : Figs. 18, 19, 24 and 25) containing a quantity of second-century pottery. A second floor (144 : Figs. 18, 19, 24 and 25) was laid over the redeposited brick-earth. The floor contained a small quantity of pottery dating to the late-second century.

In the south-east corner of the main trench a bowl-shaped pit, 40 cm. (c. 1 ft. 6 in.) deep, was cut through the floor. The 'bowl' was surround by burnt clay and contained burnt flints and tile (Fig. 18, Section A-E). This feature also appeared in the south-east extension (Fig. 19), where it was of the same depth and sloped gradually upwards to the north. The burnt stones located in the western section may have been the remains of a foundation. The shape of the pit and the burnt foundations indicate that this may have been the remains of a domestic oven of 'key-hole' shape. Only fragments of this feature were excavated and its interpretation is not, therefore, secure. A small circular pit (189) also cut the clay floor. The pit, 10-15 cm. (4-6 in.) deep, was filled with charcoal and ash and the surrounding area was fired orange-red; this feature may have been a domestic hearth. If these features have been correctly interpreted, then this excavated area may have been a kitchen. The clay floor (144) and the oven were sealed by a thick deposit of burnt brown soil (135 : Figs. 18, 19, 24 and 25) which contained no datable pottery. A thin band of chalk, (see Figs. 18 and 19) and a final clay floor (118 : Figs. 18, 19 and 25), sealed this deposit. The surface of this final floor, where it survived, was covered with a scatter of broken roofing-tiles. A sandstone quern was also recovered from this surface. A small 'box' (116 : Fig. 9, Plan) constructed of *tegulae* and box flue-tiles was set into the floor; this may have been used for the storage of fuel.

A post-hole (161 : Fig. 9 — Plan), of similar size and fill to the alignment of post-holes on the building frontage, was found in the south-east extension to the main trench. This single post-hole is the only evidence indicating the back of this possible building. During the life of this structure, the street was remetalled at least once (Street VII), (164). Only a few traces of this metalling were found, post-Roman disturbances (possibly eleventh- or thirteenth-century ploughing) and gasworks construction having effectively removed the rest of this and all traces of any other metallings. A number of shallow post-holes, possibly associated with a portico for the building, was found cutting the street surface (208, 208A, 208B, 208C and 248 : Fig. 9 — Plan). The best-preserved of these, (208 : Fig. 6), was set in a post-pit 45 cm. (1 ft. 6 in.) wide. The postvoid was filled with dark brown silt and indicated a post 15 cm. (6 in.) in diameter. The post was chocked with gravel, flints and a quern fragment. Only the lowest levels of the other post-holes survived.

Three rubbish pits may have been associated with the occupation of the building. One pit, (278 : Fig. 27; Fig. 6 — Plan), situated at the southern end of the extreme south-west extension to the main trench, contained small finds and pottery dating to the late-second century. A second rubbish pit (281 : Fig. 7, Fig. 6 — Plan) also in the same extension, contained pottery dating to the third or fourth century. The third pit (307 : Fig. 6 — Plan), located in the south-east extension to the main trench, contained pottery of an indeterminate date. In Area I only the deeply cut features survived below the massive gasworks foundations. These features were mostly rubbish pits, though a number of smaller pits may have been post-holes once associated with structures that had been completely cut away.

X. THE RUBBISH PITS (Fig. 8 — Plan)

Rubbish pit (2 : Fig. 28).	Late second- or early third-century pottery.
Rubbish pit (12 : Fig. 15).	Yielded no datable finds.
Rubbish pit (26 : Fig. 28).	Pre-Flavian or Flavian pottery.
Rubbish pit (28 : Fig. 28).	Pre-Flavian to Trajanic pottery.
Rubbish pit (31 : No Fig.)	Produced one sherd of Oxfordshire ware dated to *c.* A.D. 325-400+.
Rubbish pit (42 : No Fig.).	Contained only a few sherds of undatable pottery.
Rubbish pit (43 : Fig. 28).	Second-to fourth-century pottery.

A group of intersecting pits situated to the east of the early Roman ditches, proved to be one of the most polluted areas on the site. The pollution was so severe that it was impossible to separate one pit decisively from another. The pits, (9, 13, 14, 15, 16, 17, 18, 32 and 55) contained a homogeneous fill of light brown to black loamy silt mixed with great quantities of tar residue. Total excavation of this large pit-complex proved impossible. Only three pits were partially separated from the rest of the matrix; pit (9) yielded Oxfordshire and *éponge* wares dating to the third or fourth century or later; pit (18) contained only a few sherds of undatable coarse ware, and pit (55) produced pottery dating from the later second century to the mid-third century. The other pits yielded a mixture of pottery dating from the late-second to the fourth century or later. A second group of intersecting pits (39, 40, 41, 53 and 54.) was located in the north-east corner of the trench. An attempt was made to separate these pits, but again pollution made this impossible. However, total excavation of the disturbed area within the trench was accomplished. Only three pits from this group were partially separated from the matrix: pit (39) contained a mixture of pottery dating from the third or fourth century; pit (40) yielded pottery dating to the late-second or mid-third century, and pit (54) contained pottery of indeterminate date. The other pits contained a mixture of pottery dating from the pre-Flavian period to the fourth century or later.

XI. POSSIBLE STRUCTURAL FEATURES IN AREA I (Fig. 8)

A single post-hole (64 : Fig. 17) was found in the north-west corner of the trench. The bottom of a possible post-hole (19), cut 30 cm. (1 ft.) into the natural brick-earth and packed with flints, was found on the eastern edge of the early Roman ditches. The base of another post-hole (47) which was packed with tile fragments, *amphora* sherds and small stones, yielded pottery dating to the second century. The base of an *amphora* (61) was found with its foot set into the natural brick-earth; it appears to have been set into the floor of a Roman building and used for the storage of foodstuff. A shallow, narrow gully (50), 20 cm. (8 in.) wide and 5 cm. (2 in.) deep, aligned north-west/south-east was excavated. The gully may have been associated with the post-hole (46) and the *amphora* base (61).

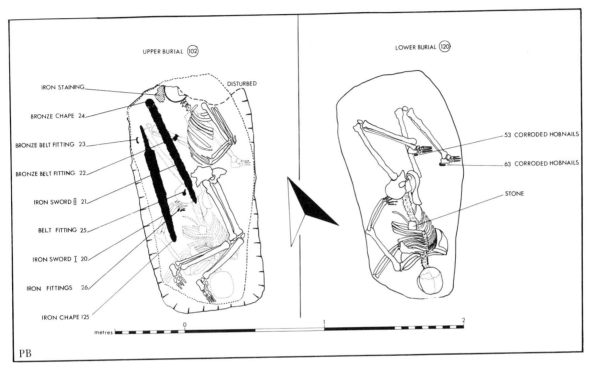

Fig. 10.   Plan of double Inhumation 'Sword' Burial.

XII. THE TRENCH SOUTH OF GAS LANE (Fig. 11, Plan and Section)

The mortared flint foundations of part of a Roman structure were found in the small trench south of Gas Lane. The trench, 12.6 m. by 3 m. (*c.* 41 ft. by *c.* 10 ft.) was cut between the walls of previous nineteenth-century flint cottages (nos. 1 and 2 Gas Lane), prior to the construction in 1976 of an extension to the nineteenth-century oast house to the east. Severe disturbance probably associated with the levelling of the area prior to the cutting of the Norman Castle ditch (3, 4, 7, 11 and 16), reduced the deposits to sub-foundation level. Only one small section of actual wall was uncovered, and no associated floors or construction-levels were found. Only in the western part was the full width of a mortared flint wall-foundation observed (12). This was 0.60 m. (*c.* 2 ft.) wide and was cut into the natural brick-earth to a depth of 0.40 m. (*c.* 1 ft. 4 in.). It may have been for an outer wall. A fragment of the same foundation (9), was located in the north-east corner of the central area of the trench. A further fragment (8) was also located in the north-east corner of the trench. This may have been the return of the outer wall, indicating perhaps that the north-east corner of the building lay just outside the north-east corner of the trench. South of the northern outer wall, the remains of another wall were located. This was completely robbed away in the extreme south-west corner (7) of the trench, and in the south-east corner of the central area. The corner of this wall was located just within the trench and was better preserved than any of the other fragments, measuring 0.55 m. (c. 2 ft.) from the lowest foundation-level to the top of the wall. The upper 15 cm. (6 in.) of the wall was faced on the inside with 2 cm. (¾ in.) of white painted plaster. A small robber trench (11), may represent an internal wall. It extended for 1.30 m. (4 ft. 3 in.) into the trench where it was completely cut away by a deep depression (16), (part of 3, 4 and 7). The wall-foundations possibly describe the corner of a Roman building consisting of at least two narrow rooms, or, more likely, two corridors surrounding and servicing other rooms. Robber trench (11) may have been a sub-division of the wider north corridor. It is just possible that this is part of a small, square Romano-Celtic temple.

Fragments of *opus signinum* flooring together with fragments of mosaic and painted plaster were found in the disturbed levels (3, 4, 7, 11 and 16). These may originally have derived from this structure. Mixed with the débris was a general collection of pottery dating from the first century to the early medieval period. A number of coins was recovered, dating to the periods A.D. 268-273 and A.D. 330-340.

Sealing these disturbed levels was a layer of light brown loam (10), perhaps plough-soil. This contained a few sherds of medieval pottery dating from the eleventh to the thirteenth century. This was in turn sealed by a deposit of crushed mortar and flint rubble (2), containing a mixture of eighteenth- and nineteenth-century pottery. The deposit may have accumulated when the bailey wall was demolished and the Keep defaced in the 1820s. A thin layer of top-soil completed the excavation sequence. The mortared flint foundations of two nineteenth-century cottages and two brick wells were sealed by the topsoil.

XIII. THE DOUBLE INHUMATION BURIAL (Fig. 9 — Plan; Fig. 10 — Plan; and Fig. 23)

In Area II a remarkable double burial, containing two skeletons, two swords and associated belt and scabbard-fittings was uncovered. (For a detailed report on the swords and fittings, see Dr. Graham Webster's report below; and for the skeletons, see the report by Dr. Peter Garrard, also below).

The grave-pit, measuring some 1.70 m. (c. 5 ft. 6 in.) by 0.90 m. (c. 3 ft.), was aligned north-east/south-west. The grave was cut through the western edge of the early Roman ditches into the natural brick-earth to a depth of 0.45 m (c. 1 ft. 6 in.). The upper levels of the grave-pit and part of the upper skeleton were cut by a modern pit (112). This made it impossible to relate the burial to any of the phases so far discussed. The upper fill of the grave contained pottery dating to the second century. The swords (cavalry *spathae*) and fittings probably date to between the mid-second and the early third century. If this dating is correct, then it is impossible that the burial took place during the life of the timber building discussed above. The nature of the double burial, with the bodies thrown in rather than properly laid out in the grave, indicates a hurried interment. The unique find of two iron swords, apparently thrown into the grave immediately after the corpses (for such important pieces of military equipment were rarely placed in Roman burials) also suggests a hurried and possibly secretive deposition. A quern fragment found in the grave-fill may also indicate a relationship between the burial and the occupation-floors.

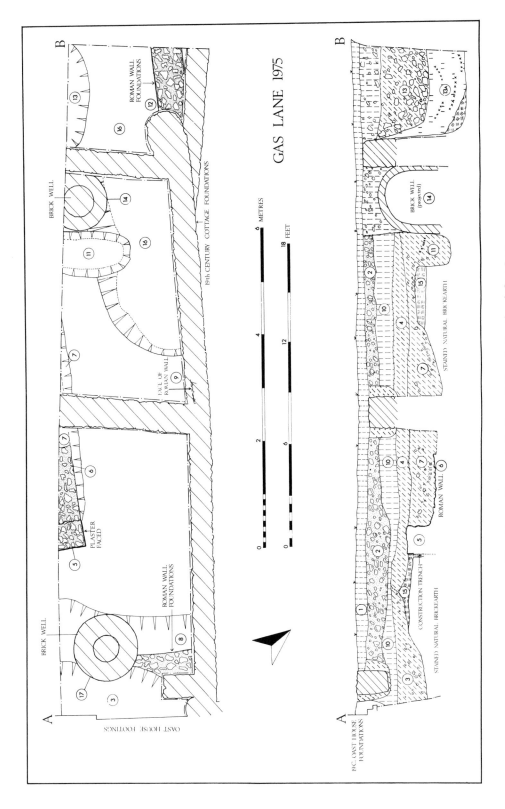

GAS LANE 1975

Fig. 11.   Plan and Section of Trench South of Gas Lane.

The upper corpse (102) was sealed by a deposit of back-brown silty loam (114, 121, 149, 153 and 175). The skeleton, that of an adult male of at least 30 years of age and about 1.73 m. (5 ft. 8½ in.) tall, was found lying on his left side with his head to the north-east and his feet to the south-west. Part of the head and the right hand had been cut away by the modern pit (112). A patch of iron-staining was found directly behind the head. The two swords and their fittings were found to the east of the upper corpse (102), overlying part of the lower skeleton (120). Both swords were intact and in their scabbards. The point of Sword II, covered by the remains of the scabbard and an ornate bronze chape (Fig. 100), was located 9 cm. (c. 4 in.) behind the head of corpse (102). The sword lay north-south and extended 0.98 m. (c 3 ft. 3 in.) from the point to the end of the tang, which was situated just below and 3 cm. (c. 1 in) to the west of the pelvis of the upper corpse. Sword I (Fig. 99) was located 9 cm. (c. 4 in.) to the east of Sword II, the tang to the north and the point with its iron chape to the south. Associated with the two swords was a number of belt-fittings. An ornate bronze belt-fitting, found 4 cm. (c. 2 in.) to the east of the tang of Sword I (Fig. 101, A). A second bronze fitting was found lying on the right humerus of the lower skeleton, 1 cm. (½ in.) to the east of Sword II. An iron fitting was found 2 cm. (1 in.) to the west of the handle of Sword II (Fig. 101, B); a further two iron objects were located 5 - 10 cm. (2 - 4 in.) to the east of Sword I, overlying the right hand of the lower corpse (Fig. 101, D and E).

The second skeleton (120), that of a male aged about 20 years and 1.815 m. (5 ft. 11½ in.) tall, was found face down with his head to the south and his legs twisted acutely to the east. The fragmentary remains of a pair of hobnailed boots were found associated with the feet of this skeleton (120), suggesting that he at least was partly clothed. No obvious cause of death came to light during the examination of the bones, but the very unusual nature of the burial could suggest murder, execution or perhaps a ritual killing as possibilities.

XIV. THE POST-ROMAN LEVELS (Area II. Fig. 13 — Plan)

In Area II, a very disturbed homogeneous layer of dark brown loam sealed all the latest Roman levels. A quantity of late Roman pottery and coins, together with eleventh- and twelfth-century pottery, were recovered from these levels. No material relating to the early or middle Saxon periods was found in Area I, II or in the trench south of Gas Lane. The same was true of Professor S.S. Frere's excavations inside the Keep itself, where apart from a few small sherds of early Saxon pottery there was the same lack of evidence (p. 48 below). It seems likely, therefore, that the area was abandoned by the fifth century, with the next phases of occupation beginning in the tenth or eleventh century, with indications of possible agricultural activity and traces of associated occupation in the form of pits and wells. In Area II, (Fig. 13, Plan), the north-east corner of the main trench and in the north-east extension, the latest Roman levels (110), were disturbed and had been sealed by a deposit of dark brown loamy silt (111, 130, 140 : Figs. 18, 20-22 and 26), containing pottery dating from the pre-Flavian period to the mid-third century or later. In the south-east corner of the main trench and in the south-east extension, the latest Roman level (118) was sealed by a similar deposit (104A, 104B, 104C, 115 : Fig. 13 — Plan, 119, 160 : Figs. 18-19 and 24-25), containing pottery dating from the pre-Flavian period to the fourth century.

The north-west and the two south-west extensions were sealed by a dark silty loam (100, 104

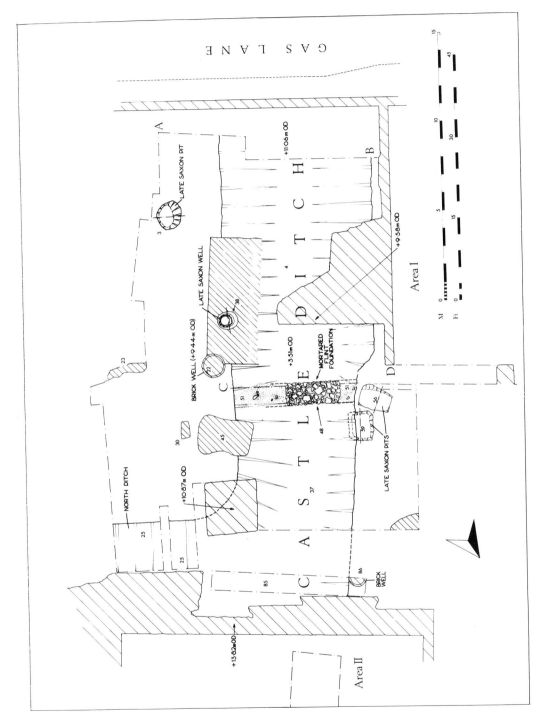

Fig. 12.   Plan of Area I — late Saxon and later Levels.

and 135 : Figs. 13 — Plan and 22). These deposits also contained a mixture of early and late Roman pottery. The latest Roman levels in the extreme south-west extension were sealed by a similar deposit (244 : Fig. 27) which contained pottery dating to the mid-second century. Eight coins dating from A.D. 270-345 were recovered from the post-Roman deposits in Area II.

XV. THE LATE SAXON PITS (Area I, Fig. 12 — Plan; Area II, Fig. 13 — Plan)

A number of late Saxon pits including two wells was located in Areas I and II. These may have been associated with the 43 or so houses mentioned in Domesday Book as having been destroyed prior to the laying out of the Royal Castle in the 1080s. In Area I (Fig. 12 — Plan), two rubbish pits were located close together on the western edge of the Castle ditch. One pit, (56 : Fig. 30) was cut by the Castle ditch and contained pottery, including a fragment of Pingsdorf ware, dating to the eleventh century (Fig. 86, no. 420). The second pit (59 : Fig. 30) was located 10 cm. (4 in.) to the west of the first. The upper levels of this pit were cut by a modern (gasworks) disturbance (49 and 58 : Fig. 15). The pit contained pottery dating to the early or mid-eleventh century and a large early Roman iron brooch (Fig. 87, no. 421). A third pit (3 : Fig. 30), also of an early mid eleventh-century date, was located east of the Castle ditch. A very interesting barrel-lined well (38 : Fig. 14) probably dating to the pre-Castle period, was found at the bottom of a large gasworks disturbance cutting the eastern edge of the Castle ditch. The uppermost levels of this pit, 1.35 m. (c. 4 ft. 6 in.) below the general clearance level and 8.09 m. (c. 26 ft. 6 in.) above O.D., consisted of two concentric circles of black tar pollution, one within the other. The innermost circle contained contaminated redeposited brick-earth. The outer ring also contained redeposited brick-earth but was less polluted. An outer discolouration suggested that the decomposed structures were set in an oval pit measuring 1.10 m. (c. 3 ft. 8 in.) by 0.95 m. (c. 3 ft.). Further excavation revealed the well-preserved remains of a circle of facing of interwoven branches surrounding a hooped wooden barrel. The pit was cut 1.32 m. (c. 4 ft. 4 in.) through the natural brick-earth and into the water-bearing gravel-terrace. The inner barrel survived to a height of 33 cm. (c. 1 ft.). This was composed of twelve vertical planks, each an average of 2 cm. (¾ in.) thick, and 17 cm. (c. 7 in.) wide, held together by three wooden hoops located 2 cm. (¾ in.), 15 cm. (6 in.) and 27 cm. (c. 11 in.) respectively from the bottom. The wooden slats were on average 6 cm. (2¼ in.) wide and 1 cm. (¼ in.) thick. The barrel was separated from the outer facing by redeposited brick-earth, probably deposited to prevent any contamination of the barrel well-chamber. The fencing was sub-circular and was constructed of double and single vertical posts on average 2 cm. (c. ¾ in.) in diameter and 0.55 m. (c. 2 ft.) long, and on average 13 cm. (c. 5 in.) apart. At least nine horizontal layers of withies were found woven around these verticals. Only one sherd of possible eleventh-century pottery was found in the well filling. A second possible barrel-lined well (152, 159 and 300 : Fig. 25) was found in Area II cutting the earlier Roman deposits in the south-east extension to the main trench. The well-shaft was cut 3.10 m. (c. 10 ft.) through the natural brick-earth and into the gravel-terrace. The lowest levels of the well (300), contained a jumbled mass of preserved wattling similar to those found in the other well (38). This deposit contained a number of intact vertical posts, on average 2 cm. (c. ¾ in.) in diameter and surviving to an average height of 0.50 m. (c. 1 ft. 8 in.). These posts lay on the circumference of the pit and were in part interwoven with at least sixteen layers of horizontal

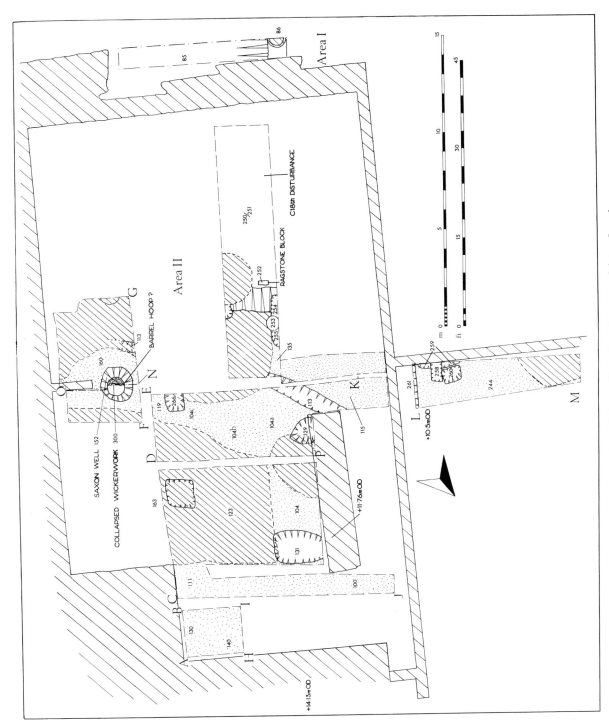

Fig. 13.   Plan of Area II — late Saxon and later Levels.

withies. This facing was filled with a mass of broken and partly decayed fragments of the upper facing. One fragment of wood, 0.50 m. (*c.* 1 ft. 8 in.) long, 4 cm. (1½ in.) wide and 2 cm. (*c.* ¾ in.) thick, may have been a fragment of hooping from a barrel. This deposit yielded early to mid-eleventh-century pottery. A layer of redeposited brick-earth sealed the organic deposit (159). This contained much residual Roman pottery, a silver *denarius* of Philip I (244-7), and part of a human foetus (Fig. 87, nos. 422-5). The upper levels of the well indicated that the barrel lining may have been extracted before the well-shaft was back-filled. The well-shaft diameter of some 1.03 m. (*c.* 3 ft. 6 in.) was widened to over 1.60 m. (*c.* 5 ft. 3 in.). These upper levels yielded quite large quantities of residual Roman pottery and a few sherds of early to mid-eleventh-century pottery.

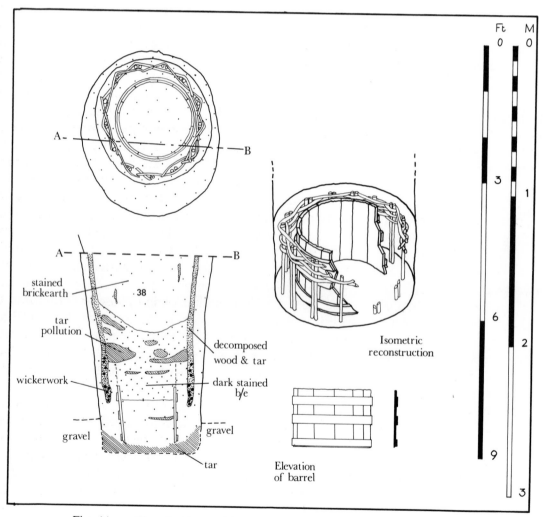

Fig. 14.   Plan, Section and isometric Reconstruction of ?late Saxon Well.

XVI. AREA III WITHIN THE NORTHERN OUTER BAILEY OF THE CASTLE (Fig. 3 — Plan)

The clearance of the gasworks foundations and rubble in Area III, (in the north-west corner of the Castle bailey), indicated that the archaeological levels had been completely destroyed, and that the surviving natural brick-earth had been badly contaminated by tar residues. Besides substantial and deeply embedded concrete foundations, three large brick tar-wells were found; these had leaked their contents over the years saturating the ground with toxic waste. No investigation of this area was therefore attempted. Only in Area I and in the small trench south of Gas Lane were features associated with the Castle excavated.

XVII. THE CASTLE DITCH (Fig. 2 — Plan, Fig. 12 — Plan)

In Area I a section of the large defensive Castle ditch (4, 4A, 4B, 4C, II and 37: Figs. 15 and 17) was excavated. A total length of some 20.50 m. (c. 67 ft. 6 in.) of ditch-fill was removed mechanically. Also the northern corner of the enclosure was located, with a small part of the return of the edge of the ditch being found (25). A small trench, 1 m. (c. 3 ft. 6 in.) wide and 8.90 m. (c. 29 ft.) long, was cut 2.6 m. (c. 8 ft. 6 in.) to the north of the main trench. The western edge of the Castle ditch (85) was found in this trench. Its position, directly below the massive and unstable foundations for part of the gasworks, did not allow total excavation. The alignment of this outer edge, however, did not seem to indicate an outer corner at this point. On the other side of the substantial gasworks foundations in Area II, a large, badly-polluted eighteenth-century disturbance (250 and 251) had effectively cut away any trace of the outer northern corner of the ditch. The position of the internal corner, however, suggests that the external ditch edge was situated just under or slightly to the north of the gasworks foundations. The natural brick-earth through which the ditch was cut is fairly water-resistant. The lowest levels of the ditch-fill (4C), a grey silt clay, may have accumulated in standing water. It is therefore suggested that at least part, if not all, of the ditch contained water at various times of the year.* The deposit yielded pottery dating to the twelfth century, a number of decorated Caen-stone blocks and a Purbeck marble column-base. These stones were probably thrown into the ditch during a construction and demolition phase and sank into the sediment at the bottom. Building-débris in quantity was found in the upper ditch-fills (4B and 4A). Cutting into this deposit, 12.5 m. (c. 41 ft.) north of the southern edge of the excavated area, was a curious mortared flint wall (Fig. 15, Section C - D and Fig. 13). During machine-clearance of the nineteenth-century back-filling (4) this wall was badly damaged. The remaining fragments of the upper parts (48 and 51) suggested that the foundations blocked the ditch completely to the level of gasworks disturbance + 9.44 m. O.D. (c. 31 ft. O.D.). At this point the ditch narrowed. The wall, 1.20 m. (c. 4 ft.) wide, was constructed of large fresh flints set in hard yellow mortar. The wall was too close to the north-west corner of the Castle defences to have been for a postern bridge and may have been constructed to regulate the level of water that collected in the ditch. The ditch silt was sealed by a deposit of grey clay (4B and 37) which contained a number of Caen-stone and sandstone blocks, but no datable finds. This

---

* The water-resistant nature of the brick-earth proved to be a considerable hindrance to excavation during the summer of 1976. The excavated ditch collected and retained water to such an extent that a pump was in continuous use.

deposit was sealed by a dump of grey loamy silt with tip-lines of fragmented mortar and building débris. This deposit was probably associated with the demolition of the Bailey wall in the late eighteenth century, or the attempted demolition of the Keep in 1817. The building débris was sealed by an homogeneous dump of dark brown loam associated with the final back-filling of the Castle ditch (4 and 11). In the small trench south of Gas Lane, levels possibly associated with the clearance of the area prior to the construction of the Royal Castle were excavated. These layers, (3, 4, 7, 11 and 17 : Fig. 11), dark brown loam mixed with Roman building débris, were possibly associated with the levelling of a Roman building (discussed above p. 43), and the use of the area for possible agricultural purposes after the construction of the Castle defences. These deposits contained pottery of the Roman period and of the eleventh to thirteenth centuries.

XVIII. OTHER MEDIEVAL AND POST-MEDIEVAL FEATURES

A number of medieval and post-medieval features was located in the small trench south of Gas Lane, and in Areas I and II. In the trench south of Gas Lane the earlier levels (3, 4, 7, 11 and 16) were sealed by a layer (10 : Fig. 11) of light brown loam. This layer contained both medieval and post-medieval pottery and may have accumulated during agricultural activity. It was sealed by a deposit of crushed mortar and flint (2), which may have been associated with the demolition of the Castle defences in the late-eighteenth and early-nineteenth centuries. Cutting and sealing this deposit were the mortared flint foundations of two cottages (formerly nos. 1 and 2 Gas Lane), and two brick wells. A rubbish pit (13) also cut into this level. In Area I two seventeenth-century pits were excavated (30 and 45 Fig 12 — Plan). These pits were probably cut at a time when a row of cottages stood on the site to the north of the Castle. Also associated with this occupation-phase were the two wells (22 and 86).

In Area II a greater number of medieval and post-medieval features was examined (Fig. 13 — Plan). In the south-west corner of the main trench a shallow gully (113) was located, cutting the upper Roman levels. This feature, possibly a field-boundary ditch, was aligned roughly north-west/south-east and was also partly located in the south-east extension to the main trench. The black loam fill of this feature contained a few sherds of pottery dated c. 1150-1170. A second small gully, again possibly a field boundary (261), was located at the eastern end of the extreme south-west extension to the main trench. This feature contained pottery dating from the mid- to late-twelfth century. In the extreme south-west extension to the main trench, a rubbish pit (259) was excavated containing thirteenth- to fifteenth-century pottery. Seven other rubbish pits were found to contain sixteenth- or seventeenth-century material, (131, 253, 254, 255, 258, 260 and 266). Many of these pits were perhaps associated with a small farm with hop fields, recorded in the City Account Book for farm rents for 1591-2. The earlier pits and features may also have been associated with agricultural activity. A large feature, which filled most of the southern extension to the main trench (250, 251 and 252) and was only partly excavated due to severe pollution, cut away all the archaeological levels in that area. This large disturbance contained a mass of organic material, mostly straw. It may have been a disused clay pit or even a pond that had been filled with farm-yard refuse. A second large feature, (123 : Fig. 18, 112, 112A, 117, 123, 133), which badly disturbed and cut away the levels in Area II, contained a mass of nineteenth-century material, and was probably associated with the gasworks.

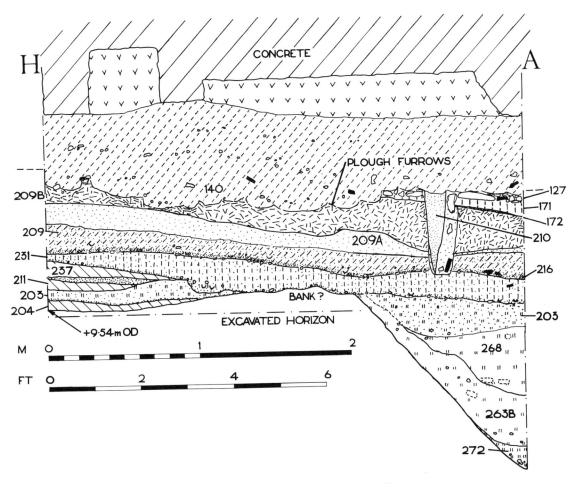

Fig. 20.   Sections H — A (Area II).

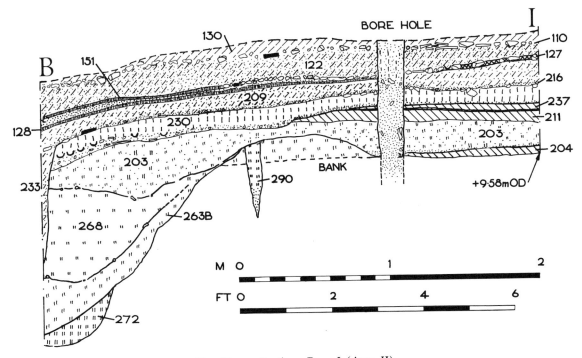

Fig. 21.   Sections B — I (Area II).

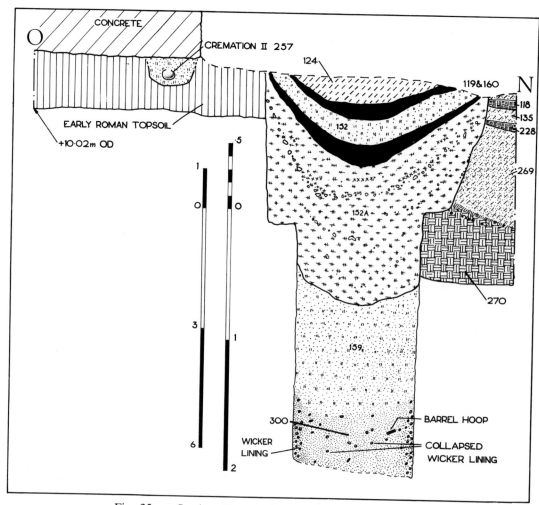

Fig. 25.   Sections O — N (late Saxon Well in Area II).

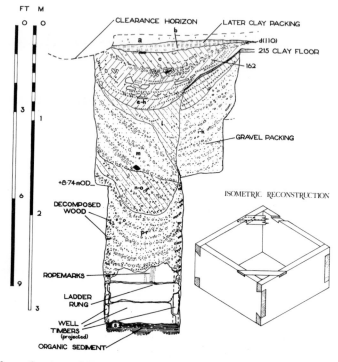

Fig. 26.   Section of Roman Well and isometric Reconstruction (Area II).

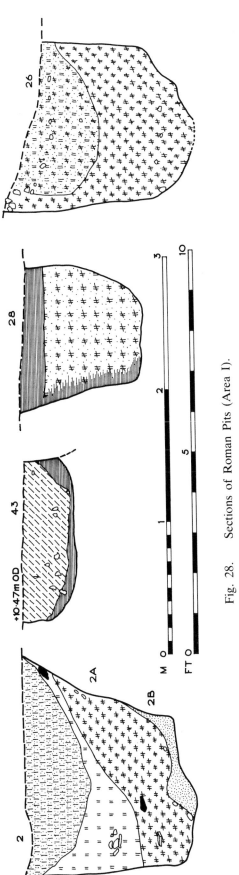

Fig. 28.   Sections of Roman Pits (Area I).

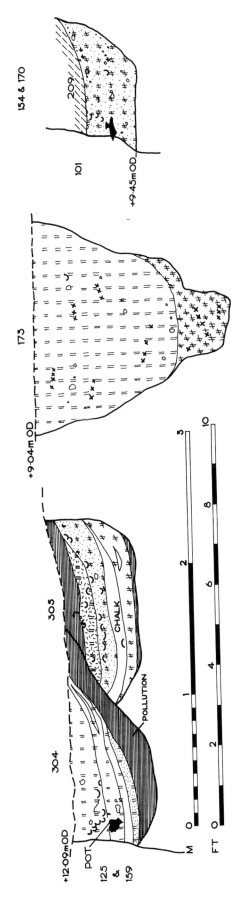

Fig. 29.   Sections of Roman Pits (Area II).

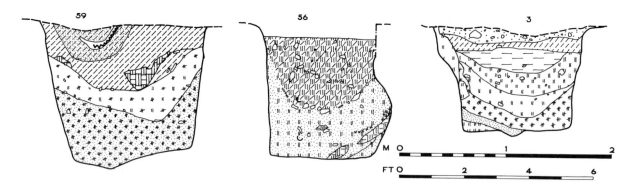

Fig. 30.   Sections of late Saxon Pits (Area I).

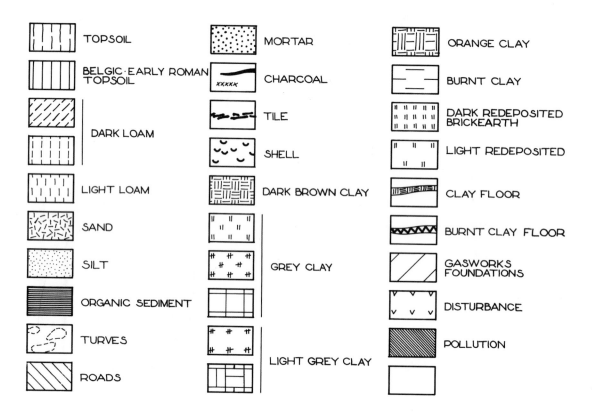

TOPSOIL	MORTAR	ORANGE CLAY
BELGIC·EARLY ROMAN TOPSOIL	CHARCOAL	BURNT CLAY
DARK LOAM	TILE	DARK REDEPOSITED BRICKEARTH
	SHELL	LIGHT REDEPOSITED
LIGHT LOAM	DARK BROWN CLAY	CLAY FLOOR
SAND	GREY CLAY	BURNT CLAY FLOOR
SILT		GASWORKS FOUNDATIONS
ORGANIC SEDIMENT	LIGHT GREY CLAY	DISTURBANCE
TURVES		POLLUTION
ROADS		

Fig. 31.   Soil Conventions.

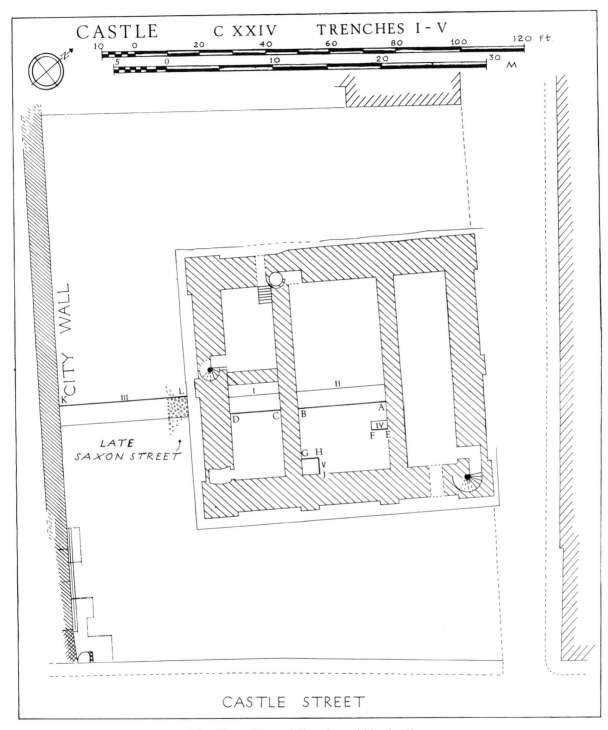

Fig. 32.   Plan of Trenches within the Keep.

EXCAVATIONS AT THE CASTLE KEEP

S.S. FRERE AND SALLY STOW[1]

Excavations took place at the Castle in 1953 and again in 1955.[2] Those of 1955 were directed to an examination of the city's defences and will be described in a subsequent volume dealing with the city wall. In 1953 also, one trench was dug between the Castle Keep and the city wall (Fig. 34); here it will be discussed only in so far as it relates to the Castle. The remaining trenches of 1953 were dug inside the Keep (Fig. 32) and form the subject of the present report.

The basement of the Keep is tripartite, being divided by two E-W cross-walls 1.68 m. (5 ft. 6 in.) wide. Because of modern rubbish accumulated in the north division, excavation was confined to the central and southern parts.

SUMMARY OF RESULTS

Where excavation extended below medieval levels, the first occupation on the site was found to be of the late-second or third century, but no obvious structures were found. The Saxon period is represented only by rubbish pits, but in the immediately pre-Castle period a thick occupation layer accumulated and several more pits were dug. The Castle was probably built at a date between c. 1100 and 1125, and wall-footings, walls and two floors of its basement were examined. By the late thirteenth to fourteenth century the building was falling into decay.

ROMAN

Only in Trench II (Fig. 33, Section A-B) was excavation taken down to the natural subsoil and here the earliest levels were Roman, not earlier than the late second century. No coherent structures were found. The earliest level, II 13, consisted of a thin layer of yellow loam and was taken to be a floor. It contained Central Gaulish samian of Antonine date (Dr 33). The floor was found only at the north end of the trench, elsewhere having been destroyed by later pits (Pits 5, 6, 7). A post-hole 6 in. square and 1 ft. deep was cut into it.

1. Miss Stow has been employed at Oxford, under a grant from the Department of the Environment, to study and prepare for publication the records of the excavations carried out between 1946 and 1957 by the Canterbury Excavation Committee under the direction of the first-named writer. Work on the Castle site was supervised by Miss M.G. Wilson.

2. Those of 1953 were coded 'C XXIV, Castle'; those of 1955 'C XXVIII, Castle' the first figures standing for the twenty-fourth and twenty-eighth season at Canterbury respectively. Excavations took place twice a year, and sometimes three times, and were numbered consecutively, individual sites being normally assigned a code letter, e.g. A or L.

Layer II 10 had likewise been largely destroyed by the later Pits 3 and 5 and was only found in the centre of the trench. It consisted of light brown soil with small pebbles, oysters and charcoal fragments, and is interpreted as the surface outside the building represented by floor 13. This layer also contained Antonine samian:

Dr 27	Central Gaulish	Hadrianic/Antonine
Dr 33	Central Gaulish	Antonine
Dr 37	Central Gaulish	A.D. 160-190 style of CETTVS

and a considerable quantity of coarse pottery which included a mortarium of the period A.D. 160-190 and a sherd of colour-coated beaker probably of early third-century date. It thus seems that II 13 and 10 are both of late second- to third-century date.

Layer II 9, consisting of grey soil with charcoal flecks which sealed II 10, was also found in Trench I (Fig. 33, Section C-D), there being the lowest level excavated (I 13). A coin of (?) Magnus Maximus (A.D. 383-88) was found in I 13 and thus I 13 and II 9 were probably deposited at the end of the fourth century. The pottery found, which included two necked jars of fourth-century date, supports this conclusion.

POST-ROMAN TO NORMAN

The layers above these deposits (I 12, II 11 and 8), although yielding for the most part only late-Roman pottery, probably cover the fifth and sixth centuries. Layer I 12, which sealed 13, consisted of black soil with burnt clay and charcoal flecks containing Roman building material and pottery of the fourth century including a flanged bowl in dark grey ware. Layer II 11, scattered cobbles and patches of yellow loam, contained one Saxon sherd and was sealed by II 8, a grey-black soil yielding Roman tile-fragments and residual pottery. Except for the occurrence of isolated sherds of Saxon pottery there is no evidence of further occupation in Trench I until the immediately pre-Castle period.

In Trench II a series of pits was found cut through the latest Roman levels (Fig. 33, Section A-B, Pits II 5, 6, 7). Of these, Pit 5 was filled with black soil becoming dark grey at the edges. A barbarous *Fel. Temp. Reparatio* coin of c. A.D. 360 could well be residual, as was clearly the coarse pottery in the pit, which was of second-century date. Pit II 7 had a shallow black filling. The only pottery recovered was a jar of early-Roman date. This pit was cut by Pit II 6, a small round rubbish-pit filled with black charcoally soil, bones and oysters. The latter produced two Saxon cooking-pot rims of approximately ninth-century date (Fig. 35, nos. 1-2) and several Saxon sherds.

PRE-CASTLE MEDIEVAL

In the immediately pre-Castle period a thick black sticky occupation-deposit containing charcoal flecks, burnt clay flecks, bones, slag and oysters accumulated over the whole area. This was found in all trenches (Fig. 33, Section C-D, I 11; Section A-B, II 6 and 7; Section E-F, IV 5; Section H-J, V 4), and suggests an increase of population in the immediate area.

It was into this layer that the Castle's foundations had been inserted. It yielded several

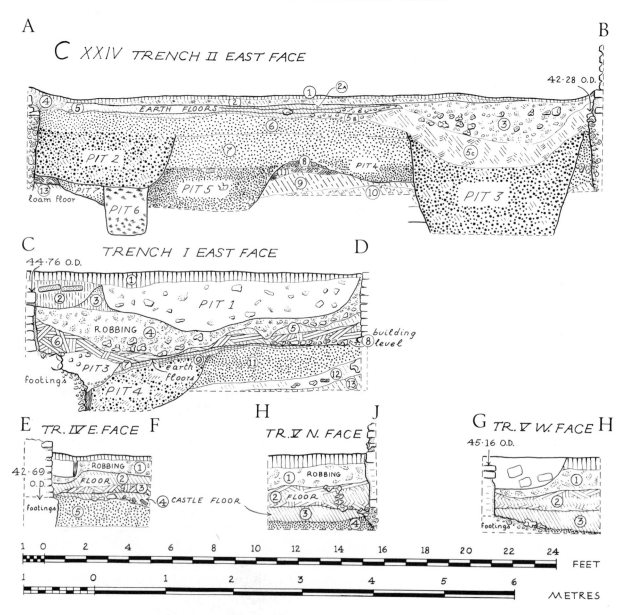

A

B

C XXIV TRENCH II EAST FACE

42·28 O.D.

④
⑤

EARTH FLOORS

②

①

②A

⑤B

③

⑥

PIT 2

⑦

⑤c

PIT 4

⑧

⑨

PIT 5

⑩

PIT 3

⑬

PIT 7

loam floor

PIT 6

C

TRENCH I EAST FACE

D

44·76 O.D.

①

②

③

PIT 1

ROBBING

④

⑤

building
level

⑥

⑧

⑨

⑦

earth
floors

⑪

PIT 3

⑫

footings

PIT 4

⑬

E TR. IV E. FACE F

H

TR. V N. FACE

J

G TR. V W. FACE H

ROBBING

①

45·16 O.D.

42·69
O.D.

FLOOR

②

③

④ CASTLE FLOOR

①

ROBBING

①

footings

⑤

②

FLOOR

②

③

③

④

footings

Fig. 33.   Section of Trenches within the Keep.

sherds of early medieval pottery which can be assigned to the mid eleventh- to early twelfth-century Groups II and III identified in the Rose Lane Report (*Arch. Cant.*, lxviii (1954), 128-38), as well as some residual Saxon pottery of earlier date. Twelve sherds were of Group II type (provisionally dated *c.* 1050-1100) and five of Group III (*c.* 1080-1150) (Fig. 35, nos. 3-25). The evidence of the pottery, though at present lacking complete precision, goes far to comfirm other evidence (p. 66) that the existing Keep was erected after 1100.

Several pits which cut through the black occupation layer but pre-dated the building of the Castle were also found (Fig. 33, Section C-D, Pit I 4; Section A-B, Pits II 4, 2, 3). Pit I 4, filled with red ash and black sticky earth, was cut into layer I 11 at the north end of the trench, but antedated the footings of the south cross-wall which were cut into it. Pit II 4 was a scoop in II 7 in the centre of the trench; the fillings were not easily distinguishable. Pit II 2 at the north end of the trench seemed to be sealed by 6 which was the upper part of the pre-Castle occupation layer. It was a black-filled pit containing lumps of yellow loam, bones, charcoal and a dump of mussel shells. It produced cooking-pot sherds of Group II or earlier and a residual Jutish cooking-pot of the fifth century (Fig. 35, no. 21). Pit II 3 was cut through layers 6 and 7. It was deep and filled with black soil and lumps of yellow loam. It yielded cooking-pots of Group III (Fig. 35, nos. 22-24) and one possibly of later type (no. 25).

These pits and the black occupation-layer were sealed by the floors of the basement of the Keep; pottery recovered from them and from the Castle building-layers should provide a *terminus post quem* for the construction of the Castle.

Documentary evidence bearing on the date of the erection of the Keep is very deficient; the problems are discussed by Dr. D.F. Renn on pp. 70-7. The pottery evidence is in agreement with a date of about or soon after 1100 (see p. 66).

THE KEEP

Walls. The walls proper were 2.79 m. (9 ft. 2 in.) thick, built of rubble with Caen-stone dressing. There is a plain chamfered plinth at the base externally (Fig. 34, Section K-L). This plinth on the south side added a further 1.12 m. (3 ft. 8 in.) of thickness and on the east side 1.68 m. (5 ft. 6 in.).

Floors. Two successive floors, belonging to the basement of the Keep, were excavated. The earlier, Floor I, extended over the footings of both the outer walls and the cross-walls (Fig. 33, Section E-F, IV 4; Sections G-H, H-J, V 3). It thus seems that the outside walls of the Keep and the cross-walls were erected at the same time. The floor consisted of yellow loam mixed with closely-packed flints *c.* 6 in. in diameter and pieces of Roman tile *c.* 8 in. across. The pottery found in Floor I consisted of a sherd of Group II and two rims with finger-printing which may be of twelfth-century date (Fig. 36, nos. 30-32).

A dark sticky occupation-layer mixed with large pebbles and Roman tile-fragments accumulated over Floor I in places (Fig. 33, Section E-F, IV 3), above which lay Floor 2 (Fig. 33, Section E-F, IV 2; Sections G-H, H-J, V 2). This floor consisted of dirty yellow-brown loam. The only pottery found in it was Fig. 36, nos. 39-40, the latter probably belonging to the later twelfth century.

In Trenches I and II the floor-levels were less clear and it was difficult to see their relationship with the walls. The earliest floor encountered in Trench I (Fig. 33, Section C-D) consisted of a 2-in. layer of loam, I 9, which was overlaid by a second loam-and-gravel floor (I 7). These surfaces probably correspond with the two floors already discussed although they are much thinner. They both sloped down into Pit I 4 and were cut away at the north end of the trench next to the south cross-wall by Pit I 3, which also cut off the top of the footings of the cross-wall. This pit was filled with black soil and a few large gravel pebbles; it yielded pottery of Group II and of Group III type (Fig. 36, nos. 41-45).

At the south end of the trench Floor I 7 was replaced for the last 1.67 m. (5 ft. 6 in.) by a flint surface (I 8) which extended up to the Keep wall. An occupation-layer of black sticky soil

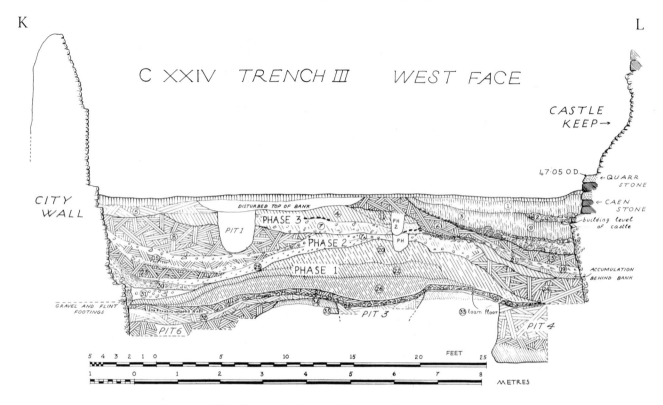

Fig. 34.   Section south-west of the Keep.

(I 6) with charcoal and burnt clay flecks overlay I 7, I 8 and Pit 3, and yielded a sherd of Group II type and another jar (Fig. 36, nos. 46-47). It was overlaid by a layer of yellow and grey sticky loam (I 5), which existed only at the south end of the trench and had been much disturbed by later robbing. A square-cut pit (Pit I 2, which did not extend to the section) was filled with material indistinguishable from I 5 and was cut through layers 6, 7 and 8; it was presumably contemporary with I 5.

In Trench II (Fig. 33, Section A-B) several floors were recognized, but again their relationship with the walls was not apparent since at the north end of the trench they were replaced by a layer of black soil (II 4), 6 in. thick, which overlay the cross-wall offset, and at the south end by a thick mortar layer (II 3) which filled a hollow which had presumably resulted from subsidence into Pit 3. The earliest floor (II 5B) consisted of earth and stones; it sank down deeply over Pit 3 and the finds from this part of it are labelled 5C. All the relevant pottery was of Group II or Group III type (Fig. 36, nos. 33-38), except one finger-printed rim which may be of early twelfth-century date (no. 37). Directly above this in the centre of the trench was another surface of gravel and earth (II 5), sealed by a yellow loam floor (II 2A) in which shell and charcoal fragments occurred. The top of this floor was somewhat disturbed in the centre of the trench where it is labelled 2. It produced pottery of the second half of the thirteenth century together with some modern glass.

TRENCH III OUTSIDE SOUTH WALL OF KEEP

The main purpose of this trench was to examine the City defences, and this aspect of the excavation will be described in a subsequent volume. The bulk of the section was occupied by tips of material forming the rampart behind the Roman city wall. Overlying the tail of this rampart was a street of late Saxon date (Fig. 34, Section K-L, 10), above which were layers associated with the Castle.

STREET

Directly above the latest Roman layer (13) was one of compact clean gravel (14) intermixed with clean yellow loam. This was clearly make-up for a cobbled surface (10) above. The cobbles ended on a straight line 1.88 m. (*c*. 6 ft. 2 in.) south of, and parallel to, the wall of the Castle by which they were cut. The street consisted of flints *c*. 6 in. in diameter, and smaller flints and pebbles. It lay to the north of and extended slightly over layer 12, which contained a sherd probably of Group II type and a Saxon tubular spout (Fig. 35, nos. 26-27).

Above the cobbled surface was a layer of dark brown fine soil with some large loose flints (9). This was probably upcast from the foundation-trench of the south wall of the Castle Keep. In addition to residual Saxon pottery it yielded two sherds (Fig. 35, no. 28) of Group II. Above this, extending 1.06 m. (3 ft. 6 in.) south from the Keep wall, was a compact level surface of building débris (2) from the Keep, the wall of which was trench-built below this level. This layer yielded a rim of Group II type.

CASTLE DESTRUCTION

Overlying and sealing the basement floors of the Keep was a thickish layer of yellow mortary débris and building material, mixed with mud and bones etc. (Fig. 33, Section C-D, I 4; Sections E-F, G-H, H-J, 1). This presumably accumulated as a result of collapses and robbings of the Castle walls. It covered the occupation levels everywhere except where modern pits and disturbance intervened, but it was not obvious in Trench II, where the ground-level had been lowered 0.91 m. (*c*. 3 ft.) below that surviving elsewhere. The only pottery recovered from the débris-layers was in Trench I 4, which yielded sherds of twelfth- and thirteenth-century date (Fig. 36, nos. 48-51).

The sole later features worthy of note uncovered in the excavations were a gully (2) at the north end of Trench I next to the wall, and a large shallow pit (Pit I 1) to the south of it (Fig. 33, Section C-D). The gully was filled with dark sticky soil and was capped with flat paving stones which looked modern. The pit contained lumps of loam and building débris from the walls, eighteenth-century bricks and modern glass.

From the pottery found in the Castle débris-layers it seems that the Keep was falling into decay probably by the second half of the thirteenth century at the latest. Documentary evidence, which provides records of expenditure on the Castle, shows that it was not being maintained in any large degree after the mid-thirteenth century and that by the fourteenth century it was in a state of very poor repair.

In 1190-1193 £177 4*s*. 1*d*. was spent on it (cf. Pipe Roll 3-4 Richard I, 112, 307; 5 Richard I,

165). For the next 20 years it was regularly repaired by the sheriff. In 1218-19 £30 was spent (cf. Pipe Roll 4 Henry III, rot. 12). In 1221 a new chamber was built beside the Keep (cf. Rot. Litt. Claus. I, 447b). In 1237-38 £47 16s. 6d. was spent on the King's Hall. After this date the amount spent on the Castle was negligible. In 1264 the Great Gateway was damaged by fire and repaired at a cost of £10 14s. 8d. Under Edwards I and II only very minor repairs were undertaken and an inquiry held in 1335 described progressive deterioration of the Castle. In 1329 the bridge had collapsed through lack of repair and in 1330 the kitchen blew down. Nothing was done to remedy this state of affairs and the total expenditure in the next 50 years was less than £2 (cf. Pipe Roll 12 Edward III, rot. 10d; 29 Edward III, rot. 11). In 1390 £200 was recorded as being set aside for repairs to the Keep. But the money never appeared and the work was not done (cf. Cal. Pat. Rolls 1392-6, 45, 240).

The Castle continued to be used throughout the fifteenth century as a prison, and £2.10s. was spent on it in 1406-7. But there are no further records of any attempt to maintain it.[3]

THE POTTERY

The majority of the pottery found sealed beneath the Castle is of types which are closely akin to those classified under Groups I, II and III in the report on some pits in Rose Lane (*Arch. Cant.*, lxviii (1954), 128 ff.). Of these Group I is pre-Conquest (probably early eleventh century), Group II can be provisionally dated *c.* 1050-1100 and Group III *c.* 1080-1150. The pottery found stratified below Lanfranc's Dormitory in the Precincts shows that Group III types had hardly appeared by the date of the erection of that building, and thus gives an approximate divide between the two.

Some sherds from the earliest floor of the basement of the Keep (nos. 30, 31, 37) are of types reminiscent of Groups II and III but with finger-printing along the top or outside of the lip. Two similar sherds (nos. 13, 14) were found below the floor. Finger-printing was absent from the vessels originally published as Groups II and III, but it occurs on two vessels in a pit below Lanfranc's Dormitory which are otherwise of Group II type, and so can be shown to appear before *c.* 1080, but was used sparingly at first. From a later floor comes a sherd (no. 40) with applied bands, a form of decoration which later became very common in the thirteenth century.

In the layers below the floors pottery of Group II amounted to 70 per cent of that present and Group III 30 per cent. In the floors themselves Group II has fallen to 50 per cent.

---

3.   This summary of documentary evidence is taken from H.M. Colvin, *The History of the King's Works* (London, 1963).

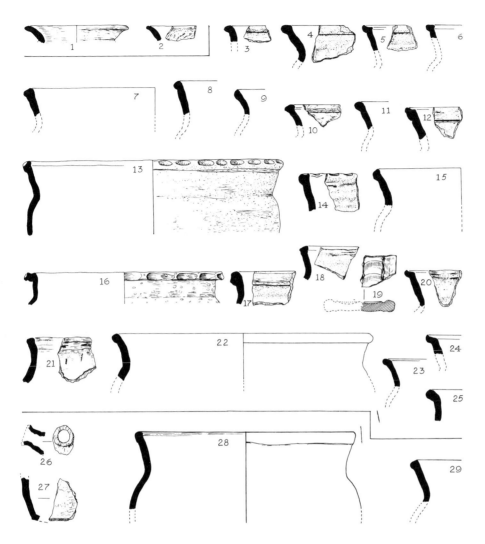

Fig. 35.   Pottery from the Keep (¼).

DESCRIPTION OF POTTERY

M.G. Wilson

Nos. 1-2 Post-Roman to Norman

FIG. 35

1.   Saxon cooking-pot in hard rather finely granular grey-black burnished ware, *c.* ninth-century. Pit II 6.

2.   As no. 1 in hard rather finely granular buff ware, grey core, Pit II 6. These sherds resemble vessels of late ninth-century date from Canterbury Lane.

Nos. 3-25 Pre-Castle medieval

3. Hard granular red-buff ware, grey core. Group II type. Also another rim similar to no. 6 in red-grey ware, and a Saxon rim as no. 1. I 11.

4-5. Hard rather finely granular light reddish ware, grey core. Group III type. II 6.

6. Hard rather finely granular grey ware. Group III type. II 6.

7. Hard granular reddish ware, two. Group II type. II 6.

8-9. As no. 7, grey. Group II types. II 6.

10. Grey ware with fine shell grit. II 6.

11. Hard granular light grey-buff ware. Group II type. II 6.

12. As no. 11, grey. II 6.

13. As no. 11, with finger-impressions on rim. Similar to Group II type save for ornament. II 6.

14. Hard granular reddish ware, grey core, with finger-impressions on rim. II 6.

15. Hard granular light grey-brown ware. Group II type. II 6.

16. Rather coarse light grey shell-gritted ware, with finger-impressions on rim. II 6. This type is different in shape and ware from Group III and is presumably early twelfth-century, if it is not a rather later stray, intrusive in this layer.

17. Hard rather finely granular dull reddish ware, grey core. IV 5.

18. As no. 17, light grey. Group II type. IV 5.

19. Jug handle fragment with finger-impressions, in hard very finely granular light grey ware, with some larger grey and white grits, covered with good pale green glaze. IV 5.

20. Hard granular grey ware. Group III type. V 4.

21. Jutish cooking pot, handmade in finely granular grey ware, rather uneven smoothly burnished surfaces. Fifth-century. Pit II 2.

22-3. Hard granular red-grey ware. Groups II (no. 22) and III types. Pit II 3.

24. As no. 22, reddish with grey core. Group III type. Pit II 3.

25. As no. 22; rim curved out; possibly later than Group III. Another rim similar to no. 33 was present. Pit II 3.

Nos. 26-9 Outside south wall of Keep

26. Saxon tubular spout, broken at both ends, in rather finely granular grey-brown ware. III 12.

27. Base sherd of cooking-pot in hard granular light grey ware, knife-trimmed at bottom. III 12. This type of smoothing is found on Group I

(pre-Conquest) and Group II vessels.

28. Hard granular grey-buff ware, (Group II type) and shoulder sherd of another cooking pot. III 9.

29. As no. 28, light grey. Group II type. III 2A.

Nos. 30-47 The Keep Floors
FIG. 36

30. Hard rather finely granular red-buff ware, grey core, with slight finger-impressions on rim. Type perhaps later than Group III. IV 4.

31. As no. 30, buff. Type perhaps later than Group III. V 3.

32. Hard granular light grey-buff ware. Group II type. V 3.

33. Hard granular reddish ware. Group II type. II 5B.

34. Hard granular grey ware. Group III type. II 5B.

35. Sherd in ware similar to no. 34, marked with scored lines. II 5B.

36. As no. 34. Akin to Group II. II 5B.

37. As no. 30. Type perhaps later than Group III. II 5C.

38. hard rather finely granular red-grey ware. Group II type. II 5C.

39. Hard granular red-buff ware, grey core. Group III type. V 2.

40. Hard rather finely granular light grey ware, with crossed finger-impressed applied strips. V 2. Both ware and the character of the strips differ from the type normal in Canterbury in the thirteenth century. For applied strips on twelfth-century pottery cf. G.C. Dunning in *Proc. Isle of Wight Nat. Hist. and Arch. Soc.,* VIII (1937).

41. Hard granular light red-grey ware. Group II type. Pit I 3.

42. As no. 41, grey. Group II type. Pit I 3.

43. As no. 41, light grey-brown. Group III type. Pit I 3.

44. As no. 41. Group II type. Pit I 3.

45. As no. 41, light grey-brown. Group III type. Pit I 3.

46-7. Hard granular grey ware. I 6.

Nos. 48-51. Castle destruction.

48. Sherd in very finely granular white ware with regular wheelmarks inside, the outside covered in good yellow glaze, from a jar in Andenne ware. Cf. Borremans et Lassance, *Archaeologia Belgica,* 32 (1956), pl. L 1-5. A whole vessel of this type was found in Canterbury with twelfth-

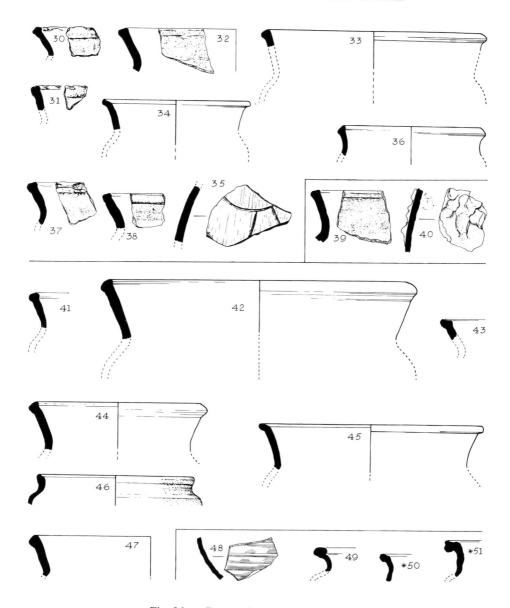

Fig. 36.   Pottery from the Keep (¼).

century pottery, smaller pieces with twelfth and
thirteenth. Twelfth to thirteenth century (Information supplied by Dr. G.C. Dunning). I 4.

49.   Hard granular reddish ware, well made. Thirteenth century. I4.

50.*   A rim of this type in granular reddish ware with
some fine shell grit. Thirteenth Century. I 4.

51.*   A rim of this type in coarse red-grey shell-
gritted ware, and a vertical finger-impressed strip
from a smaller pot. Thirteenth century. I 4.

*These two sherds were not drawn. The illustrations
are taken from the type-series.

CANTERBURY CASTLE IN THE EARLY MIDDLE AGES

D.F. Renn

We do not know exactly when the Castle at Canterbury was founded, nor when its stone keep was built, but reasonably narrow date brackets may be suggested from the documentary history and from the archaeological evidence of the structure.

FOUNDATION

Like nearly all castles in England, that at Canterbury was almost certainly a post-Conquest foundation. A castle here is mentioned in Domesday Book,[4] so that its date must be between 1066 and 1086. This castle may well have been erected originally as a temporary fort by the Normans after Canterbury had been surrendered in October 1066.[5] William the Conqueror, having left Dover, was taken ill at the 'Broken Tower' but moved on to camp elsewhere. It is not clear where this tower stood; no doubt at this time any of the Roman Saxon Shore forts would have presented at least one 'broken tower' to the invaders. But, since only one tower is mentioned, it must have been either isolated or predominant. Perhaps it was the other Roman lighthouse on the Western Heights of Dover.

The obvious route for an advance from Dover to London was along the line of the Roman road, with Canterbury at its nodal point, one day's march from the coast. Throughout the invasion it was William's habit to protect his forces by finding some existing fortification, be it prehistoric, Roman or Saxon, and adapting it to his needs by reducing its area with a new bank and ditch, so creating a smaller fortress usually adjacent to the river or sea (e.g., at Pevensey, Hastings, Dover, Wallingford and London). If the Conqueror did build such a fort at Canterbury, the obvious place was the southern angle of the Roman city, where the river and the remains of the city wall provided defences on two sides against any attack from the direction of London and also gave immediate access to the roads leading back to the Channel coast.

The Conqueror also founded a number of castles in shire towns in order to control any local unrest or to resist an invasion. The deposition of Archbishop Stigand in 1070, the arrest in 1082 of Odo, Bishop of Bayeux and a large land-holder in Kent, or the threatened Scandinavian invasion of 1083 - 85 might have been the initial cause of the building of the first Canterbury Castle. It has been argued[6] that the Dane John mound, some 250 m. (800 ft.) east-south-east of the stone keep, was the site of the original castle. The mound is now practically the only visible survivor of a group of eight or more mounds which stood to the east

4. *Domesday Book* ed. A. Farley (London, 1783), 1, f. 2r.
5. The campaign has been reconsidered in detail by D.C. Douglas, *William the Conqueror*, London, 1969, Appendix D; R.A. Brown, *The Normans and the Norman Conquest*, London and New York, 1969, 177; C. Morton and H. Muntz, *The Carmen de Hastingae Proelio of Guy, Bishop of Amiens*, Oxford, 1972 p. xlvi etc. William cannot have spent long at Canterbury; his known movements in November and December refute the tale of a month elapsing between his leaving Dover and his initial attack on London.
6. For instance: E.S. Armitage, *The Early Norman Castles of the British Isles* London, 1912, 116 - 8.

of the city on a Roman burial ground of which they probably formed part.[7] The present shape
of the Dane John is misleading, since it was heightened by over 5 m. (16 ft. 6 in.) in 1790 with
material scraped from its sides and the surrounding ditch filled in; but certainly, whatever its
pre-Conquest shape and size, it would have provided an obvious base for the *motte* of a
Norman motte and bailey Castle.[8]

Domesday Book, analysing the reduction of the number of burgesses in Canterbury
rendering to the King from 51 *T.R.E.* to 19 in 1086 says:[9]

*et xxxij. aliis qui fuerant sunt vastati xj in fossato civitatis. Et archiepiscopus habet ex eis vij, et
abbas S. Augustini aliis xiv pro excambio castelli.*

The St. Augustine's Abbey version[10] is:

*sed modo sunt xxxij burgenses minus propter escambium castelli . . . archiepiscopi vij et abbas
sei Augustini xiv et xj sunt perditi infra fossatum castelli*

Urry[11] prints two versions of a list of eleven tenants of St. Augustine's whose holdings were
exchanged with the King for the churches of St. Andrew and St. Mary *sub castellum* by 1087;
these may be the eleven holdings subsequently destroyed by the Castle ditch mentioned above,
or they may represent a separate destruction.[12] *Prima facie* this evidence suggests a ratio of
either 1:2 or 1:3 for the relative areas covered by the ditch and by the enclosed area of the first
castle, perhaps covering some 5 per cent of the populated area of Canterbury outside the
ecclesiastical precincts. Bearing in mind that the southern area seems to have been well
populated (although perhaps no-one actually lived on the Dane John), this indicates that the
Castle covered a fairly large area, perhaps 200 m. each way (4 ha.), but hardly one which
included the sites of both the Dane John *and* the stone Keep. The Dane John does not appear
to have been within the boundary of the later castle,[13] and Canterbury Castle has a number of
analogies with that of Le Mans.

That the Castle site was moved[14] to the neighbourhood of St. Mildred's church by 1089 is
clear from an incident described in the Parker Chronicle.[15] After the death of Abbot Scotland
in September 1087, the monks refused to accept Lanfranc's nominee. Some of them were
therefore imprisoned in the Castle (*in castellum duci ubique incarcere custodiri praecepit*), an
early instance of the function that Canterbury Castle was to fulfil throughout its life. The rest

7. *Archaeological Journal*, lxxxvi (1930), 236 - 7, 272 - 5; W. Urry, *Canterbury Under the Angevin Kings*,
    London, 1967, 200. This book, (hereafter cited as Urry), is essential to an understanding of the topography of
    Canterbury.
8. Such re-use has been demonstrated elsewhere, for instance at York.
9. See note 4.
10. White Book of St. Augustine's (PRO E 164/27 f. 22r). edited by A. Ballard as *An Eleventh Century Inquisition
    of St. Augustine's Canterbury* in the British Academy series of *Records of the Social and Economic History of
    England and Wales*, Oxford, 1920, IV, Part II, 7, 9.
11. PRO E 164/27 f.15v. and BM Royal MS.1B xi f. 146v. printed by Urry, p. 445.
12. Urry, 214 - 5.
13. Urry's map 2 sheet 8 indicates the likely waste area *c.* 1200.
14. A not uncommon event; see *Antiquity*, xxxiii (1959), 106 - 12.
15. Corpus Christi College Cambridge MS. 173, the Anglo-Saxon Chronicle MS.A printed in C. Plummer, *Two of
    the Anglo-Saxon Chronicles Parallel*, Oxford, 1892 - 3. The Latin edition with which we are concerned (Vol. I,
    290) was added to the chronicle after it had been removed to Canterbury from Winchester.

of the monks, expelled for their contumacy, seem to have picketed the Castle (*sub castro secus aecclesiam Sanctae Miltrudae consedisse*). But by dinner-time they became hungry and submitted to Lanfranc, whose nominee was consecrated in 1089.[16]

A charter of Anselm, which can be dated to between 1095 and 1107, refers to lands near the *castellum novem,* so that it was clearly a new site, not an extension of the old. Although the Dane John was never called the 'old Castle', its first mention in a rental of very close to the year 1200 *(vicum qui ducit uersus Danjun)*[17] shows that it was then regarded, either seriously or jokingly, as the *dunjo* or *donjon,*[18] the modern equivalent being either *motte* or keep. Another rental, at most only a few years later, refers twice to the bailey ditch (*fossa del bali*) outside Worthgate.[19]

THE STONE KEEP

Whereas the charters of 1095 - 1107 refer to the *castellum* of Canterbury, those of *c.* 1175 refer to the *turris.*[20] Armitage[21] suggested that the Keep was built in the early 1170s using the revenues confiscated from the archiepiscopal estates during the Becket quarrel, but Colvin[22] points out that in fact the revenues were fully accounted for, and no mention is made of work on the Castle, and that the small payments recorded elsewhere on the Pipe Rolls (see below) are insufficient for the building of such a large keep as Canterbury; they probably relate to some smaller works, perhaps an addition to the defences. Indeed, the local as well as the international feeling aroused by the murder of Becket in 1170 would have made any *new* show of royal power in Canterbury politically impossible. At the very least, one of Becket's hagiographers would certainly have mentioned it. Since the Castle was always a royal one, the lack of any reference to any really substantial expenditure (which in contemporary terms means over £100 per year) in the Pipe Rolls, puts the date of foundation — and indeed of substantial completion of the Keep back to before 1154 – 55, when the continuous series of the Rolls begins.

Failing documentary evidence, we next turn to the evidence of the structure itself. Built mainly of ragstone rubble, the Keep retains fragmentary courses of Caen and Quarr ashlar, the latter being predominant in the plinth courses which survive on part of the south-west face of the Keep (Fig. 46). Mr. Tatton-Brown has pointed out to me that Quarr stone is much used for string courses in eleventh-century parts of the Cathedral. The Isle of Wight escheated to the Crown between 1071 and 1101, but no doubt Quarr for a royal castle could have been obtained outside those dates.

Canterbury Keep has a number of resemblances to that at Bamburgh in Northumberland, in particular in its moulded plinth. Bamburgh is considered to have been built after 1095, perhaps

16.   W. Somner, *A History of Canterbury*, ed. N. Batteley, London, 1703, 19, tells the story slightly differently, see also Urry, 208.
17.   Chapter Archives, register H, printed by Urry, 275.
18.   *Revised Medieval Latin Word List from British and Irish Sources*, ed. R.E. Latham, Oxford, 1965, 159 s.v. *dun/jo*. For the definition, see R.A. Brown, *English Castles*, Third edition, London, 1976, 18, 32.
19.   Urry, 195, 337, 360. (Chapter Archives, register H, rental F 233, 504).
20.   *Ibid.*, 386 - 7, 423 (Charters II, III, XLVII).
21.   *Op. cit.* in note 6, 120, note 2.
22.   H.M. Colvin, *The History of the King's Works: the Middle Ages II*, London, 1963 588, note 7.

as late as the reign of Stephen;[23] like Canterbury, the Pipe Roll evidence is insufficient to support a late twelfth-century building date at Bamburgh. At Canterbury the only other ornamental detail *in situ* is the chevron carving on some of the window voussoirs, which are not closely dateable. Edward King[24] illustrates a very remarkable window with chevron carving not only on the voussoirs but also running down the tympanum, but in view of demonstrable inaccuracies elsewhere in his writings, it would be dangerous to rely on his unsupported evidence here. Heavily-carved chevron ornament occurs round hall windows at Christchurch, Durham and Sherborne Castles in the early twelfth century. When I visited Canterbury in about 1955, I photographed a loose fragment of a classic capital lying beside the remaining fragment of the moulded plinth.

Tall domed fire-places with short tapering chimney flues like those at Canterbury occur in the keeps of Norwich and Castle Rising (Norfolk, 1120s and 1130s, respectively). The central main entrance doorway at Canterbury appears to be unique in Britain, since the central doorways at Castle Sween (Argyll) and Guildford (Surrey), are placed in buttress-like projections. There is some general resemblance between Canterbury and Domfront (Orne, attributed to Henry I, 1100 - 35)[25] and the similarity of position of the secondary (north-west) doorway at Colchester (Essex) could support the hypothesis of a defensive triangle with London protecting the south-east of England in the 1080s against an attack from Scandinavia. But perhaps the vital clue lies in the positioning of the crosswalls at Canterbury. The subdivision of the interior of any large building which lacked vaulting was necessary because of the difficulty in obtaining straight timber for floor or roof joists more than say 6 m. (20 ft.) long. The internal arcades or walls are nearly always parallel to the longer axis of the building, to provide two or three long 'aisles', perhaps with a short cross-aisle at one end. Apart from Canterbury, only Corfe (Dorset, about 1105)[26] seems to have had two crosswalls at right angles to the long axis of the keep rather than parallel to it.

The early history of Rochester Castle provides some circumstantial evidence for the rebuilding of Canterbury in stone. Gundulph, Bishop of Rochester, in order to retain a valuable manor, was constrained to build a new stone castle there for the new King William II before Lanfranc's death (i.e., between 1087 - 89).[27] In 1127 King Henry I granted the custody and the constableship of the Castle to the Archbishop of Canterbury, with permission to build a tower or fortification within it, which the Archbishop had duly begun by 1129.[28] A plausible explanation is that Canterbury Castle had got its stone keep by 1127, being put up while the archbishopric was vacant between 1109 and 1114, and Henry I then mollified the archbishop for the fortification on his archiepiscopal doorstep (so to speak) by granting him a building lease in the other royal castle at Rochester. Certainly, Rochester represents a typological advance on Canterbury Keep, with a properly integrated fore-building, and the multiple steps to the window openings with half-shafted jambs used only in minor places.

So, the indirect evidence suggests that the stone keep at Canterbury was designed between about 1085 and 1125.

23.   *Ibid.*, 554 - 5, note 2.
24.   *Archaeologia*, vi (1782), pl. XXXVIII, facing p. 303.
25.   *Chronicles of the Reigns of Stephen*, London, 1889, LV, 107, 126.
26.   Royal Commission on Historic Monuments: *South-east Dorset*, London, 1970, 59.
27.   *Textus Roffensis*, ed. Hearne, Oxford, 1720, 145-8.
28.   *Regesta Regum Anglo-Normannorum* II, ed. Johnson and Cronne, Oxford, 1956, nos. 1475, 1606.

THE LATER TWELFTH AND THIRTEENTH CENTURIES

Continuous documentary evidence for work on the royal castle of Canterbury commences in the Pipe Roll for 1168 - 69 when Adeliza fitzSimon was paid five shillings a year for three years (i.e., 1167 - 69) for the exchange of land in the castle of Canterbury.[29] Over those same years money had been spent on enclosing the city and on one of its gates.[30] The payment of five shillings a year, ostensibly to Adeliza, continued regularly until at least 1214; it does not occur in the Rolls for the first few years of the reign of Henry III so far printed, but in 1230 the payment was made to Alicie de Barbecana.[31] Besides the rent, Adeliza received dwellings north of Burgate Street, which she exchanged in about 1177 for a corrody of Christchurch.[32] The land originally surrendered is described as *terra extra Wiwergate iuxta fossatum turris . . . et quia terra assumpta fuit ad efforciandum turrim extrinsecus*[33] that is, clearly an area developed as an external defence or 'barbican'. In 1234 the particulars of the farm of Canterbury specify five shillings derived from the *Barbecane qui debetur in compoto super scaecarium*,[34], probably the local double entry book-keeping.

Work on the tower of Canterbury costing £73 was paid for in 1172 - 73,[35] including material bought from St. Sepulchre's, the expenditure being 'viewed' (or vouched for) by William de Ros and Mainger. £24 was spent on the tower and castle in the following year *p' visu Maur de prendreguard*,[36] which seems to be a proper name derived perhaps from the new forework. William de Ros was 'viewing' again in 1174 - 75,[37] but the expenditure was under £6. There is then an interval of fifteen years until the beginning of the reign of Richard I, when William de Murchet provided £41-worth of stone, lime and sand for the work on the castle, 'viewed' by Baldwin Blancgernun, Ylgeri, Walter fitzWimund and Ordgar Filmes.[38] £99 worth of work was done in 1191 - 92 and was 'viewed' by William de Essetford and William Norrers, and the £69 paid in the following year was 'viewed' by Richard Deudon, William the Clerk and Henry Barate.[39] The latter two at least held land adjoining the Castle,[40] and they were probably impressed to the task for that reason.

A few pounds a year was spent on repairs for the next decade, including the *aluras* (either the wall-walk, or overhanging timber hoardings or galleries) in 1198 - 99 and on the gates in 1201 - 02.[41] £10 was spent on Canterbury and Rochester in 1213 - 14 and £30 on Canterbury in 1219.[42] In 1221 a *camera* was built beside the Keep and another beside the Castle chapel, and

29. Pipe Roll Society, *Pipe Roll* (hereafter PR), 15 Henry II, 161.
30. *PR* 13, Henry II, 196, 201; *PR* 14, Henry II, 153.
31. *PR* 14, Henry III, 110.
32. Urry, 42, 164.
33. Urry, 404, (Charter XXV).
34. Urry, 443 (Corporation Archives, Register A.2, f.64r).
35. *PR* 19, Henry II, 81, 87 - 8.
36. *PR* 20, Henry II, 6. The tempting alternative of a stone ('*maur*') forebuilding is unacceptable in the context.
37. *PR* 21, Henry II, 211.
38. *PR* 2, Richard I, 7.
39. *PR* 4, Richard I, 307; *PR* 5, Richard I, 165.
40. Urry, 116 - 7, 187.
41. *PR* I, John, 59; *PR* 4, John, 210.
42. *PR* 4 16, John, 27; *PR* Henry III, cited by Colvin (*op. cit.* in note 22, 489); *Rotuli Litterarum Clausarum*, I, 143b, 234b; II, 7b.

the tower, chapel, gates and bridges repaired.[43] The hall was repaired in 1237 - 38, and the bridges needed attention in 1253 and 1260.[44] Fire damage to the great gate cost £10 to repair in 1264, and roofing work £19 in 1268 - 71.[45] Minor repairs costing a few pounds a year continued through the reigns of Edward I and Edward II.[46]

THE ARCHITECTURE OF THE KEEP

In terms of size, the keep at Canterbury ranks quite high. At the base of the plinth, where the walls are about 40 m. (14 ft. 6 in.) thick, it measures about 30 m. x 26 m. (98 x 85 ft.) excluding the later stairs, forebuilding and gatehouse applied to its sides. This puts it below Colchester and London, but on a par with the next largest in England (Dover, Duffield, Kenilworth, Middleham, Norwich and Taunton). As Figs. 37-9 show, it has buttresses clasping the angles and on the sides: one on each of the shorter sides and two on each of the longer. The Keep is faced outside with Kentish rag sandstone rubble laid in courses with bands of flint and inside with flint with two bands of sandstone below the level of the top of the plinth. Caen stone is used as dressed ashlar around the windows and slit openings and reveals, in the string course round the buttresses (which is not continued along the intervening wall-faces) and in much of the plain courses of the plinth. The lowest courses of the plinth, especially the carved courses, and the lower steyning of the well shaft are of Quarr stone[47] (Figs. 46-7). The plinth was very substantial, being originally about 4 m. (13 ft.) high and 1.80 m. (6 ft.) proud of the wall-face (Fig. 51). Near the top were several relatively shallow chamfered courses, whilst at the base a plain vertical ashlar course is surmounted by a steeply chamfered one and topped by quadrant between fillets at right angles to each other, a sequence repeated at least once.

The interior of the keep measures about 21 m. x 17 m. (68 ft. x 55 ft.) divided into three unequal aisles by two walls about 1.50 m. (5 ft.) thick. The outer aisles each had a similar wall at right angles, which cut off a small room near the north corner but divided the southmost aisle into two equal parts. There were at least three floors, marked by substantial beam-holes, though only beam-holes for the first floor survive (Figs. 43, 47). The upper floor has largely gone (as have the cross-walls) but have been reconstructed (in dotted lines) on the drawings on the evidence of early engravings. The roofs and turrets of the reconstructed sections (Figs. 53) are entirely hypothetical, being based on those at Rochester. All three floors are linked by a spiral stair in the east angle of the Keep; another stair in the middle of the south-west wall linked basement and first floor only. The latter was so sited that the wall buttresses had to be extended to strengthen the wall, weakened by the void. This widening of the buttress was done hastily: the string course was not continued round it and the extension was stopped off with a few courses of Caen ashlar. There are slight traces of a third stair in the north-west wall linking the first and second floors, described in eighteenth-century accounts.

43. *Rotuli Litterarum Clausarum*, I, 447b.
44. *Calendar of Liberate Rolls* 1226 - 40, 342; 1251 - 60, 52, 134; *PR* 23, Henry III cited by Colvin (*op. cit.* in note 22, 589).
45. Liberate Roll 48, Henry III, *PR* 50, Henry III, cited by Colvin, as above.
46. *Ibid.* For the later history of the castle see D. Gardiner, *The Story of Canterbury Castle and the Dane John and its Manor* (1951).
47. See Tim Tatton-Brown, 'The Use of Quarr Stone in London and East Kent', *Medieval Archaeology*, xxiv (1980), 213-5.

The layout of the Keep can perhaps be best described by imagining that the original floors and doorways are still in place.

A straight ramp carrying a stair rose from the north corner along the outer face of the north-west wall to a lobby (or forebuilding) covering the doorway in the centre. This face of the keep is very dilapidated, but it is possible to demonstrate that the foundations of the forebuilding are not bonded into the keep, where the plinth was cut back to take it. Some of the Quarr stone was re-used at the level of the threshold of the main door, of which one plain jamb with a bar-hole remains (Fig. 40).

The rooms on the first floor are lit by single-light round-headed windows in four-stepped embrasures (both horizontally and vertically: see Figs. 44-7). One window retains traces of chevron decoration on its voussoirs externally, with a better-preserved fragment (perhaps a mason's reject) built into the wall nearby (Fig. 52), and another window retains evidence of reveals with rounded jambs and chamfered voussoirs, from which it is possible to compile a composite elevation and section of the openings (Fig. 50). The main central room was lit by two such windows at the far end facing the entrance. Of the two rooms to the right (south), the nearer has a large segmental-arched fireplace (the angle on the top of the voussoir is too steep for the centre to be on the springing line), in the west angle, backed with stones set in herring-bone pattern, with a domed chimney venting horizontally through flues like small loops at the corners of the buttresses (Figs. 39, 41). Recesses in the side walls of this room give access to the well-shaft and the stair to the basement respectively. Since basements were commonly used for storage, it is reasonable to identify this room as the kitchen. The further (southmost) room has three fine windows, together with an L-shaped passage in the wall ending in a deep rectangular pit with a small slit above it. There is no trace of any outlet from this pit: a hole broken through the south angle of the Keep basement shows no trace of a deep shaft. At the upper floor level above this passage are the remains of a small flint-lined pit of L-shaped plan, again without outlet. Both may have been latrines, cleaned out periodically and inconveniently, or possibly private wardrobes or treasuries; they could even be pitfalls to trap attackers thinking them to be staircases.

To the left (north) of the main entrance, the further room gave onto the main stair at the east angle linking all floors with a fireplace between the north-east windows resembling that to the west (Figs. 41, 43). A C-shaped passage linked that room to the north room; the outer wall is broken out, perhaps by a window or a door like that to be found in a similar position at Colchester and London. This room is very small and the passage barrel-vault may have been continued across its length. The wall is cut back here, perhaps to provide access to the space below by a chute and to give access to a passage in the north-west wall, which opened onto a postern door above the entrance staircase as well as to a spiral stair which rose from beside the main door to another passage running to a room contrived in the north angle of the keep (Fig. 38). We know very little of the arrangements of the upper floor, which presumably contained the private rooms, but perhaps we can regard the smaller eastern rooms of the main floor as summer and winter parlours, the one to the south overlooking the open country and that to the north, with its necessary fireplace, the city. Each had its inconveniences, however.

The basement below the floor just described was poorly lit by slits (now broken out) opening at the level of the first-floor joists in the south-east wall but shelving down very steeply within. The basement could be reached from the spiral stair in the east angle (which retains part of its original vault of Roman brick) or from the other stair to the south-west. The central aisle has a recess for access to the well-pipe at the west end; the south-east wall was broken through to provide an entrance from the building with round towers (the *camera* of 1221?) whose foundations are roughly marked out with kerbstones. The erection of this building suggests that the basement of the Keep was in frequent use, separately from the first floor perhaps as a prison.

NOTE

All the drawings that accompany this section were specially prepared by the Canterbury Archaeological Trust. They are the work of J. Bowen and L. Sartin and are the first of a series of detailed measured drawings of important medieval buildings in Canterbury that the Trust is undertaking. One of the things which is most lacking in Canterbury is an archive of accurately measured drawings of its buildings. This applies as much to Canterbury Cathedral and the buildings of Christ Church Priory as it does to the secular buildings of the City. In the past a large number of drawings of the more famous buildings have been made, but very few indeed were accurately measured and many are misleadingly inaccurate. Copies of all the drawings that have been made so far (both published and unpublished) can be seen at the National Monuments Record in London.

For a key to the present drawings see Fig. 43. It should be noted also that the dotted outline on the drawings is based on a large number of prints and drawings of the Keep made before the 1817 demolitions[48].

TIM TATTON-BROWN

48. Some of these drawings can be found in Gardiner (1951), see note 46 above.

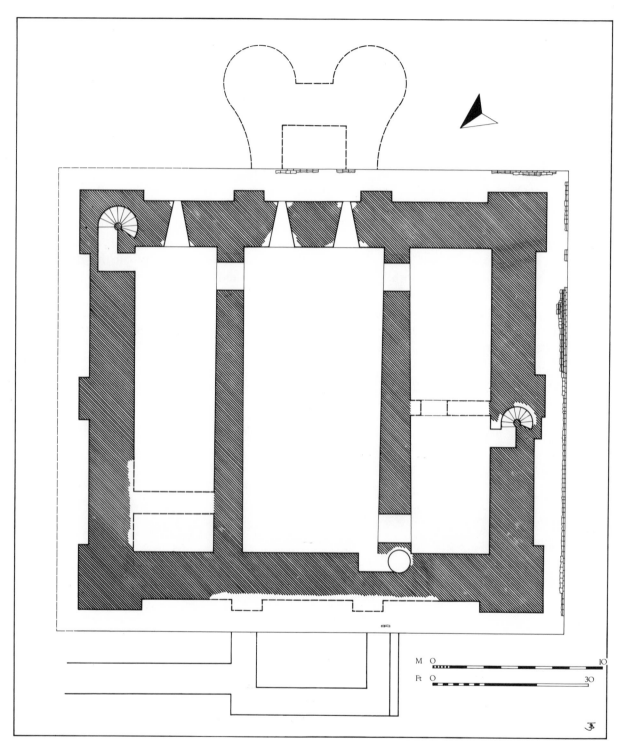

Fig. 37.   Keep — Basement Plan (1 : 50).

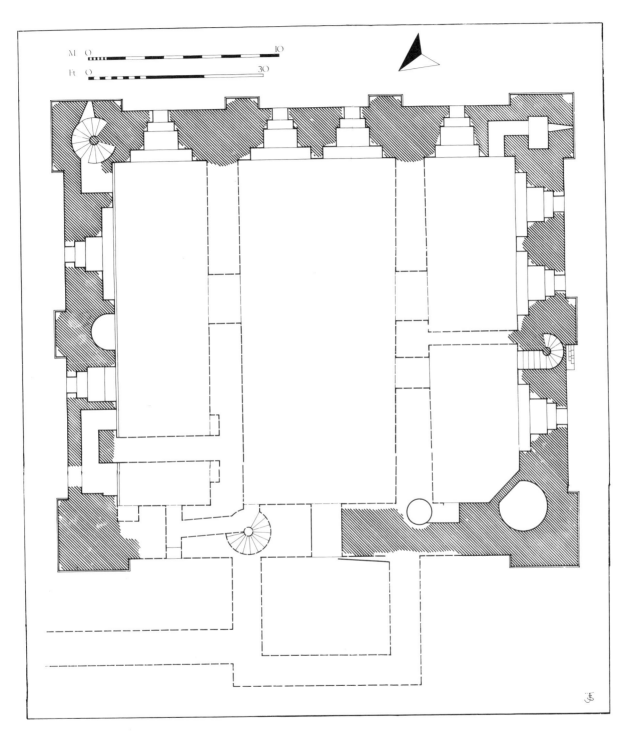

Fig. 38.   Keep — first-floor Plan.

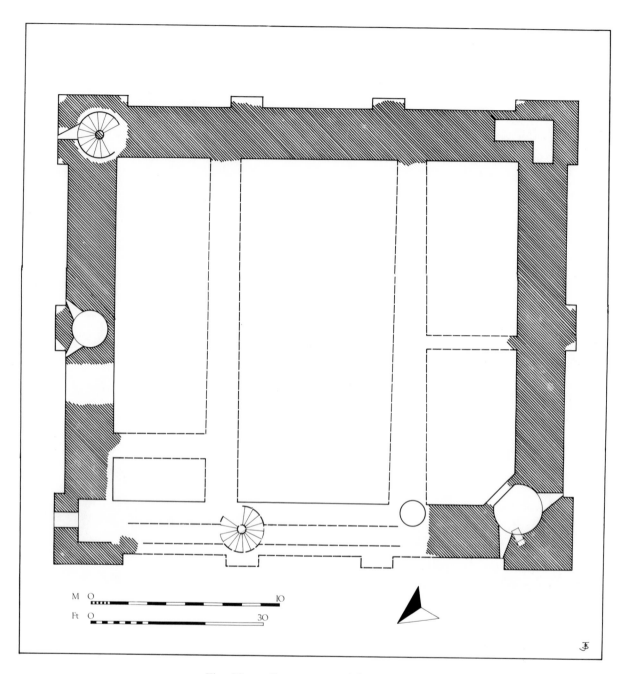

M O ⬛⬛⬛⬛⬛▬▬▬▬▬▬▬▬▬▬ 1O

Ft O ▬▬▬▬▬▬▬▬▬▬▬▬▬ 3O

Fig. 39.   Keep — second-floor Plan.

Fig. 40.   N — W external Elevation.

Fig. 41.   N — W internal Elevation.

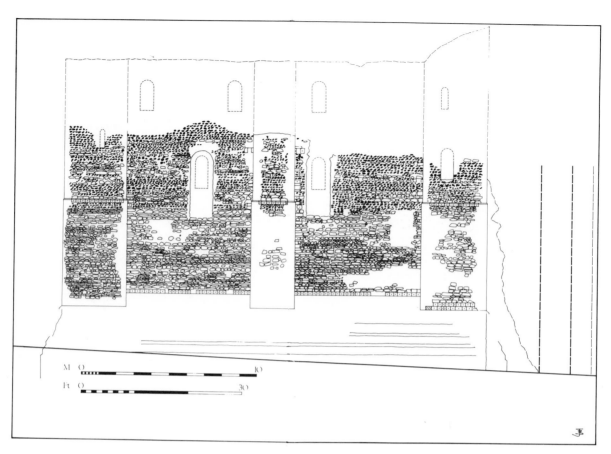

Fig. 42.   N — E external Elevation.

Fig. 43.   N — E internal Elevation.

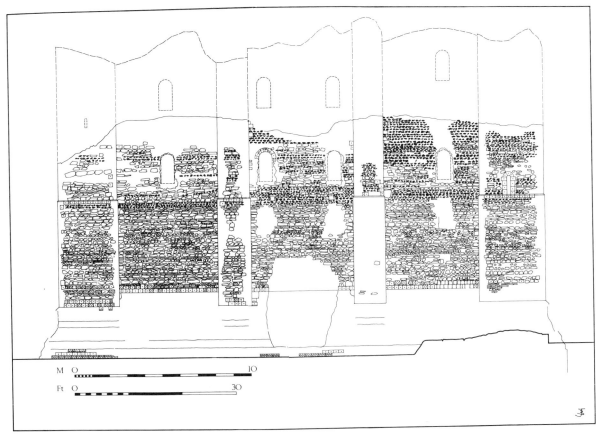

Fig. 44.   S — E external Elevation.

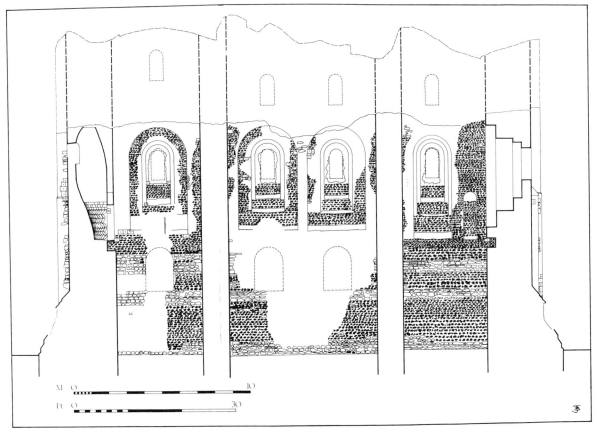

Fig. 45.   S — E internal Elevation.

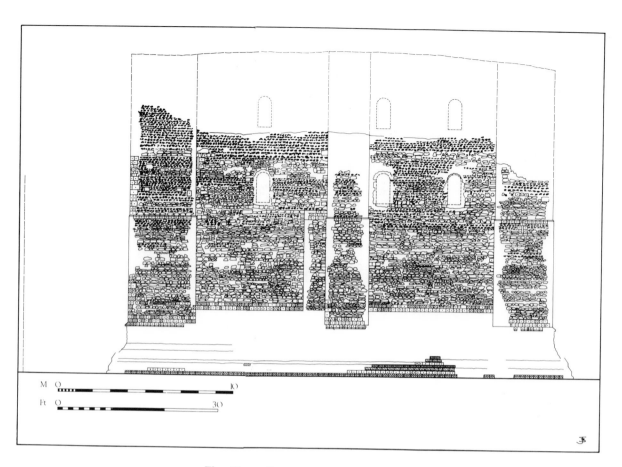

Fig. 46.   S — W external Elevation.

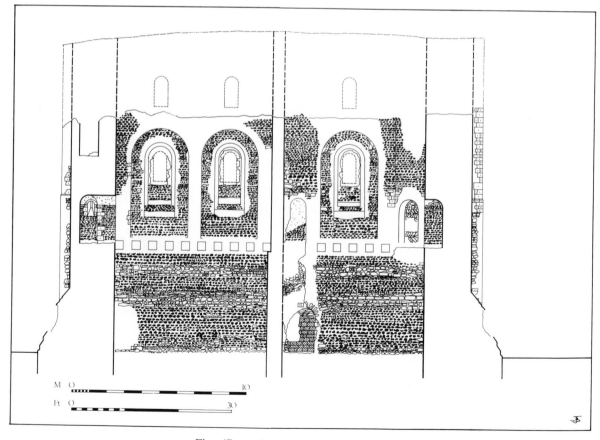

Fig. 47.   S — W internal Elevation.

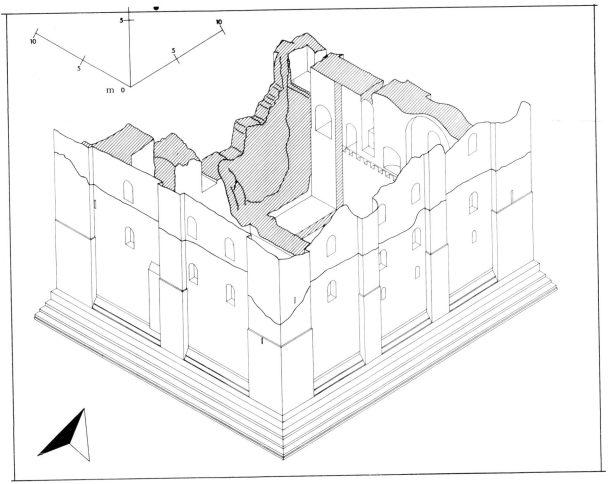

Fig. 48.   Isometric View from South.

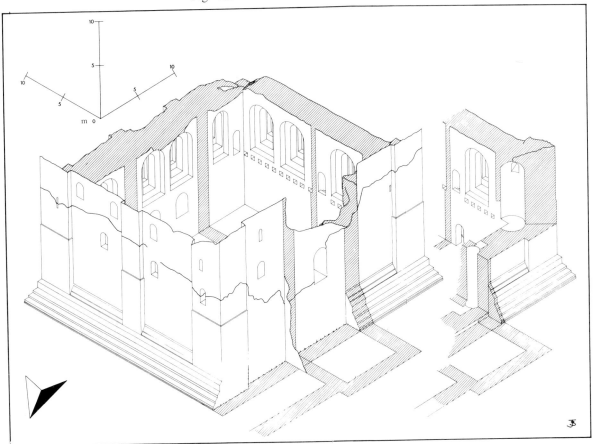

Fig. 49.   Isometric View from North.

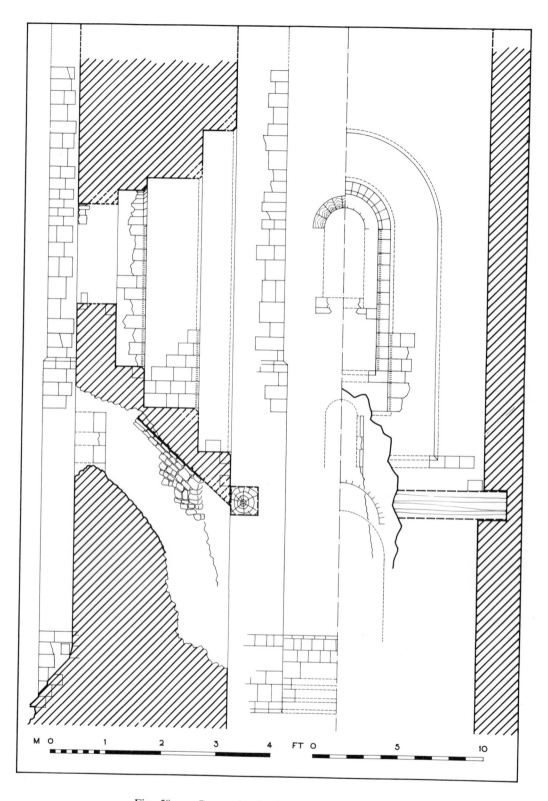

M O   1   2   3   4   FT O   5   10

Fig. 50.   Composite Section through Keep Wall.

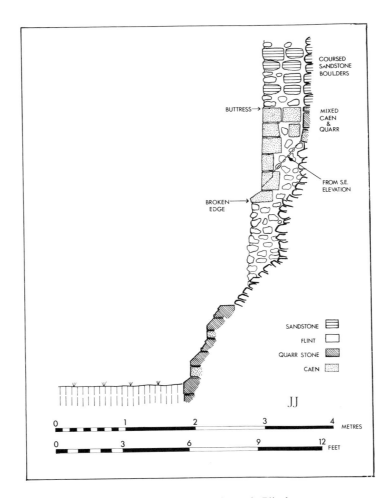

COURSED
SANDSTONE
BOULDERS

BUTTRESS →

MIXED
CAEN
&
QUARR

FROM S.E.
ELEVATION

BROKEN
EDGE

SANDSTONE

FLINT

QUARR STONE

CAEN

JJ

| 0 | 1 | 2 | 3 | 4 | METRES |

| 0 | 3 | 6 | 9 | 12 | FEET |

Fig. 51.   Section through Plinth.

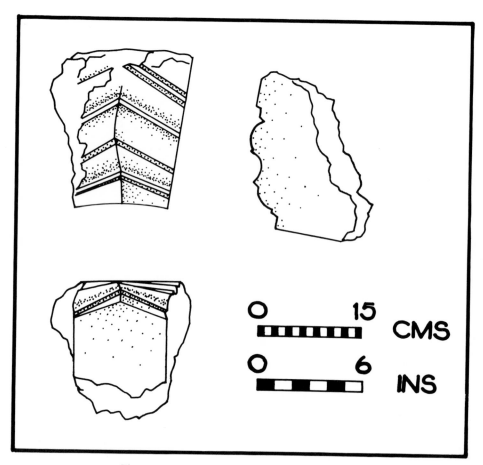

Fig. 52.   Fragment of chevroned *Voussoir*.

M 0   30   FT 0   100

Fig. 53.   Hypothetical Reconstructions of Keep Sections.

PART II

THE POTTERY

Reports edited by Nigel Macpherson-Grant

INTRODUCTION AND ACKNOWLEDGEMENTS

Though not large by urban standards the Rosemary Lane and Gas Lane excavations produced large quantities of pottery. Stratigraphically (and to a lesser extent chronologically), the two sites divided neatly into the major groups A, C, D, and G listed below, and to emphasize this point the pottery has been similarly divided. The early Roman ditch fills (A) are an important and compact unit and the associated pottery is presented in full. With the other groups the presentation has been more selective; here the only published material is from layers where a reliable sequence could be established (with the exception of some of the samian and notable imported wares). All the pottery discussed below is referred to in its stratigraphical context.

All the original, unedited, reports for the samian, fine wares and mortaria, together with detailed fabric/form analyses of the coarse wares and context-related lists of small finds, coins, stone and building materials etc., have been placed with the site records in the Royal Museum, Canterbury.

The amphorae from these excavations are still being studied; they will be incorporated into a subsequent publication.

We owe much to Mrs. Joanna Bird and Dr. C.J. Young, not only for their individual contributions, but also for all the invaluable help and advice they gave during the preparation of this report. We are also much indebted to Miss Brenda Dickinson and Mr. Brian Hartley, for the samian stamps, to Mrs. Kay Hartley, for the mortaria, and to Miss Valery Rigby, Mrs. V. Tatton-Brown and Messrs. Paul Arthur and Mark Redknap, for their respective contributions. Many thanks are also due to Dr. Kevin Greene and Richard Pollard for discussing aspects of the fine and coarse wares.

In particular we wish to thank Miss Marion Wilson for not only drawing much of the pottery from the early Roman ditches, but also for discussing some of the coarse-ware problems and for her work in preparing an initial coarse-wares form/fabric type series (the latter to be included in a future report).

Finally, the pottery draughtsmen: for their excellent drawings, many thanks are due to Mr M. Duncan, for the decorated samian, the samian stamps and the majority of the coarse wares and to Messrs. L. Sartin and J. Bowen, for the cremation group pottery and the glass flask respectively.

A. THE EARLY ROMAN DITCHES: Areas I and II.

I. *The Plain and Decorated Samian Wares* Joanna Bird

Notes: x indicates number of vessels represented. S, C and E G : South, Central and East Gaul. '2nd Century' generally indicates after *c.* A.D. 125. 'Later 2nd Century' indicates after *c.* A.D. 170. O = Oswald 1936-1937.

Layer 1:
General fill of both ditches, together with a small number of sherds from the later backfill.
Ritt 9, SG, pre-Flavian.
At least 6 x Dr 15/17, SG, pre- to early-Flavian.
4 x Dr 15/17, probably R, SG, pre- to early-Flavian.
At least 13 x Dr 18, SG, pre- to early-Flavian. Includes 3 possibly R.
Dr 15/17 or 18, SG, *c.* A.D. 55-65 (Stamp no. 6). Trimmed, ? to make lid.
Dr 15/17 or 18, SG, *c.* A.D. 50-70 (Stamp no. 9).
Dr 15/17 or 18, SG, 1st Century, (Stamp no. 17).
Dr 24/25, SG, *c.* A.D. 50-65 (Stamp no. 5).
Dr 24/25, SG, *c.* A.D. 50-65 (Stamp no. 11).
Dr 24/25, SG, *c.* A.D. 50-65 (Stamp no. 1).
4 x Dr 24/25, SG, pre-Flavian.
Dr 27g, SG, *c.* A.D. 50-60 (Stamp no. 4).
Dr 27g, SG, 1st Century (Stamp no. 16).
10 x Dr 27, SG, pre- to early-Flavian.
Dr 29, SG, pre-Flavian.
Dr 29, SG. Fragment of foliage in upper frieze. Pre- to early-Flavian.
(Fig. 54, no. 1) Dr 29, SG. The upper frieze consists of groups of arrowheads separating panels containing a rosette (similar rosettes were used by BASSVS and COELVS: Knorr 1952, Taf. 10) flanked by two birds, for which there are no exact O. parallels. The lower frieze is also divided by arrowheads into panels, containing a large rosette, used by LICINVS (Knorr 1952, Taf. 34, A), set in a corded circle (used by MODESTVS - Knorr 1952, Taf. 43, L - and other

potters) with tendrils. For a generally similar style, cf. Knorr 1952, Taf. 48, by PASS(I)ENVS, and Knorr 1952, Taf. 43, F by MODESTVS. *c.* A.D. 55-75.
Dr 29, SG. Dog (?), in a double medallion in the lower frieze. Pre- to early-Flavian.
Dr 30, SG, *c.* A.D. 45-60 (see Layer 73).
Dr 37, SG, early- to mid-Flavian.
Dr 37, CG, Antonine.
Dr 31, CG, Antonine.

Layer 7:
Later backfill sealing both ditches.
Dr 18, SG, Nero to early-Flavian.
Dr 27g, SG, second half 1st Century.
Dr 27, SG, Nero to early-Flavian (= pot in Layer 57).
SG sherd, probably Dr 18, 1st Century.
Dr 31, CG, Antonine, very abraded.

Layer 10:
General fill of both ditches, together with a few sherds from the later backfill.
4 x Dr 15/17 (1 probably R), SG, pre- to early-Flavian.
Dr 15/17 or 18, SG, *c.* A.D. 45-65 (Stamp no. 3.).
2 x Dr 15/17R or 18R, SG, pre- to early-Flavian (1 incompletely slipped).
Dr 18R, SG, *c.* A.D. 60-70 (Stamp no. 7).
6 x Dr 18, SG, pre- to early-Flavian (1 cream slipped below red on rim).
2 x Dr 27, SG, 1st Century.
Dr 29, SG, pre- to early-Flavian.
Dr 29, SG. Scroll in upper frieze, with ears of corn and an unusual circle motif used as a terminal. *c.* A.D. 50-70.
Dr 30, SG, *c.* A.D. 45-60 (see Layer 73).
Dr 31, CG, Antonine.
Dr 44, EG, later-2nd to early-3rd Century.

Layer 33:
Deposit in recut ditch.
Dr 15/17, SG, pre- to early-Flavian.
Dr 15/17R or 18R, SG, pre- to early-Flavian.
At least 2 x Dr 27, SG, 1st Century.
Dr 24/25, SG, pre-Flavian.
Dr 33, CG, 2nd Century (intrusive).
4 SG, 1 CG sherds.

Layer 36:   Later backfill sealing both ditches.
               Dr 18(R), SG, Flavian or pre-Flavian.

Layer 57:   Later backfill sealing both ditches.
               Dr 15/17R or 18R, SG, pre- to early-Flavian.
               Dr 18 probably, SG, Nero to early-Flavian.
               Dr 18, SG, 1st Century.
               Dr 27 probably, SG, 1st Century (Stamp no. 15).
               Dr 27, SG, Nero to early-Flavian (= pot in Layer 7).
               3 x Dr 27, SG, pre-Flavian.
               Dr 29, SG, with fragment of scroll in upper frieze; pre- to early-Flavian.
               Dr 33, CG or EG, Antonine probably (Stamp no. 14); worn foot.
               At least 2 x Dr 31, CG, Antonine.
               Dr 37, CG, with fragment of scroll and leaf; Antonine.
               Dr 37, EG, later-2nd to early-3rd Century.
               Walters 79, probably CG, later-2nd Century; burnt.
               Large closed form (e.g. Déch 68, 72), CG, Antonine.
               SG sherd, 1st Century.

Layer 57A: Description as Layer 57.
               At least 4 x Dr 15/17, SG, pre-Flavian.
               At least 8 x Dr 18, SG, pre-Flavian.
               Dr 18R, SG, pre-Flavian.
               Ritt 8, SG, pre-Flavian.
               Ritt 9, SG, pre-Flavian.
               Dr 24/25, SG, pre-Flavian.
               Dr 15/17 or 18, SG, c. A.D. 65-90, (Stamp no. 13).
               3 x Dr 27, SG, pre- to early-Flavian.
               Dr 33, CG, 2nd Century.
               Dr 37, CG; the decoration includes a trilobe motif. Hadrianic to early-Antonine.

Layer 57C: Deposit in recut ditch.
               Dr 15/17R, SG, pre-Flavian.
               SG sherd, 1st Century.

Layer 57A/D: Occupational backfill in recut ditch.
               3 x Dr 15/17, SG, pre-Flavian.
               Dr 18R, SG, pre-Flavian.
               Dr 18 probably, SG, pre-Flavian.
               Dr 18/31, CG, early- 2nd Century.

Dr 24/25, SG, c. A.D. 50-70 (Stamp no. 8).
Dr 24/25, SG, pre-Flavian.
3 or 4 x Dr 27, SG, pre- to early-Flavian.

Layer 57D: Description as Layer 57A/D.
               2 x Dr 15/17, SG, pre-Flavian.
               Dr 18, SG, second half 1st Century.
               Dr 24/25, SG, pre-Flavian.
               Ritt 8, 9 or Dr 24/25, SG, pre-Flavian.
               2 x Dr 27, SG, pre- to early-Flavian.
               Dr 29, SG, gadroons in the lower frieze; pre-Flavian.

Layer 70:   Later backfill sealing both ditches.
               Dr 31, CG, Antonine.

Layer 71:   Description as Layer 70.
               SG sherd, probably Dr 18, second half 1st Century; rivet hole.

Layer 72:   Occupation backfill in recut ditch.
               Dr 24/25, SG, pre-Flavian.
               Ritt 12 probably, SG, pre-Flavian.
(Fig. 54, no.2). Dr 30, SG. The large goose is 0.2320, the small one similar to 0.2286. SG 30s are rarely signed or stamped, and it is usually impossible to assign them to a single workshop; the general style of this piece is similar to the work of potters such as MODESTVS and the OFFICINA LICINIANA. c. A.D. 45-60.
               Dr 30, CG. The ovolo is probably one used by MEDETVS-RANTO of Les Martres (Stanfield and Simpson 1958, Pl. 30, no. 365). c. A.D. 100-125.

Layer 73:   Description as Layer 72.
               Ritt 12, SG, pre-Flavian.
               Dr 27g, SG, probably pre-Flavian.
               Dr 30, SG. A bowl from Mainz attributed to CALVS (Knorr 1952, Taf. 70, G), has all the motifs, and is probably from the same mould. The figure is Hermet 1934, Pl. 20, no. 124, the dog is Hermet 1934, Pl. 26, no. 19. c. A.D. 45-60. (Sherds from Layers 1 and 10).

Layer 74:   Description as Layers 72 and 73.
               Dr 15/17, SG, c. A.D. 45-60 (Stamp no. 10); worn foot.
               Dr 18R, SG, c. A.D. 45-65 (Stamp no.

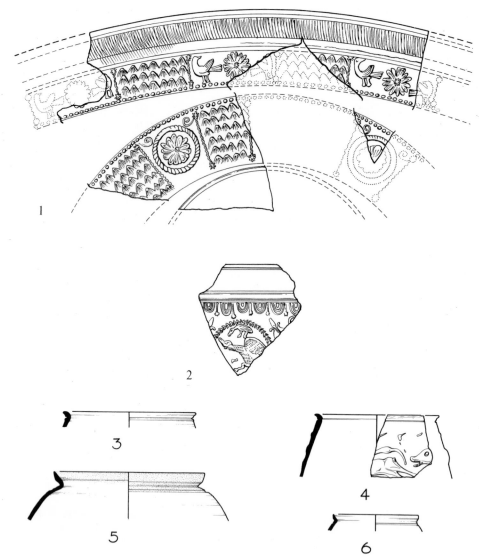

Fig. 54.   Area I : Ditch : Nos. 1-2 The decorated Samian (½); nos. 3-4 Colour-coated Wares; no. 5 Fine White Wares; no. 6 Central Gaulish lead-glazed Ware (¼).

12); unworn.
Dr 16, SG, Claudio-Neronian.
Dr 24/25, SG, c. A.D. 50-70 (Stamp no. 8). Unworn foot with three notches.
SG sherd, 1st Century.
(74 - intrusive, Dr 40, 'black samian', CG, Antonine. Worn foot).

Layer 75:   Occupation backfill in primary ditch.
Dr 18, SG, pre-Flavian.
Dr 15/17, SG, pre- to early-Flavian.

Dr 27, SG, Flavian.
SG sherd, 1st Century.

Layer 76:   Description as Layer 75.
Dr 18R, SG, c. A.D. 45-65 (Stamp no. 2); unworn.
Dr 18, SG, pre-Flavian.
Dr 27, SG, pre- to early-Flavian.

Layer 77:   Primary ditch fill.
Dr 18, probably R, SG, pre- to early-Flavian.

Layer 79:   Occupation backfill in recut ditch.
            Dr 18, SG, pre-Flavian.

Layer 80:   Description as Layer 79.
            Dr 15/17R or 18R, SG, pre-Flavian.

Layer 82:   Fill of recut ditch.
            Dr 15/17R or 18R, SG, pre-Flavian.

Layer 267: Area I material from both ditches.
            3 x Dr 27 (2g), SG, later 1st Century.
            2 x Dr 15/17, SG, pre- or early-Flavian.
            3 x Dr 18, SG, pre- or early-Flavian.

Layer 263A: Early Roman Ditches (Primary Ditch).
            Area II.
            Dr 18, SG, Flavian-Trajanic.

The samian from the Canterbury early Roman ditch consists of a very large quantity of first-century material with a small amount of later wares, dating probably after *c.* A.D. 170; the date of this early phase is almost certainly pre-Flavian and probably before *c.* A.D. 65. This is confirmed by the samian stamps and by the Gallo-Belgic and early imported fine wares.

For a summary discussion of the samian from the Rosemary Lane and Gas Lane sites, see Section F, Part XI.

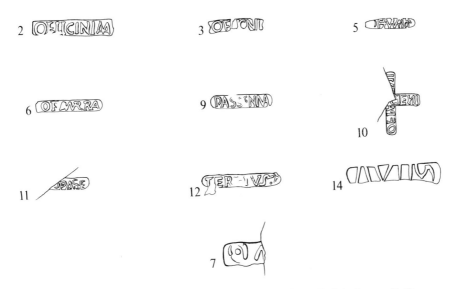

Fig. 55.   Area I : Ditch : samian Stamps; 7 : Gallo-Belgic Stamp (1:1).

II. *Stamped samian.* Brenda Dickinson
and B.R. Hartley.

Fig. 55, p.

1. FIRMO on Dr 24/25. Die 15a, FIRMO I, La Graufesenque.[2] The stamp is known from Hofheim and Usk, and was used on forms Ritt 8 and 9. *c* A.D. 50-65. Layer 1.

2. OFLICINIANA on Dr 18R. Die 3b, LICINVS, La Graufesenque.[2] There is no dating evidence for this particular stamp, but LICINVS' general range is *c.* A.D. 45-65. (Layer 76).

[1] Indicates a stamp known at the pottery.
[2] Indicates a stamp not itself known at the pottery but used by a potter of whom other stamps are known there.
[3] Pottery inferred from distribution, fabric or other factors.

3. OFLICNI on Dr 15/17 or 18. Die 20a, LICINVS, La Graufesenque.[2] There are two examples of the stamp from Camulodunum and it may also have been used on form Ritt I. *c.* A.D. 45-65. (Layer 10).

4. OFMODES on Dr 27g. Die 4b, MODESTVS I, La Graufesenque.[2] This stamp appears at Camulodunum and was used on form Dr 24/25. The modified version (4b) is in the Colchester Pottery Shop II. *c.* A.D. 50-60. (Layer 1).

5. OFMVRRAN on Dr 24/25. Die 8h, MVRRANVS, La Graufesenque.[2] There are four examples of this stamp from Camulodunum and it occurs on forms Dr 24/25 and Ritt 8. *c.* A.D. 50-65 (Layer 1).

6. OF.MVRRA on Dr 15/17 or 18. Die 10c, MVRRANVS, La Graufesenque.[2] This stamp occurs in the group from Cirencester Fort Ditch and, three times, in Colchester Pottery Shop I. *c.* A.D. 55-65. (Layer 1).

7. [OFNIG]RI on Dr 18R. Die 2a, NIGER II, La Graufesenque.[1] Although this stamp has been noted from the Nijmegan fortress and Rottweil-Hochmauren, it is basically pre-Flavian, as its presence at Fishbourne (in Period I) and the Strutts Park site at Little Chester attests. *c.* A.D. 60-70. (Layer 10).

8. PASSEN PA[SSEN] both on Dr 24/25. Two examples Die 16b, PASS(I)ENVS, La Graufesenque.[2] There is no dating evidence for the stamp, but the potter's range is *c.* A.D. 50-70. (Layer 74; Layer 57 A/D).

9. PASSENMA on Dr 15/17 or 18. Die 31a, PASS(1)ENVS, La Graufesenque.[1] This stamp is known from Baginton (2), Broxtowe, Hofheim and Usk. *c.* A.D. 50-70. (Layer I).

10. OF.PASSIENI[22] *retr.* (impressed twice) on Dr 15/17. Die 40a, PASS(I)ENVS, La Graufesenque.[2] The stamp appears in the pre-Flavian cemeteries at Nijmegan, at Usk and or Verulamium (Period I). *c.* A.D. 45-60. (Layer 74).

11. OP SIE on Dr 24/25. Die 53a, PASS(I)ENVS, La Graufesenque.[1] This stamp, used mainly on forms Dr 24/25 and Ritt 8, is known from Metchley. *c.* A.D. 50-65. (Layer I).

12. TERTIVS.F on Dr 18R. Die IIc, TERTIUS II, La Graufesenque.[2] An uncommon stamp of a Claudio-Neronian potter, whose other stamps occur at Camulodunum, Hofheim andUbbergen and on forms Dr 17 and Ritt 8. The decoration of a bowl of form Dr 29 stamped by him suggests a date of *c.* A.D. 45-65. (Layer 74).

13. OFVITALI on Dr 15/17 or 18. Probably Die 5b, VITALIS II, La Graufesenque.[2] The appearance of this stamp at the Nijmegen fortress (2) and at Rottweil suggests that it is basically pre-Flavian, but VITALIS probably started work *c.* A.D. 65, and a date *c.* A.D. 65-90 is possible for the stamp. (Layer 57A).

14. VII on Dr 33. Illiterate Die 482, Central or East Gaulish.[3] This stamp, not previously recorded, is unlikely to be literate. The style of the lettering suggests Antonine date. (Layer 57).

15. [ ] V probably, on Dr 27. Presumably South Gaulish and 1st Century. (Layer 57).

16. [ ]AN on Dr 27g. South Gaulish and 1st Century. (Layer 1).

17. OF[ ] on Dr 15/17 or 18. South Gaulish and 1st Century. (Layer 1).

The closing date for this assemblage should be within a few years of A.D. 60 either way — more probably after than before, especially if the last identified stamp is indeed VITALIS II.

III. *The Gallo-Belgic Imports.* Valery Rigby.

Layer I: Excavated material from both ditches.
a) Matching rim sherds from a platter, Camulodunum form 16, in terra nigra (TN). Hard pale blue-grey fine-grained paste; dark blue-grey surfaces; highly polished interior, less glossy faceted exterior finish. Imported. Possibly dates to the Claudian period but more likely to date to *c.* A.D. 60-85.
b) Foot-ring from a large platter in TR 2. Tiberio-Claudian. Imported.
c) Base sherd from a large platter, possibly form I, in micaceous TN. The form and fabric were in production from the late Augustan period possibly into the Claudian period. An import,

the precise location of the potteries concerned is not known, possibly central Gaul.

d) Fragment of a platter with a broad, shallow footring in TR (cf. Rigby 1973, figs. 1-3). Pre-Flavian.

Layers 1, 10,   Material from the fill of both ditches.
57 A/D and 76: Several body sherds from the lower section of a beaker with a sharply carinated shoulder, Holwerda type 26a. Dark brown fine-grained sand-free micaceous ware; densely grey-black exterior surface, with a smoothly polished finish. (Holwerda 1941, Pl. VII, 236). Probably an import from the Rhineland or possibly Bavay. Beakers of this type were made in several different fabrics ranging from the very thin black 'eggshell' imports, to coarse-grained sandy ware, presumably of 'local' origin, but all were given dark glossy external finishes. This example is fine-textured, so is probably imported. Little is known of these beakers in Britain for unless stamped or fairly complete they tend to be ignored. The best examples are from burials found sites in the Rhineland, below Mainz; they appear to date from the Tiberian to early-Flavian periods.

Layer 57 A/D: Occupation material from the recut ditch.
Base sherds from a platter with a foot-ring, probably Camulodunum form 14 in TN. Hard, dense sand-free paste, pale blue, with sparse grey grog grits; the surfaces shade from dove-grey to the more usual grey-blue colour and have a polished finish; the pale areas are streaked with grey from the grog inclusions. Imported c. A.D. 45-70.

Layer 74:
(Fig. 55A, no. 7)   Description as Layer 57 A/D.
The base from a platter, Camulodunum form 16, in a fabric which is border-line between TN and an imitation. Light khaki-grey fine-grained sand-free paste, with grey ferrous inclusions, accidental; with dark grey-black micaceous surfaces, worn and flaked so that no original finish survives. The central stamp is an illiterate mark and no other examples from this particular die have been identified. Marks in a similar style on both TN and coarse ware are known from Camulodunum, e.g. 228, 229 and 254, none apparently stratified. c. A.D. 50-85.

Layer 76:   Occupation backfill of primary ditch.
Base sherd from a platter with a broad foot-ring, probably Camulodunum form 3 or 5, in TR 1. Pre-Claudian, an import from Gallia-Belgica.

Comments:

Some of the TN sherds from Layers 1a, 57 A/D and 74 cannot predate A.D. 50 at the earliest, while two of them are more likely to be Neronian or Nero-Vespasianic in date. Few of the Gallo-Belgic imports from excavations in Canterbury are definitely pre-Conquest in date, but two sherds of TR and one of micaceous TN, from Layers 76, IOIS and I respectively, are from vessels manufactured in the late-Augustan or Tiberian periods suggesting that trade may have begun around A.D. 20.

IV. *Fine Wares*. Joanna Bird, Dr. C.J. Young and Paul Arthur.

Colour-Coated Wares. (J.B.)

A full context-related catalogue of the early Roman colour-coat wares was jointly compiled by Mrs. Bird and Dr. Young. For the reasons given in the introduction (see p. 89), only the section concerning the early Roman ditches is published in detail. (See also Section F. XIII, p. 163).

Layer 1:   Fill of both ditches together with a small number of sherds from the later backfill.
Lyons ware cup (Greene 1972, Fig. 1; form 1.1-2). Yellowish-cream fabric drab brown colour-coat, rough casting

(very sparse on interior).
Pre-Flavian.

Sherds of 4 Lyons ware beakers (Greene 1972, Figs. 2 and 3, form 20). All have yellowish-cream fabrics and external rough-casting of coarse whitish quartz grits. Colour-coats are: (i) orange-brown, some fine rough-casting on interior; (ii) reddish-brown (now almost completely gone), some fine rough-casting on interior; (iii) drab brownish-black, some internal rough-casting; (iv) reddish-brown, smooth interior. Pre- or very early- Flavian.

(Fig. 54, no. 3) Beaker with cornice rim. Fine off-white fabric, brownish-grey colour-coat. Source uncertain; perhaps an import from the Cologne region, or an early Nene Valley product. Antonine.

Layer 10:   Description as Layer 1.
Lyons ware beaker (Greene 1972, Figs. 2 and 3, form 20). Yellowish-cream fabric, drab brownish-black colour-coat, whitish coarse grit rough-casting (coarse on exterior, fine on interior). Pre- or very early-Flavian.

Beaker sherd. Fine orange fabric, grey core; matt purplish-brown colour-coat with grog rough-casting on exterior. Probably a Colchester product; late-1st to early-2nd century.
Beaker, cornice rim. Fine, off-white fabric, brownish-black colour-coat, fine rough-casting on exterior. Cologne region or Nene Valley. Antonine.
Beaker, with barbotine decoration. Hard fine cream fabric with sparse red and brown inclusions, brownish-black colour-coat. Nene Valley probably; Antonine — early-3rd century.

Layer 57 & 57A: Later backfill sealing both ditches.
(Fig. 54, no. 4) Beaker with barbotine stag and hound. Fine off-white fabric, some dark inclusions, purplish-brown colour-coat. Probably Nene Valley, Antonine to early-3rd century.

Layer 57D: Occupation backfill in recut ditch.
Lyons ware cup (Greene 1972, fig. 2,

form 5); with applied raspberry roundel and part of a plain motif. Cream fabric, drab brown colour-coat. Pre-Flavian.
Beaker sherd. Hard fine orange fabric, grey core; quartz grit rough-casting on exterior. Source unknown, possibly an import. 1st or 2nd century probably.

Layer 74:   Description as Layer 57D.
Lyons ware beaker, (Greene 1972, figs. 2 and 3, form 20). Yellowish-cream fabric, drab brown colour-coat, whitish quartz rough-casting (coarse on exterior fine on interior). Pre- or very early-Flavian.

Note: Lyons ware ceased to be made c. 70 A.D., though the beakers probably continued a little later.

Fine White Wares (J.B.)

Layer 1:   Fill of both ditches together with a small number of sherds from the later backfill.
(Fig. 54, no. 5) Rim, ovoid beaker, fine pinkish-white fabric, cream surfaces; orange-red paint on rim and shoulder. Probably manufactured in south-east England, and Flavian-Trajanic in date.

Layer 10:   Description as Layer I.
Beaker, probably ovoid in form. Fine off-white ware with blobs of rustication. Probably manufactured in south-east England and Flavian-Trajanic in date.

Roman Lead-Glazed Pottery (P.A.)

Layer 267:   Occupation backfill.
(Fig. 54, no. 6) Rim sherd of a pre-Flavian, CG beaker, in a slightly micaceous hard white fabric with other sparse inclusions. The surfaces are covered with a greenish-yellow lead glaze. (See p.   Layer 233).

Oxfordshire Ware. (C.J.Y.)

Layer 57:   Later backfill sealing both ditches.
1 bowl body sherd, C22, c. A.D. 240–400+.
Layer 57A: Description as Layer 57.
2 bowl bases, one very heavily burnt.

'A l'éponge' Ware (J.B.)

Layer 57:   Later backfill sealing both ditches.
                Foot-ring fragment of bowl in pale yel-
                low fabric with some brown inclusions
                and yellowish-orange colour-coat. Prob-
                ably 'à l'éponge' ware (Fulford 1977,
                45–47), of 4th century date.

Lamp (J.B.)

Layer 57D: Occupation backfill into recut ditch.
                Fragment of lamp (for form, cf. Bailey
                1963, Pl. 7). Fine off-white fabric, un-
                even orange slip on exterior. Probably
                Italian; 1st Century, burnt over the
                fracture.

V. *The Coarse Wares.* (N.C.M.-G.)

Introduction.

All the coarse wares from each section are illustrated (unless otherwise stated), and are presented in an overall, continuous, number sequence. Each item is a straightforward description; detailed discussion of distribution and parallels have been reserved for forthcoming form and fabric type-series publications.

The individual pot descriptions are fairly detailed, since it is felt that conventional descriptions are too simplistic and a bare illustrated catalogue not adequate. In particular, the more unusual fabrics are dealt with as fully as it is possible using the eye alone. Where a variable colour description is used, e.g., 'dirty grey/brown-pink', the first group is the dominant colour. Grogged fabrics can be considered as the traditional local 'Belgic' ware.

Area I Ditch: Primary and recut phases. (Figs. 56-9).

1. RLP (77).   Butt-beaker in fairly soft brown grogged ware, with dark grey surfaces. Exterior and rim, inside to angle, burnished.

2. RLP (33).   Jar in soft brown grogged ware with dirty-grey/pink-brown surfaces. Exterior burnished. Worn. Base has slight foot-ring.

3. RLP (57C).   Jar with fabric and burnish as 2.

4. RLP (33).   Jar with cordoned neck in grey grogged ware with darker grey surfaces. Rim and body, above shoulder, lightly burnished.

5. RLP (57B).   Jar in fairly hard dark brown grogged ware with dark grey lightly burnished surfaces. Well formed and finished.

6. RLP (57C).   Jar with cordoned shoulder in grey grogged ware. Grey surfaces.

7. RLP (57C).   Jar in fairly hard grey grogged ware, with dirty-grey/brown-pink exterior surface. Rim and external surface smoothed. An original oval hole through neck.

8. RLP (267).   Widemouthed jar/bowl in dirty grey fairly soft grogged ware. Surfaces mainly grey. Exterior body smoothed — neck, rim and interior lightly burnished. Shoulder panel decorated with tooled cross-hatching.

9. RLP (57D).   Jar in dark grey grogged ware with small voids on both surfaces. Rim|and neck|lightly burnished. Shoulder decoration of ? coarse rouletting.

10. RLP (75/76). Jar. in grey slightly sandy ware. Numerous small voids inside. Rim, and neck above shoulder groove, burnished. Faint vertical finger-nail impressions below groove.

11. RLP (267)   Small jar/beaker in grey fairly soft grogged ware, with chocolate-brown sandwich to core. Grey surfaces. Rim and neck lightly burnished. Shoulder decorated with neat finger-nail impressions.

12. RLP (267).   As 11, but ware brown with grey/dirty buff surfaces. Decoration and burnish poorly executed.

13. RLP (57D).   Small jar/beaker in hard dark grey ware, with tight-packed grog. Rim and exterior burnished.

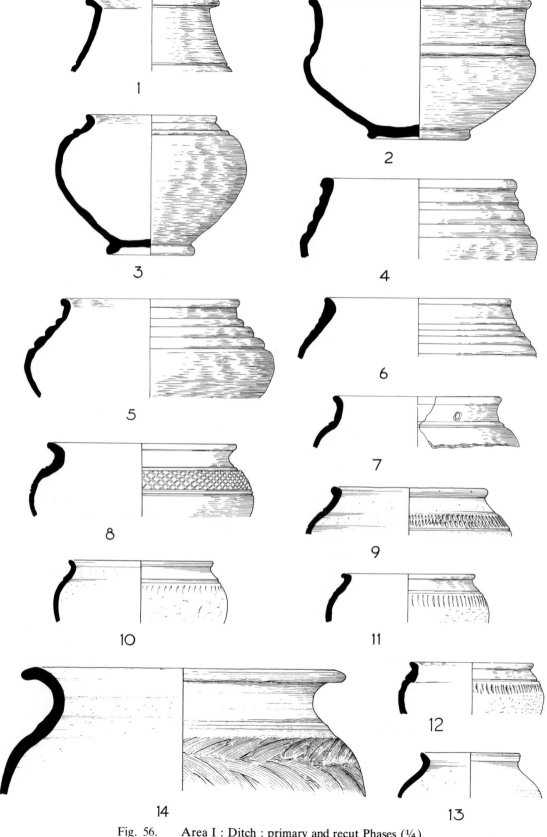

Fig. 56.   Area I : Ditch : primary and recut Phases (¼).

14. RLP (75/76). Large jar in coarse light grey grogged ware, with pink-brown and grey surfaces. Fabric contains small black grits, ill-sorted and varying in size up to 3 mm. Fine brush or twig striations on shoulder.

15. RLP (267). Jar in very soft buff-pink grogged ware. The grog is finely crushed (1 mm. max.) and bright pink. Surfaces dirty brown-grey. Bead rim lightly burnished. Body coarsely combed except for a basal panel. Worn.

16. RLP (267). Jar in black fairly soft flint and grog-tempered ware, with a thin dirty brown sandwich to core, weathering deep pink. Surfaces dark grey/drab buff-pink. The burnt flint and red-brown grog temper is fairly coarsely crushed (2.5 mm. max.), but well-mixed and fairly open-spaced, showing as a clear but not dominant 'sparkle' on the surfaces. Chalk grains of similar size are also present. The rim and upper shoulder have been smoothed — the rest of the body roughly wiped vertically and then lightly combed horizontally. A distinctive fabric.

17. RLP (57D). Jar in dark grey, fairly soft, grogged ware with drab grey-brown surfaces. Rim and neck smoothed. Coarse irregular horizontal combing on body below shoulder. Poorly made.

18. RLP (57D). Jar in light grey crisp hard grogged ware. Rim and neck roughly smoothed. Fine diagonal brush strokes on body. Exterior sooted.

19. RLP (57D). Light grey grogged ware with dirty buff-grey surfaces. Rim and upper neck slightly burnished; horizontal combing below.

20. RLP (74). Jar in grey grogged ware, with exterior roughly burnished.

21. RLP (75). Jar in brown, fairly soft grogged ware with grey/dark grey surfaces. Rim and exterior lightly burnished.

22. RLP (267). Jar in soft black grogged ware with a 1 mm. deep chocolate-brown lining below the interior surface. Exterior black, with neck and rim roughly burnished. Body decorated with fine diagonal brush strokes.

23. RLP (57D). Jar with simple, thickened upright rim. Ware fairly hard, dark grey and grogged. Patchy surface colours from black to light grey. Shoulder ledge, neck and rim smoothed and partially burnished. Rough untreated body.

24. RLP (267). Small jar in fairly hard grey grogged ware with dirty brown-grey surfaces. Body finely combed below lightly smoothed rim and neck.

25. RLP (57D). Small jar in brown fairly soft grogged ware with drab brown-grey surfaces. Neck smoothed. Rim lightly burnished. Horizontal combing from the shoulder down.

26. RLP (57D). Jar in dark grey grogged ware with patchy drab grey-buff surfaces. Neck, and rim inside to angle, roughly burnished. Body lightly combed vertically.

27. RLP (57D). Jar in fairly hard grey grogged ware with grey/pink-grey surfaces. Rim and neck burnished. Junction between neck and body marked by single row small, spaced, oval impressions. Remainder of body lightly striated with faint vertical brush strokes.

28. RLP (73). Jar in fairly hard light grey grogged ware with grey/dirty brown surfaces. Rim and neck smoothed. Decoration and body treatment as 27.

29. RLP (57C). Jar with ware as 28, but with thin brown sandwich to core and dark grey/pink-brown surfaces. Rim, neck and cordons lightly burnished, lower body smoothed. Latter roughly decorated with faint tooled lines. Fabric contains occasional grains of maroon haematite (up to 2 mm.).

30. RLP (57AD). Coarse hard grey grogged ware with dirty grey-buff surfaces. Some small voids on all surfaces.

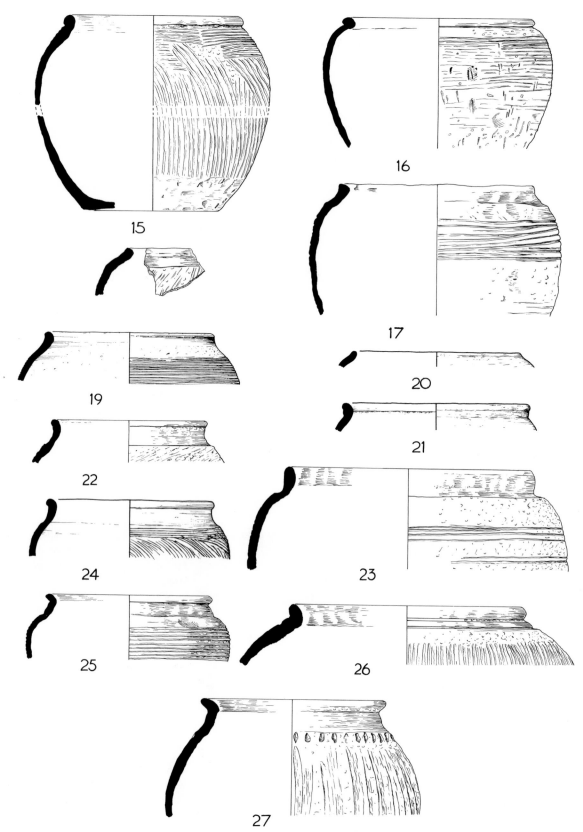

Fig. 57.   Area I : Ditch : primary and recut Phases (¼).

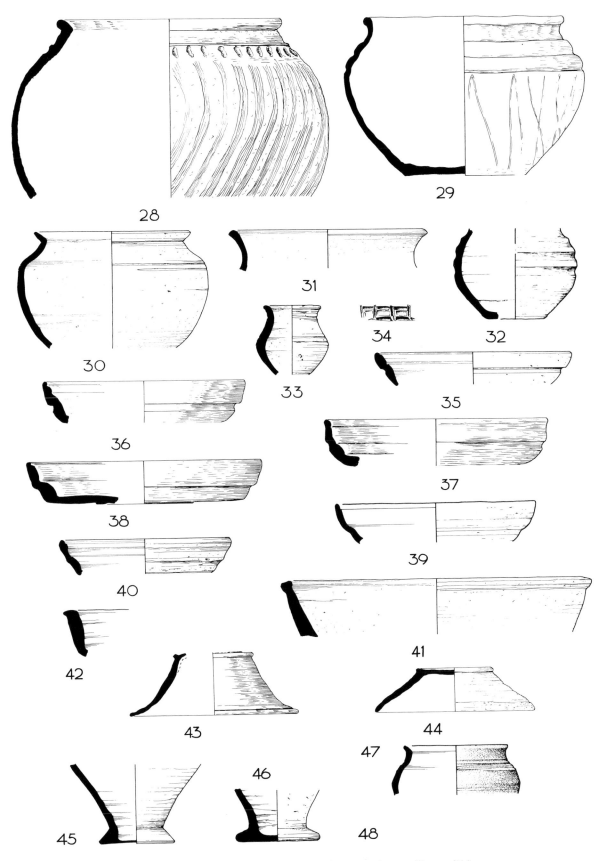

Fig. 58.   Area I : Ditch : primary and recut Phases (¼).

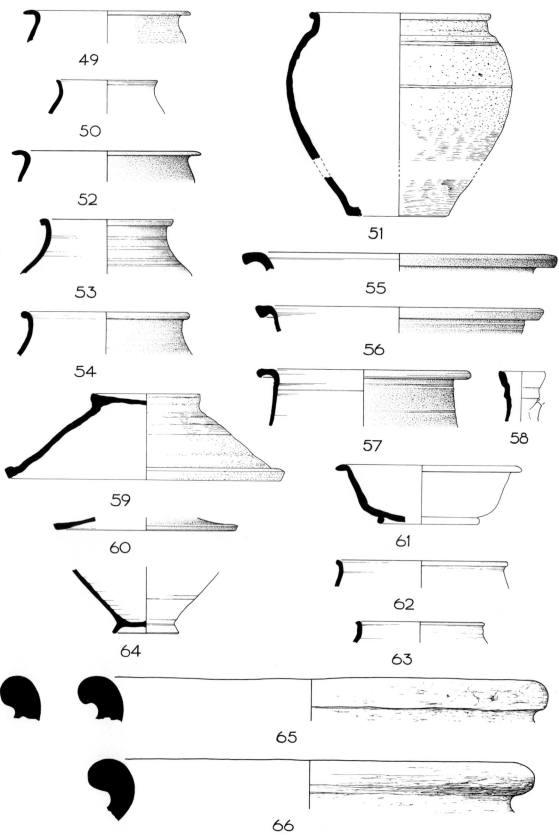

49

50

52

51

53

55

54

56

57

58

59

60

61

62

64

63

65

66

Fig. 59.   Area I : Ditch : nos. 49-64 primary and recut Phases; nos. 65-66 later backfill Phases (¼).

Incomplete grooves on shoulder. Lower body roughly burnished.

31. RLP (75/76). Jar in grey, slightly sandy ware. Dark grey to black surfaces. Rim and neck burnished.

32. RLP (267). Small vessel with cordoned shoulder in soft dirty brown-grey grogged ware, with thin brown sandwich to core. Exterior grey, interior dirty brown. The whole exterior tooled smooth, with the cordons highlighted by the burnished grooves between.

33. RLP (57D). Small pot in coarsely grogged dark grey ware. Some voids on all surfaces. Rim and exterior lightly burnished — rather more strongly below soft carination.

34. RLP (57AD). Coarsely cut stamp or potter's mark on burnished shoulder of large combed jar. Dark grey coarse grogged ware.

35. RLP (75/76). Platter in dark grey/black grogged ware. Medium sand content (in the fractures), with occasional angular grits (c. 1 mm.).

36. RLP (75). Platter in grey grogged ware with dark grey surfaces. Lower body and interior partially burnished.

37. RLP (267). Platter in dirty grey-buff, fairly hard, grogged ware with buff surfaces. Lower body and interior treated as 36.

38. RLP (267). Platter with ware and treatment as 36.

39. RLP (267). Platter in soft brown grogged ware, with colouring and surface treatment as 36.

40. RLP (74). Platter in black slightly micaceous ware with small sand content. Grey-buff surfaces. ?covered with a buff slip.

41. RLP (57C). Dish or plate in coarse grey grogged ware. Fabric is slightly micaceous; scatter of small grits (up to 1 mm.). Exterior burnished below incipient shoulder.

42. RLP (74). Shallow dish or plate with a diameter similar to the platter series, in hard light grey grogged ware with grey-buff surfaces.

43. RLP (57D). Lid in grey fairly hard grogged ware with drab grey surfaces. Interior smoothed, exterior lightly burnished.

44. RLP (57D). Lid in fairly hard, grey, finely grogged ware with grey-buff surfaces. Upper surface burnished down to a c. 2 mm. untreated band above lip. Horizontal burnishing originally done on fairly soft surface giving a slightly channelled 'terracette' finish. Fabric contains occasional milky quartz and chalk grits.

45. RLP (57AD). Base in fairly hard grey grogged ware with dark grey surfaces. Burnished exterior. Well made.

46. RLP (57D). Pedestal base in chocolate-brown grogged ware, with dark grey surfaces. Burnished exterior, particularly foot.

47. RLP (57D). Small jar in dark grey sandy ware.

48. RLP (74). Colour-coat beaker in smooth dark grey ware, with pink-orange and buff-brown exterior. Faint rouletted decoration covered by worn pink-cream colour-coat. Fabric micaceous — also profusely speckled with grey or brick-red ?haematite grains (up to 1 mm.).

49. RLP (267). Beaker/small jar in smooth grey ware — slightly micaceous.

50. RLP (57D). Carinated beaker in hard, smooth dark grey ware, burnished outside with rather rough interior below burnished lip.

51. RLP (267). Jar in coarsely sanded grey ware with brown sandwich to core, below dark grey surfaces. Incised horizontal line on shoulder and at max. girth. Lower body roughly burnished/scraped; traces of light burnish on rim and neck.

52. RLP (267). Jar in grey sandy ware — possibly beaker.

53. RLP (57AD). Jar in red-brown sandy ware, with grey surfaces. Horizontal, spaced, tooled lines on neck.

54. RLP (57AD). Jar in dull red sandy ware, with thin buff-grey core and surfaces. Tooled horizontal lines on shoulder.

55. RLP (33). ? Bowl in finely sanded brown ware with dark grey surfaces.

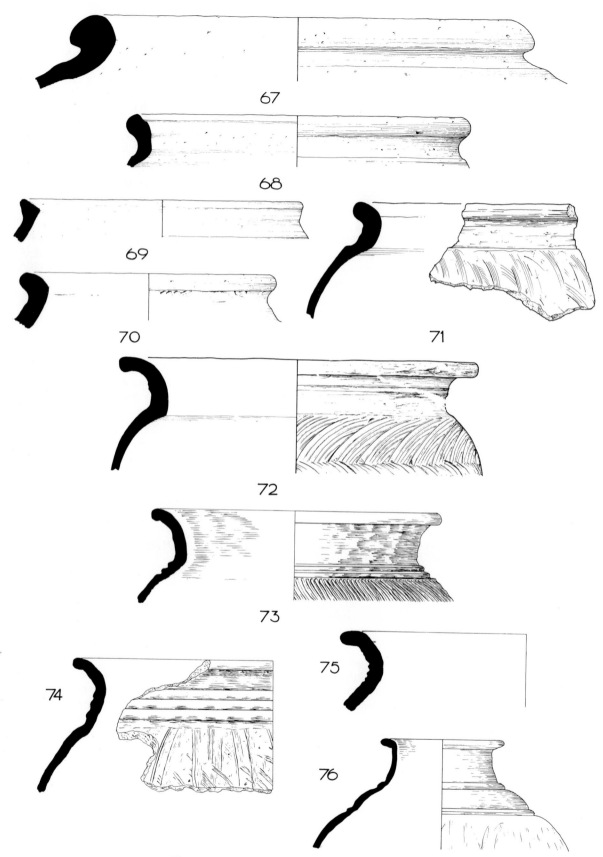

67

68

69

70

71

72

73

74

75

76

Fig. 60.   Area I : Ditch : later backfill Phases (¼).

56. RLP (57D). Flanged-rim bowl in buff-grey sandy ware.

57. RLP (57D). As 56 in coarsely sanded grey ware.

58. RLP (76). Flagon in pink-buff sandy ware; occasional fine chalk grits.

59. RLP (75). Lid in finely sanded dirty grey ware with brown sandwich to core and dark grey surfaces.

60. RLP (74). Lid in hard, finely sanded grey ware.

61. RLP (73). Bowl with foot-ring in finely sanded grey ware with marked buff sandwich to the core, and dark grey surfaces. Rim and interior tooled smooth.

62. RLP (76). Beaker/small jar in orange micaceous, finely sanded ware; thin pink core. Traces of pink-red slip. Worn.

63. RLP (75). As 62 for ware. Worn burnished pink slip.

64. RLP (75). Base in pale grey-buff ware with buff-cream surfaces. Moderate sand content.

Area I Ditch: Later backfill phases. (Figs. 60-68).

65. RLP (57). Rim sherd from large storage jar in brown, soft, coarsely grogged ware. Fabric contains occasional flint grits. Rim smoothed. Worn.

66. RLP (1). As 65, but in grey grogged ware, with grey-orange surfaces. Neck and rim lightly burnished.

67. RLP (10). Very large storage jar in coarse grey grogged ware. Grits are large (4–6 mm.) and profuse. Worn, but rim and incipient shoulder burnished.

68. RLP (57). Large jar in buff-grey grogged ware. Fairly high mica content; several grits of flint and ironstone (3 mm.). Surfaces orange-buff. Slight recess inside rim, which is burnished.

69. RLP (1). Jar in grey grogged ware with dark grey/black lightly burnished surfaces. Rim with slight internal recess.

70. RLP (1). Jar in buff-grey grogged ware with dark grey/buff burnished surfaces. Fabric friable and partially laminated.

71. RLP (1). Large jar in dark grey/black grogged ware; buff-grey surfaces. The grog-temper is profuse and black or buff. Rim and neck burnished. Body lightly combed.

72. RLP (10). Large jar in fairly hard dark brown coarse grogged ware with grey/buff-brown surfaces. Neck and rim interior roughly burnished. Shoulder combed. Fabric contains occasional large chalk grit (c. 7 mm.).

73. RLP (57A). Jar in fairly hard grogged ware with a thin buff-brown lining below exterior surface. Surfaces fired dark-light grey/pink/drab brown-pink. Rim and neck burnished. Combing below cordons.

74. RLP (13). Large jar in light grey fairly hard grogged ware. Surfaces dark grey/pink-brown. Rim and neck smoothed. Body decorated with fine brush strokes.

75. RLP (14). Large, fairly thick-walled jar in grey medium-hard grogged ware. Rim and neck smoothed; neck grooved rather than cordoned. Body decorated with fine comb/brush strokes.

76. RLP (1). Jar in grey fairly hard grogged ware with dirty buff-grey surfaces. Fabric contains occasional chalk grains (up to 1 cm.). Worn overall burnish.

77. RLP (57A). Jar in dark grey fairly soft grogged ware with dark grey/dirty buff surfaces. Rim, shoulder and cordons burnished. Roughly decorated with a shoulder panel of tooled cross-hatching.

78. RLP (57A). Jar in dirty grey, soft, grogged ware with thin, light chocolate-brown sandwich — tingeing surfaces dirty grey-pink. Rim and exterior lightly burnished. The formation of the shoulder mouldings is clearly marked by internal finger-presses. Well-made, thin-walled product.

79. RLP (57A). Jar in grey fairly hard grogged ware, with darker grey surfaces. Rim and exterior tooled smooth giving a matt finish.

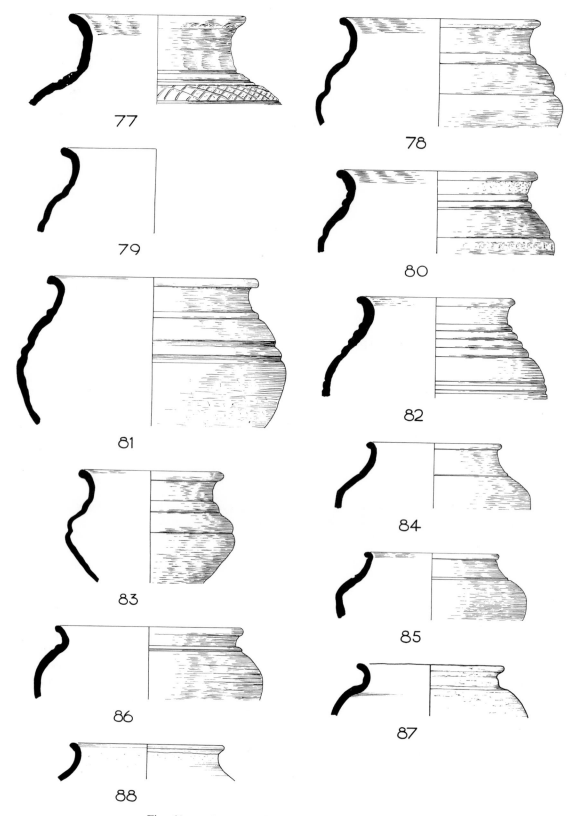

Fig. 61.   Area I : Ditch : later backfill Phases (¼).

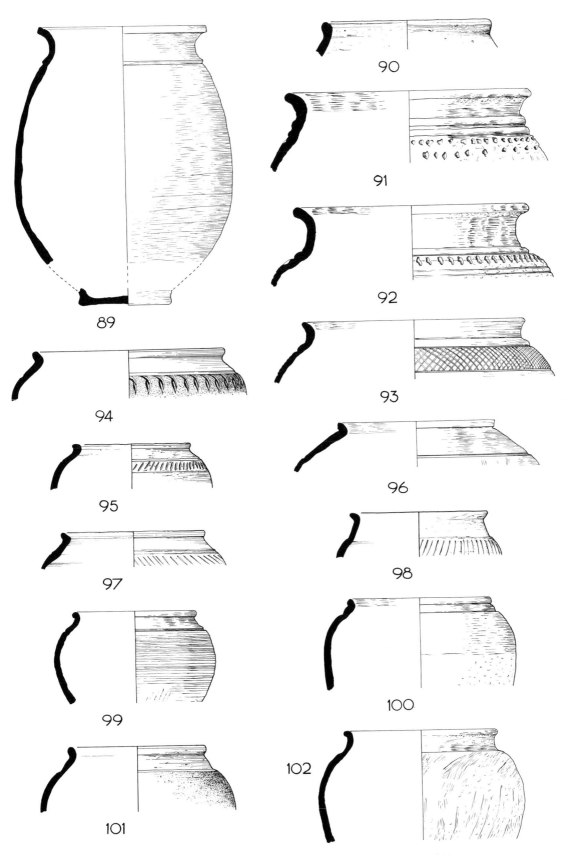

89

90

91

92

93

94

95

96

97

98

99

100

101

102

Fig. 62.   Area I : Ditch : later backfill Phases (¼).

80. RLP (57A). Jar in grey fairly soft grogged ware with dirty grey surfaces — drab chocolate-brown on the rim. Latter and exterior lightly burnished.

81. RLP (1). Jar in dark grey, fairly hard, finely grogged ware with dark grey/dirty buff surfaces. Lightly burnished; single groove inside rim.

82. RLP (1). Jar in fairly hard light grey grogged ware with a brown-pink lining below grey exterior surface. Rim and outside smoothed.

83. RLP (1). Well-made thin-walled jar in brown soft grogged ware with brown-pink/grey surfaces. Interior smoothed, exterior lightly/burnished. Single groove inside rim.

84. RLP (1). Jar in fairly hard grey-buff grogged ware. Exterior and rim lightly burnished.

85. RLP (57). Small jar/beaker in smooth black ware, with pale grey sandwich to core; grey surfaces. Lip and exterior burnished silver grey. Sparse-finely micaceous fabric.

86. RLP (57A). Small jar in light grey fairly hard grogged ware with pink-brown lining to core and drab chocolate-brown/dark grey surfaces. Rim and exterior lightly burnished.

87. RLP (1). Jar in fairly hard grey grogged ware with buff-grey surfaces. Rim Rim and body burnished. Incipient neck cordon. Worn.

88. RLP (57A). Jar in coarse grey ware, slightly micaceous, with light chocolate-brown surfaces. Rim and shoulder burnished.

89. RLP (1). Ovoid ? flagon in grey fairly soft grogged ware with predominantly pink exterior surfaces; grey internally. ? originally handled — the distinctive surface colouration is normally associated locally with handled flagons. Single groove inside lip, cordon at base of neck, and an untidy zone of incised horizontal lines on lower body. Overall body smoothed, upper portion more markedly.

90. RLP (57). Jar in grey grogged ware. Little mica. Lip and exterior burnished.

91. RLP (57A). Jar in hard light grey grogged ware. Rim and incipient neck cordons burnished. Decorated with two irregular rows of small roughly heart-shaped impressions above fine vertical brushstrokes.

92. RLP (1). Jar in dark grey fairly soft grogged ware with dark grey/black surfaces. Rim, neck and shoulder cordon burnished. Single row of small oval impressions below cordon, impressed into an already horizontally combed body.

93. RLP (1). Jar in black fairly hard grogged ware with dirty buff/dark grey surfaces. Interior smoothed; rim, neck and cordon burnished. Shoulder panel of tooled cross-hatch decoration.

94. RLP (1). Beaker in hard grey grogged ware. Thin, well-made product, burnished on upper shoulder and rim; smoothed inside. Decoration may be rouletted.

95. RLP (10). Jar in soft dull brown grogged ware, with dark grey surfaces. Light burnish on neck and rim. Single band of diagonal finger-nail impressions on shoulder.

96. RLP (57A). Beaker in dirty grey, fairly hard, finely grogged ware with dark grey surfaces. Exterior and rim burnished — internally down to rim/body angle.

97. RLP (57). Jar in dark grey grogged ware with black surfaces; lightly burnished on rim and neck. Below shoulder groove a band of thin incised diagonal lines.

98. RLP (1). Beaker in soft dirty grey grogged ware with darker dirty grey-brown surfaces. Fabric contains an irregular scatter of small chalk grains (up to 0.50 mm.). Rim and neck smoothed. Slightly diagonal incised line decoration on shoulder.

99. RLP (1). Small jar in black, fairly soft grogged ware with a 2 mm. dark brown lining beneath the interior surface. Surfaces grey. Rim and neck smoothed. Body decorated with fine horizontal combing — smudged near the base.

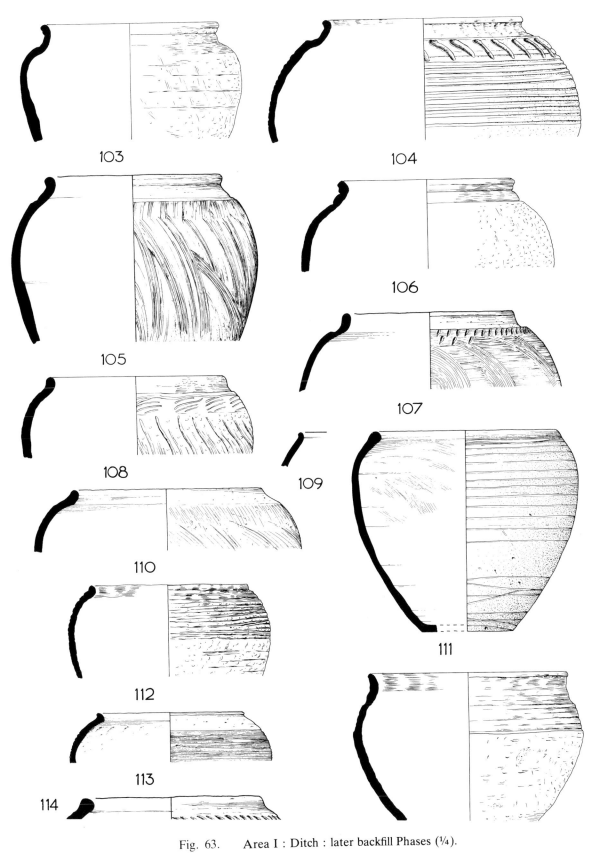

Fig. 63.   Area I : Ditch : later backfill Phases (¼).

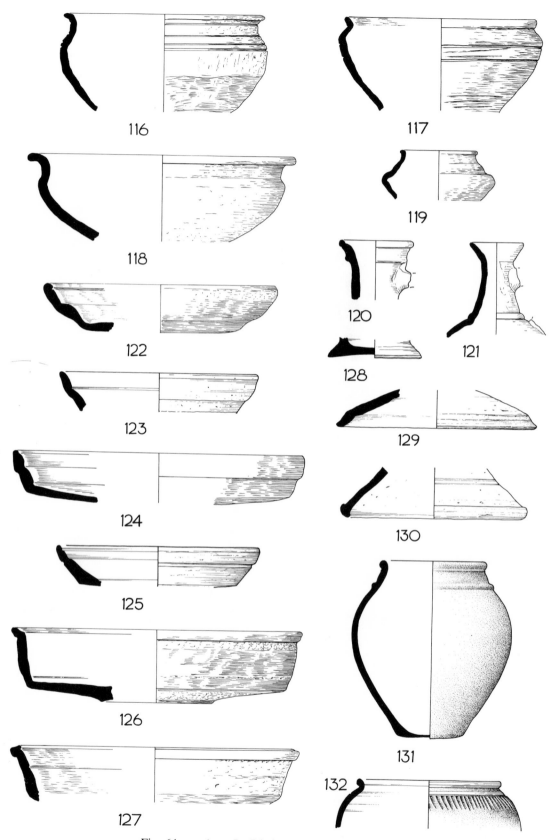

Fig. 64.   Area I : Ditch : later backfill Phases (¼).

100. RLP (1). Jar in fairly soft black grogged ware with dirty-grey surfaces. Rim, neck and internal bevel lightly burnished — body untreated.

101. RLP (1). Jar in grey-brown grogged ware, with dark grey surfaces. Burnished on rim and neck only. Well made.

102. RLP (1). Jar in black fairly soft grogged ware with grey/dirty buff-brown surfaces. Rim and neck roughly burnished; body decorated with very fine brush strokes.

103. RLP (57A). Jar in dirty grey soft grogged ware with drab grey/buff surfaces. A few shallow voids where organic matter has burnt or leached out. Shoulder slightly sooted. Neck and rim smoothed.

104. RLP (57A). Jar in fairly hard buff-grey coarsely sanded ware with buff-orange surfaces; exterior has occasional black/light grey patches. The oxidation process extends 1–2 mm. into the core from both surfaces. Rim and neck smoothed. Body decorated with rough horizontal combing, overlain at the shoulder by short diagonal strokes.

105. RLP (1). (Not illustrated). Jar in grogged ware with form similar to 101 but larger; body decorated with fine brush strokes.

106. RLP (57A). Jar in grey fairly soft coarsely grogged ware. Dirty grey surfaces. Fabric contains occasional grits of ? flint, milky quartz and chalk grains (2–3 mm.). Neck and rim tooled smooth. Body untreated and slightly sooted.

107. RLP (1). Jar in black grogged ware, with black surfaces. Rough burnish on neck and rim. Remainder of body decorated with fine horizontal comb/brush strokes - overlain by spaced, downward curving combed swags. The sharply defined shoulder is further enhanced by neat diagonal impressions.

108. RLP (1). Small jar in black fairly hard grogged ware with dirty brown/ dark grey surfaces. Rim and neck lightly burnished. Body roughly decorated with brush strokes.

109. RLP (10). Small jar/beaker in soft dark brown grogged ware with dirty grey surfaces. Rim and exterior lightly burnished.

110. RLP (1). Jar in grey coarsely grogged ware. Body below shoulder combed/ brushed with light diagonal strokes.

111. RLP (57A). Jar in finely sanded grey ware. Incised decoration in two zones of spaced horizontal lines — poorly executed at base.

112. RLP (57A). Neat fairly thin-walled jar in dark grey grogged ware; moderately hard. Dark grey/buff-grey surfaces. Rim and upper shoulder irregularly burnished. Body horizontally covered with brush/comb decoration. Several voids (max. 4 mm.).

113. RLP (1). Small jar in dark grey grogged ware with buff-grey surfaces. Lip and shoulder burnished above fine horizontal combing.

114. RLP (1E). Jar in dark dirty grey grogged ware. Rim and neck lightly burnished above diagonal combing on body. Fabric contains occasional chalk grains (up to 1 mm.).

115. RLP (57A). Wide-mouthed jar/deep bowl in fairly hard brown-grey grogged ware, with dark grey/dirty buff-grey surfaces. Rim, neck and shoulder roughly burnished. Body untreated.

116. RLP (57A). Bowl in brown fairly soft grogged ware with dirty grey surfaces. Rim and neck very lightly smoothed — shoulder emphasized by irregular grooves. The lower body has been firmly, but roughly burnished giving a slightly tripartite profile.

117. RLP (57A). Bowl with high carinated shoulder in dirty grey, fairly soft, finely grogged ware. Irregular, horizontal tooled lines below shoulder.

118. RLP (57). Bowl in brown fairly hard ware; some fine sand and partially tempered with grog. Pale red-brown lining beneath grey/pink-brown

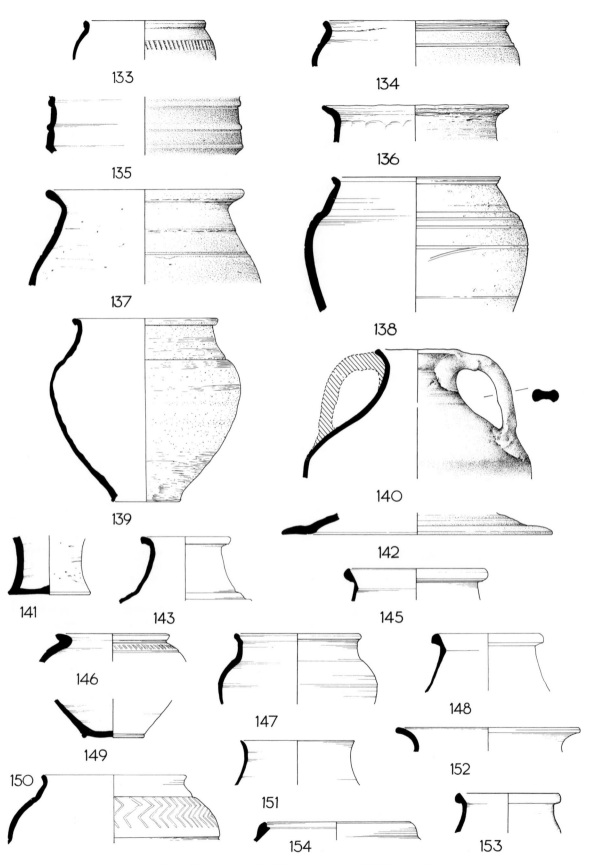

Fig. 65.   Area I : Ditch : later backfill Phases (¼).

exterior surface. Body smoothed; rim burnished, also single 'highlights' on shoulder and neck.

119. RLP (71). Small pot with incipient neck cordon and exaggerated, slightly flattened shoulder. Grey fairly soft grogged ware with dirty grey surfaces. Exterior lightly burnished.

120 RLP (1). Flagon in grey fairly hard grogged ware with worn pink-red surfaces — the oxidation extending 1 mm. into the fabric. Traces of worn exterior burnish. Narrow straphandle missing.

121. RLP (1). Flagon in chocolate-brown, soft grogged ware with worn pink-brown surfaces. Narrow tubular neck. ? Rod-handle missing.

122. RLP (57A). Platter in soft chocolate-brown grogged ware with dirty grey surfaces. Light burnish internally and outside on the base and below overhang.

123. RLP (57A). Platter in fairly soft drab brown ware.

124. RLP (1). Platter in dark grey-brown, soft, grogged ware with dirty grey surfaces. Fabric contains occasional chalk inclusions. Worn overall burnish.

125. RLP (1). Platter in fairly soft brown grogged ware, with dirty grey burnished surfaces.

126. RLP (57A). Heavy platter/dish in ware and colouring as 125. But fabric contains uneven scatter of chalk grains (up to 1.50 mm.). Roughly finished with light internal burnishings — mostly on the floor; the external burnish is confined to the lower wall only — leaving a 2 cm. untreated band to the rim. Poorly formed slightly 'pedestalled' base with incipient footring. The treatment of base and burnish copies the normal platter characteristics.

127. RLP (57A). Plate/dish in black soft, grogged ware with dark grey/buff-orange surfaces. Slight laminar tendency in the fabric.

128. RLP (57A). Pedestal base in chocolate-brown/ grey grogged ware. Upper surface of foot burnished.

129. RLP (57A). Lid in coarse drab brown ware with dark grey surfaces. Slight sand and mica content.

130. RLP (1). Lid in pink-brown grogged ware. Base of lid nicely moulded and burnished.

131. RLP (1). Jar in dark grey sandy ware.

132. RLP (1). Beaker in hard, dark grey, finely sanded ware. Burnished on neck and rim. A diagonal rouletted band on shoulder. Well-made.

133. RLP (10). Small beaker in red-brown sandy ware with buff-brown surfaces. Decoration as 132.

134. RLP (57D). Beaker/small jar in grey sandy ware. Shoulder cordon.

135. RLP (10/1E). Carinated jar/bowl in fairly hard finely sanded dirty grey ware, with thin buff sandwich to core. All surfaces smoothed and partially burnished. Worn.

136. RLP (1). Jar in finely sanded grey ware. Lightly burnished exterior below rim. ? Hand-made.

137. RLP (1). Large jar with incipient cordons, in finely sanded grey ware. Fabric contains an ill-sorted admixture of brown-red grog and some grits (up to 1 mm.). Worn burnish on exterior and inside rim.

138. RLP (1). Jar in grey grogged ware with buff-grey surfaces. Fabric contains a little sand and the occasional rounded grit (1–2 mm.). Four incised horizontal lines spaced down body.

139. RLP (57). Jar in brown-red sandy ware with grey surfaces. Neck and rim 'highlighted' by spaced, horizontal, lightly tooled lines.

140. RLP (1). Flagon in fairly soft red-brown sandy ware with buff-grey surfaces. Fabric has a tendency to laminate. Strap-handle with slightly raised edges and roughly trimmed with a knife, particularly at junction with body. ? Originally two handled.

141. RLP (57A). Pedestal base in finely sanded grey ware.

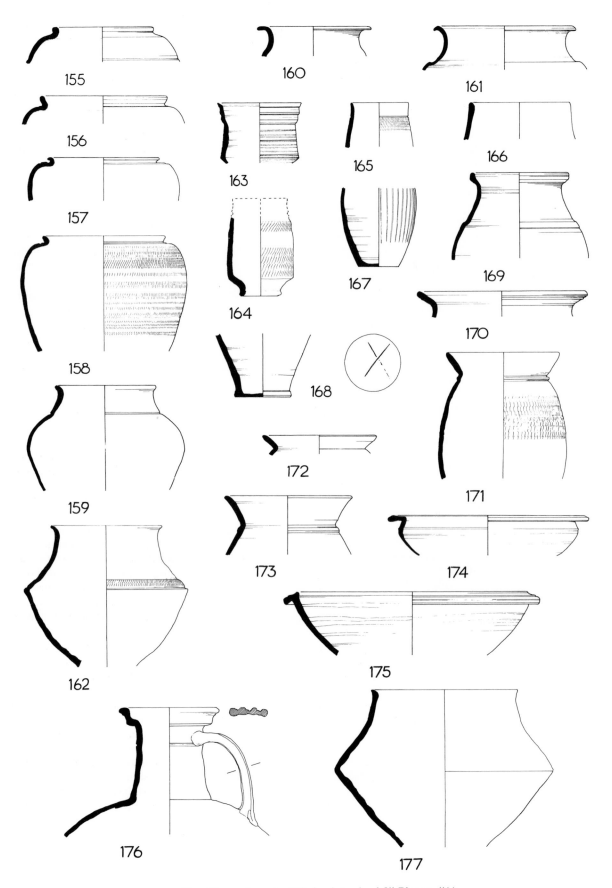

Fig. 66.   Area I : Ditch : later backfill Phases (¼).

142. RLP (57A).   Lid in dark grey sandy ware. Occasional large grits — one of chalk (5 mm.).

143. RLP (57A).   Beaker in fairly soft, grey, finely sanded ware with a distinctive close-textured appearance on the untreated surfaces. Dirty brown-pink sandwich to the core; same colour for the internal surface. Exterior dark grey and burnished.

144. RLP (1).   (Not illustrated). Lid with ware as I42.

145. RLP (1).   Butt-beaker in fine, hard, dirty-cream ware with buff-pink surfaces. Fabric where the surface is burnished occasionally streaked with red (? from grog/haematite inclusions). Finely micaceous. Burnished on exterior and internal chamfer. Body sherds belonging to this vessel show panels of fine rouletting.

146. RLP (1).   Beaker in soft white-cream ware. Fabric contains small specks of bright red grog/haematite, occasional sand grits and lumps of grey, unmixed clay. Worn rouletted panel on shoulder.

147. RLP (1).   Pink, micaceous, finely sanded ware with thin black core. Traces of pink-red slip. Worn.

148. RLP (57).   Butt-beaker in hard fine pink-cream ware — tinged grey where burnished. Fabric contains a fairly sparse mixture of fine mica black sand and, rarely, fine chalk grains. (Max. size for sand or chalk 0.025 mm.). The fabric also contains fine grains of haematite/grog, which when burnished give very characteristic dark pink-brown streaks to the surface. Exterior and cupped inner rim burnished.

149. RLP (57).   Flagon base in dirty pink ware; grey core and dull orange-red surfaces. The fabric is fairly micaceous, contains a little sand, some specks of chalk and the occasional large haematite grit (6 mm.). Cream colour-coat.

150. RLP (57AD/73). Jar in smooth brown-grey ware with orange/buff brown exterior surface – burnished. Worn shoulder decoration of faint zig-zag lines in cream-white paint. Fabric micaceous.

151. RLP (57A).   Carinated beaker in soft smooth red-brown ware with thin black core. Buff-grey surfaces with traces of pink-brown slip. Originally burnished. Fabric is mottled with small specks of red-brown grog/haematite; fair mica content.

152. RLP (57).   Smooth grey ware with buff-orange ? slip. Exterior burnished. Fine incised lines inside the rim.

153. RLP (36).   Butt-beaker in smooth drab buff-grey ware. Micaceous.

154. RLP (1).   Closed-form jar with inner lid recess, in hard grey ware with very slight mica content. ? Traces of an external black burnished slip.

155. RLP (7).   Beaker in smooth dark grey ware with grey-buff surfaces; exterior burnished. Worn.

156. RLP (10).   Beaker with ware as 155.

157. RLP (1).   Squat beaker in fairly hard smooth grey ware with light grey/dirty buff surfaces. Fabric finely micaceous. Body decorated overall with worn horizontal rouletting.

158. RLP (57A).   Beaker in smooth dark grey ware with lighter grey-buff surfaces. Fine, well-made product with rouletting on body and rim edge.

159. RLP (57A).   Small jar in smooth brown ware; grey surfaces. Fabric mottled and pimpled with darker grey/buff-brown grog/haematite – burnished flat on the exterior, but left lumpy inside.

160. RLP (7).   Beaker in fairly soft smooth grey-buff ware with light grey core. Buff slip overall, burnished on rim and exterior. Fabric mottled as 159. Low mica content. Worn.

161. RLP (10).   Jar in pink ware with thin grey core and surfaces. Fabric mottled. Burnished exterior and rim.

162. RLP (57A).   Carinated beaker in smooth buff-grey ware with light grey core and grey surfaces. Slightly micaceous. Worn exterior burnish, originally

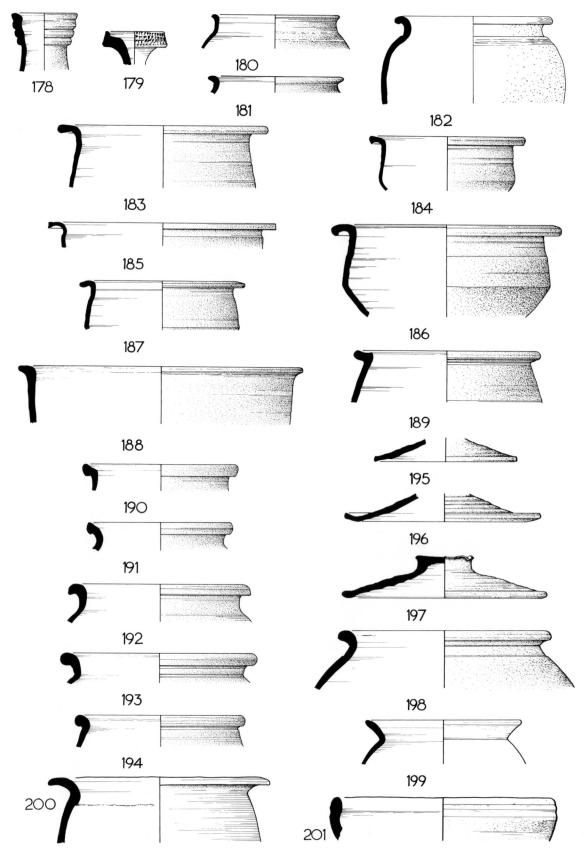

Fig. 67.   Area I : Ditch : later backfill Phases (¼).

163. RLP (10).   high. Single rouletted band immediately above shoulder.
     Cup in smooth brown-pink ware with thin black core and dark grey surfaces. Fabric very finely sanded and slightly micaceous. Decorated with bands of small fine rouletting.

164. RLP (57A).   Beaker in hard smooth grey ware with thin pale grey core. Roulette decorated.

165. RLP (57).   Beaker with form and ware close to 164.

166. RLP (57).   Beaker with ware as 164–5.

167. RLP (57).   Base of small beaker in rather coarse soft pink ware, with black core and dark-grey surfaces. Decorated with vertical tooled lines.

168. RLP (57).   Base in smooth hard dark grey ware, with potter's mark.

169. RLP (1).   Butt-beaker in smooth hard grey ware. Some mica. Exterior and rim burnished dark grey.

170. RLP (70).   Beaker in smooth dark grey ware mottled with profuse, but ill-sorted black grog/haematite.

171. RLP (57).   Poppy-head beaker in fairly hard smooth light grey ware, with thin brown core and grey surfaces. Exterior burnished. Single cordon at junction of neck and body. Rouletted panel on lower shoulder.

172. RLP (10).   Poppy-head beaker in smooth grey ware. Low mica content.

173. RLP (10).   Poppy-head beaker in hard smooth grey micaceous ware. Worn orange-buff slip? Burnished exterior and rim. A fine product.

174. RLP (10).   Fine shallow bowl with flanged rim in smooth hard grey ware. Slightly micaceous.

175. RLP (57A).   Bowl with flanged and reeded rim. Fairly hard smooth buff-grey ware. Fairly high mica content.

176. RLP (57A).   Flagon in hard, fairly smooth dirty mauve-grey ware, with the exterior fired pink-red, the oxidation extending generally to half the wall thickness. The fabric is finely micaceous and contains a fine black sand (not visually dominant) and an uneven scatter of ? haematite grains (av. 1 mm.). Rather worn cream colour-coat over exterior, and thinly into the cupped rim. Nicely moulded four-ribbed strap-handle.

177. RLP (57A).   Carinated beaker in fairly hard buff-pink sandy ware. The black sand shows clearly against the ware matrix – open-spaced and unevenly sized – (max. 1 mm., usually 0.50 mm.). Fabric also contains a little clear quartz and occasional red-brown haematite/grog grains.

178. RLP (1).   Flagon in hard sandy white-buff ware with cream-white surfaces. Occasional ironstone grits (1–2 mm.).

179. RLP (10).   Flagon in hard finely sanded orange ware. Overlapping square-toothed rouletting on collar.

180. RLP (10).   Small jar in hard finely sanded grey ware. Rim, neck and shoulder streak burnished.

181. RLP (57).   Small jar in grey sandy ware.

182. RLP (57).   Jar in fairly hard red-brown sandy ware with grey/pink-brown surfaces. Slight burnish on rim and a narrow 'highlight' on the shoulder, otherwise untreated.

183. RLP (1).   Flanged-rim bowl in dark grey sandy ware. Hard.

184. RLP (1).   Flanged-rim bowl in light grey sandy ware.

185. RLP (57A).   Flanged-rim bowl in grey sandy ware, with buff-grey surfaces.

186. RLP (57A).   Carinated bowl with flanged rim in brown-red sandy ware with grey surfaces.

187. RLP (57A).   Flanged-rim bowl in grey sandy ware.

188. RLP (1).   Bowl with simple everted rim in buff-grey sandy ware. Rim and interior burnished.

189. RLP (1).   Jar in grey sandy ware. Rim lid recessed.

190. RLP (57).   Jar in buff-pink sandy ware with grey surfaces.

191. RLP (57).   Jar as 190 - but sand finer.

192. RLP (57).   Jar in dark grey sandy ware. Lip and shoulder burnished.

193. RLP (57).   Jar in light grey sandy ware with darker surfaces.

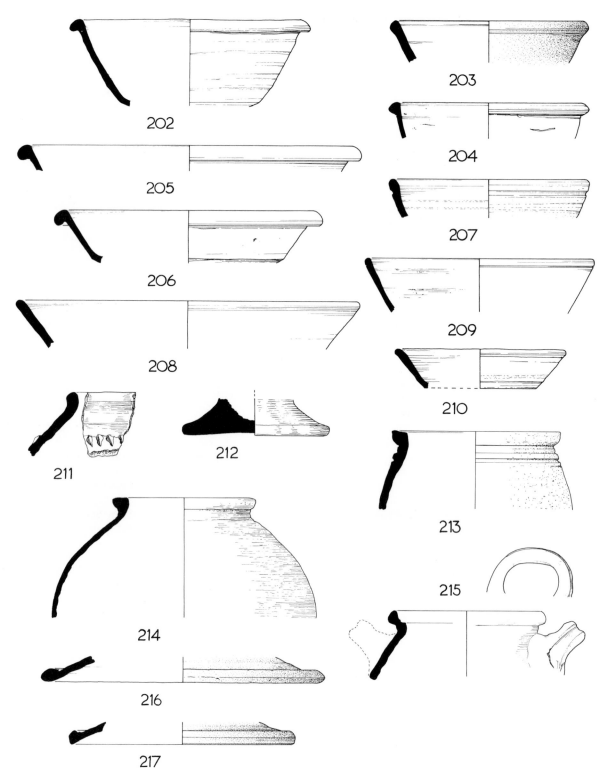

Fig. 68.   Area I : Ditch : nos. 202-210.   Area II : Ditch : nos. 211-217 (¼).

194. RLP (57).   Jar in hard dark-grey sandy ware. Rim burnished in facets.

195. RLP (57).   Small lid in hard buff-grey sandy ware with dark grey surfaces.

196. RLP (57A).   Lid in hard red sandy ware with black core and grey surfaces.

197. RLP (1).   Lid in soft chocolate-brown medium-sandy ware with some larger rounded grits (c. 2 mm.). Ware has a tendency to flake and is slightly laminated. Upper surface smoothed.

198. RLP (1).   Jar in coarse grey sandy ware.

199. RLP (57).   Jar in hard, finely sanded grey ware, with rim and shoulder originally burnished.

200. RLP (36).   Jar in sandy ware with dark grey core, with think pale grey sandwich beneath grey surfaces. Fabric contains irregular scatter of small milky quartz grains (0.05 mm.). Shoulder and rim interior down to body junction burnished. Probably BB1.

201. RLP (10).   Dish in hard finely sanded light grey ware with darker grey surfaces. Burnished – exterior less so. Single groove below rim. Copying BB2?

202. RLP (7).   Bowl in grey sandy ware. Copying BB1/2.

203. RLP (57).   Dish in grey sandy ware. BB2 or copy.

204. RLP (1).   Bowl in dark grey sandy ware. Worn overall burnish. ? BB2.

205. RLP (57).   Bowl in hard finely sanded light grey ware. BB2.

206. RLP (57).   Bowl in dirty grey finely sanded ware with brown sandwich to core and grey burnished surfaces. Fabric speckled with minute ? quartz grains (0.01 mm. or less). Probably BB2.

207. RLP (10).   Dish in buff-grey finely sanded ware. Micaceous. Occasional grit (1 mm.). Rim burnished – body streak burnished. Probably BB2.

208. RLP (57).   Dish in finely sanded grey ware with thin light brown sandwich to core. Burnished. BB2.

209. RLP (57).   Dish in fairly soft black finely sanded ware; thin brown sandwich to core and grey surfaces. Fabric contains an ill-sorted, open-spaced scatter of milky quartz grits (up to 0.05 mm.). BB2?

210. RLP (57).   Dish in grey finely sanded ware with brown and black double sandwich to core: dark grey surfaces – burnished. Fabric contains a moderate but ill-sorted quantity of milky quartz grits – as 209. BB1?

Area II Ditch: Primary and recut phases. (Fig. 68).

211. RLP (263).   Jar in fairly hard light grey grogged ware. Neck and rim smoothed. Shoulder decorated with probably single row of neat impressions.

212. RLP (263A).   Large, heavy pedestal base in chocolate-brown densely grogged ware; dirty grey-brown surfaces. Upper surface lightly burnished.

213. RLP (263).   Jar in hard, crisp, light-grey sandy ware. Exterior sooted.

214. RLP (268).   Jar in fairly hard light grey sandy ware with thin brown sandwich to core; grey surfaces. ? Traces of pale grey slip on body. Rim–top smoothed.

215. RLP (263).   Two-handled jar in fairly smooth buff-pink ware. The grit content is fine, fairly evenly mixed and not dominant, visually consisting of fine black sand, some mica, chalk (max. 1 mm.) and ? some haematite.

216. RLP (263B).   Lid in coarse dark grey sandy ware.

217. RLP (263B).   Lid in sandy grey ware.

Discussion

The whole Area I ditch sequence, incorporating both the primary and recut phases and the later and disturbed backfills should be considered as one complete process, with the main infill activity occurring during the second half of the first century, the ditch being left open to receive a gradual deposition of material up to the mid-third century at the earliest, and probably continuing into the fourth century.

Using the samian and fine wares evidence (see Sections I – IV above), this overall statement can be further refined:

1. All the material from the primary and recut phases (Nos. 1–64) has been presented as one group because they are sealed by the backfill immediately following the recut (Layers 57A/D, 57D, 62, 72–4, 79, 80, 267). The bulk of the samian accompanying these layers indicates a Flavian date, but the presence of a little Central Gaulish samian must, of necessity, give a *terminus post quem* of *c.* A.D. 125.

2. Within this date-ceiling the pottery from the primary ditch and the actual recut can, however, be dated more specifically to the pre-Flavian and Flavian periods – the majority probably being before *c.* A.D. 65.
   (Nos. 1–7, 10, 14, 15, 21, 29, 31, 35, 41, 55.).

3. Much of the pottery from the later and disturbed backfills is, again, almost certainly of first-century date, but the increased presence of Central Gaulish samian and the appearance of BB2 wares and Oxford region products introduce a cautionary note.

The dating of the Area II ditch sequence is less certain, with only a small quantity of pottery recovered, and virtually no samian. Though both the primary and recut ditches are likely to be first-century, the date ceiling is early second century.

B. THE VESSELS FROM THE CREMATIONS.
(See Fig. 7 – Plan; Figs. 69–70 Pottery).

(The letter in brackets indicates the particular vessel in the group).

Cremation Group I

Layer 156: (A): Glass flask. (V.T.-B.)
Flask with bulbous body, cylindrical neck constricted at the base, flaring rim folded upwards, inwards and downwards. Greenish-yellow with many small bubbles in the metal. A little white enamel-like weathering and iridescence. Broken and mended; part of rim and upper part of neck missing. Height: 16.65 cm.
Parallels for this type of flask date from the fourth century or later.[1] However, bulbous jugs with a con-

striction at the base of the neck but without the flaring rims, have been found in first-century contexts.[2] A two-handled flask in Canterbury Museum from Bourne Park, Bishopsbourne, near Canterbury,[3] is also similar but again lacks the flaring rim. The present flask therefore, has features in common with contemporary vessels, but as yet no exact parallels are known at this early date.

(B): Jar containing cremation, in fairly hard grey grog-tempered ware, with patchy grey/buff-grey exterior surface, interior reduced grey. Rim, lip and exterior roughly burnished. Incipient cordon at base of neck. (N.C.M.-G.)

(C): Samian dish. (See Samian Report p. 126). (J.B.) Dr 36 CG, early — mid-2nd Century; unworn foot.

References:

1. Isings (1957), 161 from 133; Vanderhoeven (1958) 28 ff., no. 26. pl. XXIII.6.
2. Isings (1957), 69 ff., form 52.
3. Canterbury Museum (Cat. No. 704.9). I am indebted to Dr. D.B. Harden who brought this flask to my attention and indeed helped with all the parallels quoted here.

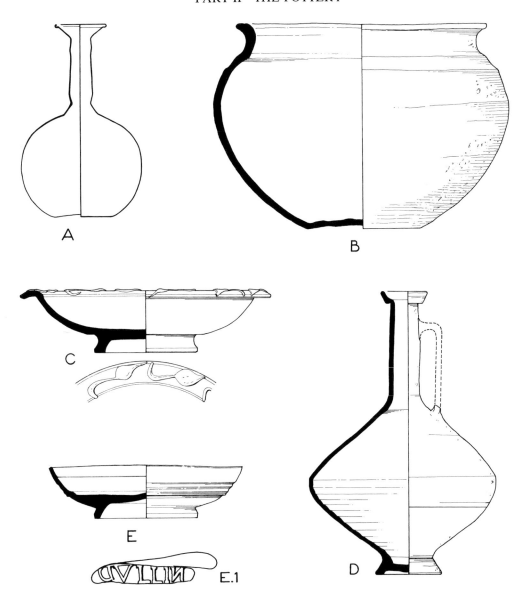

Fig. 69.   Vessels from Cremation Group I (¼); stamp (1:1).

(D): Flask, complete except for the single handle and a few body sherds. Hard micaceous orange-brown fabric, abundant fine white inclusions (probably quartz sand), and sparse large lime fragments; the exterior has a dull red slip burnished vertically on the neck and horizontally around the body. The form is close to Camulodunum form 135 (Hawkes and Hull 1947), and it is likely that the potter was trying to copy the *terra rubra* type. The rim of the Canterbury vessel is closer to the first-century one- and two-handled flagons of 'Hofheim' type (e.g. Gose 1950, types 360, 362–364; Camulodunum form 136 etc.); flagons with similar rims were produced for example, in first-century kilns at Eccles, Kent (Detsicas 1977, esp. fig. 3.2, no. 39). The fabric suggests a fairly local origin. Camul-

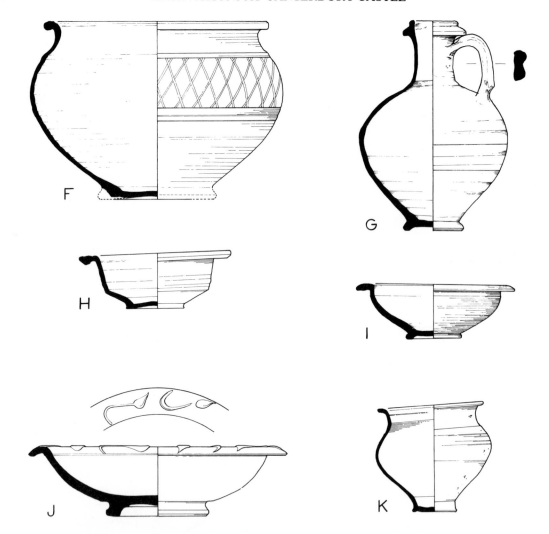

Fig. 70.   Vessels from Cremation Group II (¼).

odunum form 135 should probably be dated Tiberio-Claudian and this vessel is likely to be Claudio-Neronian in date (J.B. and V.R.).

(E): Samian platter; with bird bones. (See Section C. VII. The Stamped Samian – No. 22 stamped by IVLLINVS).

Layer 157:   *Cremation pit backfill*
Dr 30, SG. Flavian probably.
Dr 35 probably, SG. Flavian.
3 × Dr 18, SG; 1st Century. (J.B.)

Cremation Group II

Layer 257: (A): Cremation pit backfill.

Dr 30, SG. Double-bordered ovolo. Formal arrangement of toothed foliage motifs with stag; narrow wreath arcading. Pre- to early-Flavian. (= Pot in Layers 152, 159 and 164).
Dr 37, SG; Flavian.
2 × Dr 18, SG; Flavian.
Dr 36, SG; Flavian. (J.B.).

(F): Jar containing cremation in hard, dirty grey-buff sandy ware with grey surfaces. Reeded rim. Panel of burnished trellis decoration on shoulder. (N.C.M-G.)

(G): Small flagon in finely sanded pink-buff ware. Fabric contains occasional grits of dark red grog (up to 3 mm.). (N.C.M.-G.)

(H): Small flanged-rim bowl in light grey sandy ware, with darker grey surfaces. Rim reeded. (N.C.M.-G.)

(I): Bowl, almost complete, imitating samian Dr 35 but undecorated. Fine micaceous drab-buff fabric with greyish core; pale orange-red slip, burnished except under rim. Now heavily worn, especially on the interior; graffito under the base. Probably made in south-east England in the late-1st or early-2nd century (for a discussion of fine ware production of this date in the London area, see Marsh 1978). (J.B.)

(J): Samian platter. (See Samian Report p. 128).
Dr 36, CG, early to mid-2nd Century. Worn foot. (J.B.)

(K): Small jar in fairly hard, smooth grey ware with darker grey core. Fabric very slightly micaceous, body bears worn light burnish. (N.C.M.-G.)

C. OTHER ROMAN LEVELS

VI. *The Plain and Decorated Samian Wares* (J.B.)

Layer 101:   Timber well, general fill.
3 × Dr 15/17, SG, pre-Flavian.
Dr 18, SG, pre- to early-Flavian.
2 × Dr 18/31, SG, Flavian-Trajanic.
Dr 24/25, SG, pre-Flavian.
At least 6 × Dr 27 (1 27g), SG, pre- to early- Flavian.
Dr 27g, SG, Neronian or early-Flavian. (Stamp no. 40).
Dr 29 (= pot in Layer 230 below q.v.) Rosette stamp. Dish form, CG, Antonine. (Stamp no. 47).

(Fig. 71, no. 1)   Dr 37, CG. In the style of the CINNAMVS group; the ovolo and large leaf are shown on Stanfield and Simpson 1958, Pl. 162, no. 58; the circle on no. 61. c. A.D. 150–180. (= pot in Layer 101E below).

(Fig. 71, no. 2)   Dr 37, CG, in the style of DOECCVS of Lezoux. The ovolo and beads are shown on Stanfield and Simpson 1958, Pl. 147, no. 1; the vase on Pl. 147, no. 6; the small dog on Pl. 148, no. 21 and the figure and the small wreath on Pl. 149, nos. 27 and 28 c. A.D. 160-190/200. (= pot in Layer 101C below).

Dr 37 (= pot in Layer 279 below, q.v.) Dr 30, CG. The fabric suggests the work of the QVINTILIANVS group; the ovolo may be that on Stanfield and Simpson 1958, pl. 71, no. 31. Hadrianic to early-Antonine.
2 × Dr 30, CG, Antonine.
Dr 36, CG, 2nd century.
2 × Dr 33, CG, later-2nd century.
Rim, probably jar (as Déch 72), CG, Antonine.
Base, jar (as Déch 68, 72), CG, Antonine.
Dr 38, CG, Antonine.
Bowl, CG, Antonine.
Walters 79R, CG, later-2nd century.
Dr 31R, CG, later-2nd century.
Dr 18/31, CG, early-2nd century.
At least 9 × Dr 18/31 or 31 (probably mostly the latter), CG, later-2nd century.
Dr 18/31 or 31, EG, later-2nd to early-3rd century.
2 × Dr 33, EG (1 unstamped), later-2nd to mid-3rd century.
Dr 38, EG, Antonine to early-3rd century.
Curle 21, EG, later-2nd to mid-3rd century.
Mortarium sherd, EG and probably the Argonne, later-2nd to 3rd century or later.

Layer 101C: Material over floor sealing well.
Dr 37 (= pot in 101 above q.v., style of DOECCVS).

Layer 101E: Upper well shaft fill.
Dr 37 (= pot in 101 above q.v., style of CINNAMVS group).

Layer 101H: Latest infilling of well.
2 × Dr 18/31 or 31, CG, later-2nd century.
Dr 33, EG, unstamped; late-2nd to mid-3rd century.

Layer 101I: Intact gravel packing - well construction(?).
Dr 31R, CG, later-2nd century.

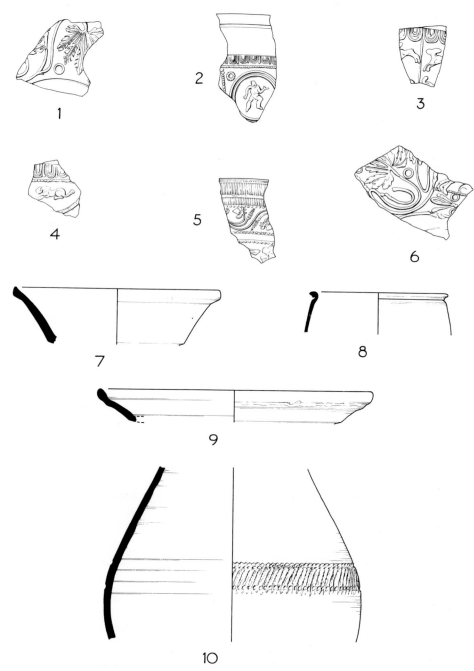

Fig. 71.   Other Roman levels : nos. 1-6 The decorated Samian (½).
(1-2 : Layer 101; 3 : Layer 104; 4 : Layer 106; 5 : Layer 242; 6 : Layer 278);
no. 7   *Terra nigra* (Layer 266) (¼);
no. 8   Colour-coated Ware (Layer 177) (¼);
no. 9   Colour-coated Ware (Layer 242) (¼);
no. 10   Oxfordshire Ware (Layer 262) (¼);

Layer 101J: Intact gravel packing - well con-
struction.(?).
Dr 18, SG, Flavian.
Dr 35, SG, Flavian.

Layer 101L: Lower backfill deposits in well.
Dr 18, SG, Flavian-Trajanic.
2 × Dr 27, SG, Flavian-Trajanic.

Layer 101M: Lower backfill deposits in well.
Dr 31, CG, Antonine.

Layer 101P: Lower well shaft fill.
Dr 18/31 or 31, CG, Antonine.
Dr 38, CG, later-2nd century.

Layer 101S: Well: basal fill.
Curle 11, SG, Flavian.
Dr 18, SG, Flavian.
Dr 27, SG, pre- or early-Flavian.
Dr 33, SG, Flavian.
Dr 33, CG, 2nd century.
Dr 31, CG, later-2nd century.
4 SG and 4 CG sherds, 1st to 2nd
century.

Layer 102: Double inhumation grave fill.
Dr 15/17, SG, pre-Flavian.
Dr 18, SG, 1st century.
2 or 3 × Dr 27 (1 27g), SG, Flavian.
2 SG sherds, 1st century.

Layer 103: Latest deposit of possible Roman
ploughsoil.
Dr 15/17, SG, pre-Flavian.
Dr 27, SG, 1st century.
2 × Dr 33, CG, Antonine.
Dr 37, CG, freestyle scene with
horse and boar, Antonine.
2 SG, 2 CG, 1 C/EG sherds. 1st
to late-2nd or early-3rd century.

Layer 104: Deposit sealing latest Roman levels.
(Fig. 71, no. 3) Dr 37, EG. There is no apparent
exact parallel for the four-banded
ovolo, but it is likely to be a later
Trier product: cf. Fölzer 1913, Taf-
eln 19–24 (Taf. 20, no. 11, has the
animal). Early-to mid-3rd century.

Layer 104A: Dr 29, SG; panels with saltires
containing corded and triple motifs
and narrow wreath festoons. Pre-
or early-Flavian = Layer 171 below.

Layer 105: Possible Roman ploughsoil.
Dr 15/17 or 18, SG, c. A.D. 80–95
(Stamp no. 39).

2 × Dr 18, SG, Flavian.
2 SG sherds.

Layer 106: Possible Roman ploughsoil.
2 × Dr 27, SG, 1st century.
(Fig. 71, no, 4) Dr 30, CG. The ovolo and large
beads were used by DOECCVS
(Stanfield and Simpson 1958, Pl.
147, no. 1.), the beads, lion and
corded festoon by CASVRIVS
(Stanfield and Simpson 1958, Pl.
134, no. 31; Pl. 135, no. 41). c.
A.D. 160–190/200.
Walters 79, CG, later-2nd century.
2 × Dr 33, CG, Antonine.
Dr 18/31, CG, 2nd Century.
Dr 38, C/EG, later-2nd century.
Dr 33, EG, later-2nd to mid-3rd
century.
2 SG and 2 CG sherds, 1st to 2nd
century.
SG sherd, 1st century.

Layer 110: Timber building: (North) latest
floor.
Dr 18, SG, 1st century, burnt.
Dr 27, SG, Flavian-Trajanic.
Dr 37, joins a sherd in Layer 279,
see below.
Dr 37, CG. There is apparently no
exact parallel for the ovolo; the
border on a bowl of this date re-
calls the work of Potter X–6.
Hadrianic to early-Antonine.
Dr 36, CG, early-2nd century.
Dr 33, EG, later-2nd to early-3rd
century.
1 SG, 1 CG sherds, 1st to 2nd century.

Layer 121: Double inhumation: grave backfill.
Dr 30 (= pot in 235 below, q.v.)

Layer 122: Timber building (North), layer over
phase II floor.
Dr 29, SG, pre-Flavian.
Dr 18/31 or 31, CG, 2nd century.

Layer 127: Timber building (North), phase II
floor.
Dr 15/17 or 18, SG, Neronian or
early-Flavian (Stamp no. 41).
Dr 18, SG, Flavian.
Dr 35, CG, early-2nd century.
Dr 18/31, CG, early-2nd century.

Layer 128:   Timber building (North) primary floor.
Dr 29, SG. Upper frieze scroll with acorn terminals and trilobe pendants. Pre-Flavian.
Dr 42 (Curle 15 type) with handles; CG, early - to mid-2nd century.
Dr 36, CG, 2nd century.
3 SG sherds, 1st century.

Layer 128A: Timber building (North) primary floor.
SG sherd, 1st century.

Layer 156:   See Cremation Group 1 (pp. 120-2 and Fig. 69, nos. C, E) (Stamp no. 22).

Layer 158:   Timber building (South), levelling prior to floor II.
2 × Dr 15/17, SG, pre-Flavian.
Dr 18, SG, Flavian.
Dr 35, SG, Flavian.
Dr 18/31, CG, c. A.D. 145–160 (Stamp no. 34).
Dr 33, SG, Flavian-Trajanic.

Layer 161A: Dr 29, SG. Similar upper friezes were used by FELIX and MVRRANVS (Knorr 1952, Tafn. 23, A, and 44, C). Band of arrowheads was used by MASCLVS (Knorr 1952, Taf. 36, C,D) and, with a similar lower frieze, by CARVS (Knorr 1919, Taf. 20, F). Lower frieze is in the general style of much of PASSIENVS's work. c. A.D. 50–65.
Dr 30, SG. Panels with grass motifs and coarse tendrils. Flavian (probably = Layer 100).

Layer 168:   Dr 29 (= Layer 161A).

Layer 171:   Timber building (North) occupation over primary floor.
Dr 15/17 or 18, SG, Flavian (Stamp no. 42).
Dr 15/17, SG, pre-Flavian.
2 × Dr 27 (1g), SG, later-1st century.
Dr 18R or 15/17R, SG, pre- or early-Flavian.
Dr 29 (= pot in 104A above, q.v.)
Dr 42, (Curle 15), with handles, CG, early - to mid-2nd century.
Dr 36 probably, CG, 2nd century.

Dr 18/31, CG, 2nd century.
3 SG sherds, 1st century.

Layer 175:   Double inhumation, grave fill.
Dr 18/31, CG, early - to mid-2nd century.

Layer 177:   Early road ditch fill.
Dr 18/31, SG, Flavian-Trajanic.
Dr 29, SG. Lower frieze of gadroons below wreath of palmettes; c. A.D. 70–85.
Dr 37, CG. Panels with ? male figure, and fish in festoon; Antonine.
Dr 33, CG, c. A.D. 150–180 (Stamp no. 33).

Layer 179:   Early road ditch fill.
SG sherd, 1st century.

Layer 180:   Deposit sealing primary Roman road.
SG sherd, pre-Flavian.

Layer 200:   Early road ditch fill.
Dr 37, SG. Scroll above chevron wreath, above scroll with small frilly leaves winding over medallions containing an eagle: as Atkinson 1914, pl. 8, no. 45; c. A.D. 70–85.
2 × Dr 15/17, SG, pre- or early-Flavian.
Dr 37, SG, chevron wreath at base; Flavian.
3 × Dr 18, SG, Flavian.
Dr 27 probably, SG, 1st century.
Dr 18/31, CG, early-2nd century.

Layer 201:   Deposit sealing primary Roman road.
2 × Dr 15/17, SG, pre- or early-Flavian.
Dr 18, SG, pre- or early-Flavian.

Layer 203:   Deposit sealing primary road and other early features.
Dr 18, SG, Flavian.
Dr 27, SG, Flavian.
2 SG sherds, 1st century.

Layer 209:   Timber buildings (North), dump under primary floor.
Dr 18, SG, c. A.D. 75–90 (Stamp no. 35).
Dr 37, SG. Rosette tongued ovolo,

? foliage, Flavian.
Dr 33, SG, Flavian.
2 × Dr 35, SG, Flavian.
3 × Dr 27, SG, Flavian.
4 × Dr 18, SG, Flavian-Trajanic.

Layer 209A: Timber building (North), dump under primary floor.
Dr 15/17 or 18, SG (Stamp no. 31).
Dr 37, SG. Small figure beneath heavy wreath arcade, coarse wavy line verticals, columns: cf. Hermet 1934, pl. 86; Grimes 1930, figs. 38, 39, c. A.D. 80–110.
Dr 18, SG, Flavian-Trajanic.

Layer 212: Timber building (North), dump over phase II floor.
Dr 18, SG, Flavian-Trajanic.
Dr 18/31, CG, early-2nd century.

Layer 213: Timber building (North), phase II floor.
Dr 15/17, SG, pre-Flavian.
Dr 18R, SG, later-1st century.

Layer 214: Timber building (North), levelling prior to phase II floor.
SG sherd, 1st century.

Layer 215: Timber building (North), primary floor.
Dr 27g, SG, 1st century.
Dr 46, CG, early-2nd century.

Layer 218: Pit fill.
Dr 37, SG. Dolphin under wreath scroll, in the general style of GERMANVS. Flavian.
Dr 27g, SG, Flavian.
3 × Dr 15/17, SG, pre- to early-Flavian
2 × Dr 18, SG, Flavian.
Dr 36, SG, Flavian.
Dr 18/31, CG, early-2nd century.
Dr 42 with barbotine, CG, early-2nd century.

Layer 220: Possible Roman ploughsoil.
Dr 18, SG, Flavian-Trajanic.
Dr 18/31, CG, early- to mid-2nd century.
2 × Dr 27, CG, early- to mid-2nd century.
Dr 37, CG, early- to mid-2nd century.
2 × Dr 33, CG, 2nd century.

Dr 18/31 or 31, CG, c. A.D. 125–155 (Stamp no. 19).

Layer 221: Early Roman road ditch fill.
Dr 15/17, SG, pre-Flavian.
Dr 18, SG, Flavian.
Dr 27, SG, Flavian.

Layer 227: Early Roman road ditch fill.
At least 2 × Dr 27, SG, pre- or early-Flavian.
Dr 15/17 or 18, SG, pre-Flavian.

Layer 229: Pit fill.
Dr 27, SG, ? Flavian. (Stamp no. 45).
Dr 29 (= pot in Layer 161A above, q.v.).
Dr 29, SG, gadroons in lower frieze, pre-Flavian.
Dr 18, SG, pre-Flavian.
2 × Dr 35, SG, pre- to early-Flavian.

Layer 230: Ritt 12, probably SG, pre-Flavian.
Dr 29, SG. Upper frieze scroll with palmettes, winding over arrowheads; wreath of toothed leaves in lower frieze. c. A.D. 70–85 (= Layer 101 above).
Dr 37, SG. Scroll with pointed leaves. Flavian.
Dr 37, CG. Beaded circles in place of ovolo (cf. Stanfield and Simpson 1958, Pl. 35, no. 413, attributed to IOENALIS) c. A.D. 100–125.
Dr 42, CG, early 2nd century.
Dr 15/17 (R), SG, pre-Flavian.
Dr 24/25, SG, pre-Flavian.
Dr 36, CG, early 2nd century.
Dech 67, SG, Flavian.
At least 4 × Dr 27, SG, Flavian-Trajanic.
At least 8 × Dr 18, SG, pre-Flavian to Flavian-Trajanic.
(2 stamps, nos. 20 and 30).

Layer 233: Pit fill.
Dr 27, SG, pre- or early-Flavian.
SG sherd, 1st century.

Layer 235: Possible Roman ploughsoil.
Dr 30, SG, wreath scroll over guide-line, corded motif, small

bird; pre-Flavian (= pot in Layer 121 above.).

Dr 37, CG; small warrior; early-2nd century.

2 × Dr 18/31, CG, 2nd century.

Layer 239:

Possible Roman ploughsoil.
Dr 29, SG, pre- or early-Flavian.
Dr 37, SG, Flavian.
Curle 15, SG, pre-Flavian.
Dr 15/17, SG, pre-Flavian.
Dr 27, SG, 1st century.
Dr 18R, SG, Flavian-Trajanic.
Dr 18/31, CG, c. A.D. 150–180 (Stamp no. 18).
2 × Dr 18/31, CG, 2nd century.
2 × Dr 33, CG, 2nd century.
Several SG and CG sherds.

Layer 242:

Pit fill.
Ritt 9, SG, pre-Flavian.
2 × Dr 24/25, SG, pre-Flavian.
Dr 18 (?), SG, c. A.D. 45–65 (Stamp no. 23).
Dr 15/17, SG, pre-Flavian, (= pot in Layer 161A).
Dr 29, SG, Flavian.

(Fig. 71, no. 5)

Dr 29, SG. Upper frieze scroll with corded motifs and spurred buds. Lower frieze wreath festoon with ? eagle: cf. Hermet 1934, pl. 57, nos. 3, 13. Pre- or early-Flavian.
Dr 37, SG; hare with arrow on tendril (as Knorr 1952, Taf. 83, A, by SEVERVS); Flavian.
Dr 33, CG, 2nd century.
2 × Dr 27 (1 27g), SG, Flavian.
Dr 18R, SG, pre- or early-Flavian.
Curle 15, CG, early-2nd century.
Dr 27, CG, early-2nd century.
Dr 37 probably, CG, early-2nd century.
2 × Dr 18/31, CG, early- to mid-2nd century.
2 × Dr 18/31, CG, early- to mid-2nd century.

Layer 246:

Deposit sealing primary road.
Dr 15/17(R), SG, pre- or early-Flavian.
2 CG sherds, 2nd century.

Layer 256:

Possible Roman ploughsoil.
2 × Dr 18, SG, Flavian-Trajanic.
Déch 72 type, incised decoration,

CG, Antonine.
2 × Dr 33, CG, Antonine.

Layers 257 & 257A: see Cremation Group II (pp.122-3 and Fig. 70, no. J).

Layer 262:

Possible Roman field ditch.
Dr 37, CG, signed (see p. 131 and Fig. 72, no. 48).

Layer 264:

Road ditch fills.
Dr 29, SG; scroll in upper frieze, pre-Flavian.
Dr 18, SG, pre-Flavian.
Dr 15, SG, Claudian probably.
2 × Dr 15/17, SG, pre-Flavian.
? Ritt 9, SG, pre-Flavian.
3 × Dr 27, SG, pre- or early-Flavian.
2 × Dr 33, CG, Antonine.
Several SG sherds, 1st century.

Layer 269:

Pit fill.
2 × Dr 27, SG, Flavian.
Dr 37, SG, Flavian.
3 × Dr 18, SG, pre- to early-Flavian.
Dr 35, burnt.
Dr 37, CG, early-2nd century.

Layer 270:

Pit fill.
Dr 37, SG, blurred double bordered ovolo; Flavian-Trajanic.
Dr 42 (Curle 15) with handles, CG, early- to mid-2nd century.
Dr 18/31, CG, early-2nd century.
Dr 27, unstamped, CG, early- to mid-2nd century.
Dr 36, CG, early-2nd century.
Several SG and 2 CG sherds, 1st to 2nd century.

Layer 275:

Early road ditch.
Dr 18, SG, pre- or early-Flavian.
Dr 15/17, SG, pre-Flavian.

Layer 278:
(Fig. 71, no. 6)

Pit fill.
Dr 37, CG, in the style of SACER: a closely similar bowl is shown on Stanfield and Simpson, 1958, pl. 83, no. 12, and has the divided arcade with horse and triple motif, similar large leaves and the corded motif; c. A.D. 125–150.

Layer 279:

Dr 37, CG, with ovolo used by SACER-ATTIANVS group (Stanfield and Simpson 1958, Pl. 85, no. 6). *c*. A.D. 125–150.

Dr 37, CG; no ovolo. Surface is very abraded, but traces of a panel design with fine beaded borders. Single festoons containing a bird or harpy, and a ? Caryatid survive; foliage at base. Hadrianic-early Antonine (= Layers 101 and 110).

Dr 29, SG; upper frieze scroll with acorns, circles, corded motifs and leaves; lower frieze gadroons. Pre-Flavian.

Dr 42 (Curle 15), with handles, CG. Early to mid-2nd century.

2 × Dr 15/17, SG, pre-Flavian.

Dr 15/17R, SG, pre-Flavian.

Dr 37, SG, Flavian.

Dr 37, CG, 2nd century.

Dr 36, CG, 2nd century.

Curle 11, CG, early 2nd century

Curle 11, SG, Flavian-Trajanic.

2 × Dr 27, SG Flavian.

5 × Dr 18, SG, Flavian-Trajanic.

3 × Dr 18/31 or 31, CG, 2nd century. (Stamp, no. 37).

Layer 286:   Early road ditch fill.
Dr 29, SG, upper frieze scroll with double leaves and large rosettes: cf. Knorr 1919, Taf. 49, A, D, by MACCARVS. Pre-Flavian.

Layer 288:   Early road ditch fill.
SG sherd, 1st century.

Layer 303:   Period II road, ditch fill.
Dr 37, SG; small rosette tongued ovolo above chevron wreath; *c*. A.D. 70–85.
Dr 37, SG, large double bordered ovolo; Flavian.
Ritt 8 or 9, SG, pre-Flavian.
2 or 3 × Dr 15/17, SG, pre-Flavian.
3 × Dr 27, SG, Flavian.
Dr 36, SG, Flavian.
3 × Dr 18, SG, Flavian.
Dr 27g, SG, *c*. A.D. 60–75 (Stamp no. 27).

For a summary discussion of the samian from the Rosemary Lane and Gas Lane sites, see Section F, Part XIII.

VII.   *The Stamped Samian* (B.D.)

Fig. 72.

18.   AL[BVCI] on Dr 18/31. Die 6a, ALBVCIANVS II, Lezoux.[1] This stamp appears at Birrens and in the material from the Worcester fire. It was commonly used on form 80, and occasionally on form 79. *c*. A.D. 150–180. RLP (239).

19.   AVITVSF on Dr 18/31 or 31. Die 7a, AVITVS III, Lezoux.[2] This stamp was used only on forms 18/31, 18/31R and 31. It occurs at sites on the Antonine wall and at Corbridge. *c*. A.D. 125–155. RLP (220).

20.   CARILLFE on Dr 15/17 or 18. Die Ia, CARILLVS II, La Graufesenque.[2] CARILLVS began work under Nero, but the record for this stamp is entirely Flavian. It was quite frequently used on form 29. Dated sites include Caersws, the Nijmegen fortress and Rottweil. *c*. A.D. 70–85. RLP (230).

21.   [D]OVIICCVS on Dr 33. Die IIe, DO(V)ECCVS I, Lezoux.[2] This stamp is common at sites in northern Britain founded, or reoccupied,

c. A.D. 160. *c*. A.D. 165–200. RLP (222).

22.   IVLLI on Dr 15/17. Die 7a IVLLINVS I of La Graufesenque.[1] The site dating for him is entirely Flavian, and this particular stamp is known from sites such as Butzbach, Corbridge and Inchtuthil. *c*. A.D. 75–95. RLP (156D) (See Cremation Group I. Fig. 16 No. E.1)

23.   [L]IC∧VS on Dr 18(?). Die 46a, LICINVS, La Graufesenque.[2] Although there is no dating evidence for this particular stamp, LICINVS other work belongs to the Claudio-Neronian period. Several of his stamps are in a group of vessels of *c*. A.D. 50–60 at Narbonne and others come from Colchester Pottery Shops. *c*. A.D. 46–65. RLP (242).

---

[1]   Indicates a stamp known at the pottery.

[2]   Indicates a stamp not itself known at the potter but used by a potter of whom other stamps are known there.

[3]   Pottery inferred from distribution, fabric or other factors.

Fig. 72. Other Roman levels : samian Stamps (1:1).

24. MARTIM on Walters 80. Die 1b, MARTIVS IV, Lezoux.[1] The record for this stamp includes sites on Hadrian's Wall, Malton and the Brougham cemetery. c. A.D. 155–185. RLP (100).

25. OFMODESTI on Dr 15/17 or 18. Die 2b, MODESTVS I, La Graufesenque.[2] There are no dated contexts for this stamp, but MODESTVS general rante is c. A.D. 50–70. RLP (4).

26. OFMODES on Ritt 8 or 9 or Dr 24/25. Die 4b, MODESTVS I, (see RLP I, Belgic ditch, no. 4 in stamps report: same die). RLP (159).

27. OFMOI⟨⟩ on Dr 27g. Die 9a', MODESTVS I, La Graufesenque.[1] As there are several examples of this stamp at Flavian foundations, the die is likely to have been in use rather longer than MODESTVS others, but it was also used on forms 24/25 and Ritt 8. c. A.D. 60-75. RLP (303).

28. OFM M on Dr 27. Die 9j, MOMMO, La Grau-

fesenque.² This stamp occurs at Castleford and Heddernheim, so should date *c.* A.D. 60–75. RLP (164).

29. [M]V+TVʎʌI. on Dr 38 or 44. Die 3a, MVXT-VLLVS, Lezoux.² This stamp is common at sites in northern Britain reoccupied *c.* A.D. 160. One of his other stamps is in an early-Antonine group at Castleford. *c.* A.D. 140–170. RLP (U/S).

30. [OFN]GRI on Dr 15/17 or 18. Die 3b, NIGER II, La Graufesenque (3b'). A stamp from a die which underwent four modifications. The original version here is not common and does not appear in dated contexts, but the evidence for the modified versions (forms 24/25 and Ritt 8 and 9) suggests a Neronian date, though there is one example from the Nijmegen fortress. *c.* A.D. 55–70. RLP (230).

31. [PASSEN]MA on Dr 15/17 or 18. Die 31a probably, PASS(I)ENVS (see RLP I., Belgic ditch, no. 9 in stamps report: same die probably). RLP (209A).

32. [PA]TERNIM on Dr 31. Die 1b, PATERNVS III, Lezoux.¹ One of this potter's less common stamps, used mainly on moulds for form 68. His work occurs in a pottery shop at Castleford burnt down in the 140s. Another of his stamps appears on the same mould as one of IANVARIS II. *c.* A.D. 135–150. RLP (56).

33. REGALIS on Dr 33. Die 5a, REGALIS I, Lezoux.¹ The dating evidence for this potter comes mainly from his forms. This particular stamp was used on forms 27, 31R, 79/80 and Ludowici Tg. *c.* A.D. 150–180. RLP (177).

34. [R I]IOGEN[:I] on Dr 18/31. Die 2b, REO-GENVS, Lezoux.² Unlike most of this potter's other stamps, this one is not known from the Antonine Wall. It is, however, relatively common in the Rhineland, and occurs once on form 27. *c.* A.D. 145–160. RLP (158).

35. SECVNDV[SF] on Dr 18. Die 25a, SECVN-DVS II, La Graufesenque.¹ The site record for this stamp includes Camelon and the Nijmegen fortress. *c.* A.D. 75–90 RLP (209).

36. SEXTIM on Dr 33. Die 2b, SEXTVS II, Lezoux. SEXTVS IIs output consists mainly of forms 27 and 33. There are seven examples of this stamp from the Castleford Pottery shop. *c.* A.D. 130–160. RLP (U/S).

37. SOLLEMNI OF on Dr 33a or 46. Die 2a, SOL-LEMNIS I, Lezoux.¹ Several of SOLLEMNIS's stamps, including this one, appear on form 27. His work is known from the Birdoswald Alley,

the Castleford Pottery shop and sites in the Rhineland. *c.* A.D. 130–150. RLP (279).

38. VIRTHV[SFE] on Dr 15/17 or 18. Die 4a, VIR-THVS of La Graufesenque.² This stamp appears in Period I at Valkenburg ZH and was occasionally used on form 24/25. VIRTHVSs forms include 16 and Ritt 1R. *c.* A.D. 50–65. RLP (U/S).

39. OF.VIT in a panel with swallowtail ends, on Dr 15/17 or 18. Die 8h', VITALIS II, La Graufesenque.² The die gave OF VITA in a panel with rounded ends, before modification. Both dies seem to have only been used in the Flavian period, and the original version (8h) appears twice at Newstead. *c.* A.D. 80–95. RLP (105).

40.]VʜK or ʌʌʜɅ on Dr 27g. Unidentifiable, South Gaul, Neronian or early-Flavian. RLP (101).

41. Ô·Fʠ on Dr 15/17 or 18. Unidentifiable, South Gaul, Neronian or early-Flavian. RLP (127).

42. ʔĹʈ◟ on Dr 15/17 or 18. Unidentifiable, South Gaul, Flavian. RLP (171).

43. ʌO[or]Oʋʅ on Dr 31. Unidentifiable, Central Gaul, Antonine. RLP (176).

44. Illegible and *bis. imp.* on Dr 24/25. South Gaul Neronian. RLP (196).

45. Illegible and *bis. imp.* on Dr 27. South Gaulish and Flavian, probably. RLP (229).

46.]M. on Dr 18/31. Unidentifiable. Les Martres-des-Veyre, Hadrianic or early-Antonine. RLP (278).

47. Rosette stamp on dish form, Lezoux, Antonine. RLP (101).

48. *Decorated Ware*
Dr 37, Central Gaulish, with panelled decoration. The fragmentary cursive signature ATTIA *retr.* below the decoration belongs to ATTIA-NVS II of Lezoux, who used the tree (Rogers, 1974, type N7), four-petalled rosette (*ibid.*, type C23) and astragalus across the panel border. The rather square ovolo and the seated Diana (Déchelette 1904, no. 68) are apparently not known for him. *c.* A.D. 125–145. RLP (262).

VIII. *Fine Wares*

The Gallo-Belgic Imports (V.R.)

Layer 101S: Roman well, sump deposit. Rim sherd from a cup (cf. Rigby 1973, Fig. 4, no. 38) in TR 1 (B), very worn. Late Augustan-Tiberian.

Layer 119: Deposit sealing latest Roman levels.

Base sherd from a platter in underfired TN.

Layer 163:   Medieval pit fill.
Rim sherd from a platter. Camulodunum form 14; in typical TN with a dark blue-black polished finish. An import from Gallia Belgica. Claudio-Neronian.

Layer 201:   Deposit sealing primary Roman road. Laminated rim-sherd from a small moulded platter, Camulodunum form 8 in typical TN. An import from Gallia Belgica. Tiberian-Neronian.

Layer 242:   Pit fill.
Rim sherd from a platter, Camulodunum form 14 in TN, faceted finish on the outside. Probably an import, but possibly made in south-east Britain. Claudio-Neronian.

(Fig. 71, no. 9) Rim sherd from a Gallo-Belgic beaker with a pedestal base, Camulodunum form 74, in TR 1 (A). Cream ware with an external red slip confined to the external visible surface. Tiberio-Claudian.

The rim from a pedestal beaker, Camulodunum form 74, in TR 1 (A). Claudian at the latest. Imported. (Possibly same vessel as above).

Layer 266:   Medieval pit; Layer 274: Early Roman road ditch; Layer 275: Early Roman road ditch fill.

(Fig. 71, no. 7) Two rims and a body sherd from a bowl with a footring, Camulodunum form 52 B, in micaceous TN. Under x30 magnification the fabrics appear identical and should be from the same vessel. Claudian at the latest. A rare form. The only examples from Britain to date are from Camulodunum itself, sixteen examples, eight in post-Conquest contexts; the King Harry Lane Cemetery, St. Albans, the only example from a burial; and Pucker-idge-Braughing, Herts.

Roman Lead Glazed Pottery (P.A.)

Layer 233:   Pit fill.
Body sherd, probably from a globular beaker. The fabric and glaze are similar to that from Layer 267 (p.   ), although this sherd only has glaze on the exterior

surface. The two may have originally belonged to the same vessel. Pre-Flavian and Central Gaulish.

Other Wares (J.B.)

Layer 104:   Deposit sealing latest Roman levels. Dish rim, burnt but a reddish fabric and colour-coat. Probably a variety of 'Pompeian Red' ware, dating generally within the 1st Century. (Peacock 1977). Worn.

Layer 177:   Early Roman road ditch.
(Fig.71, no. 8) Beaker with cornice rim in fine hard orange fabric with slightly darker matt colour-coat. Central Gaul probably, early-2nd century.

Beaker sherd in fine slightly micaceous pink fabric with greyish exterior; the exterior is decorated with rows of lightly impressed corded chevrons, to resemble imbrication? Imported and presumably 1st. century.

Late Roman Fine Wares (C.J.Y.)

For Corpus of Late Roman Fine Wares – see pp. 160-3.

Layer 103:   Latest deposit of possible Roman ploughsoil.
Oxford Parchment ware body sherd of P9, *c.* A.D. 240-400+; C31, *c.* A.D. 300-400+; 2 enclosed-vessel body sherds, 2 bowl body sherds.
Eponge one body sherd of Fulford 1977, Fig. 3, 1 for form.
Hadham one body sherd.
Nene Valley one beaker base, one 'castor box' lid.
Rhineland Sherds from pitcher (see separate report by Mrs. Bird).

Layer 127:   Timber building (North) phase II floor.
Oxford one sherd parchment ware bowl, P24 *c.* A.D. 240-400+. (? Intrusive).

Layer 151:   Description as Layer 127.
Oxford one enclosed vessel body sherd (intrusive).

Layer 161:   Disturbed level.
Oxford one bowl body sherd.

Layer 171:   *Oxford* Three enclosed-vessel body sherds, One bowl body sherd.

Layer 175: Double inhumation, grave backfill. *Oxford* C75, *c.* A.D. 325–400+.

Layer 262: Possible Roman field ditch.
(Fig. 71, no. 10) *Oxford* Ten body sherds of a large flagon, with wide rouletted band; two C77, *c.* A.D. 325-400+; one bowl base sherd; two bowl body sherds.

Layer 270: Pit fill. *Oxford* one enclosed-vessel body sherd; one bowl base sherd.

Imports from Germany (J.B.)

Layer 103: Latest deposit of possible Roman ploughsoil.
Flagon sherd in hard orange-buff fabric with some brownish inclusions, and a marbled yellowish-orange colour-coat on the exterior. Probably an import from Germany (cf. Gose 1950, forms 277, 278 and 280), Later 3rd-4th century.
Flagon sherd in similar fabric, but with blackish-buff marbling on the exterior and white overpaint. Probably an import from Germany (cf. Gose 1950, form 272). Later 3rd to 4th century.

IX. *The Coarse Wares* (N.C.M.-G.).

Levels sealing Period I Road and associated features. (Fig. 73).

218. RLP (203). Base with foot-ring in finely grogged dark grey ware with chocolate-brown/black surfaces. Underside of base, within foot-ring, has been incised — ? potter's mark.

219. RLP (203). Platter in grey grogged ware. Body burnished inside and exterior above carination.

220. RLP (203). Beaker in fine orange-pink ware with ? grey slip on rim. Lip highly burnished.

Period II Road: Ditch fills. (Figs. 73–4).

221. RLP (264). Jar in black, partially flint-tempered ware with grey surfaces.

Shoulder and rim lightly burnished. Fairly fine horizontal combing on lower shoulder.

222. RLP (177). Jar in fairly hard grey grogged ware with grey-buff surfaces. Body decorated with fairly fine horizontal combing.

223. RLP (200). Beaker in dark brown, soft, grogged ware, with dark grey-brown surfaces. Rim and exterior burnished.

224. RLP (177). Jar in dark grey finely grogged ware with drab dark brown surfaces.

225. RLP (264). Flagon in fairly soft dark brown grogged ware, with buff-grey surfaces. Smoothed.

226. RLP (264). Beaker in thin, fairly soft, finely grogged ware with dirty grey/buff surfaces. Rim and exterior burnished. Some small voids (up to 1 mm.).

227. RLP (177). Platter in fairly hard dirty grey grogged ware; drab dark brown surfaces. Internally lightly burnished. Numerous small voids on all surfaces.

228. RLP (303). Lid in brown coarsely grogged ware with dirty grey surfaces.

229. RLP (264). Presumed lid in grey coarsely grogged ware, with dirty buff-grey surfaces. Lightly burnished lumpy surface.

230. RLP (200). Beaker/small jar in finely sanded brown ware; grey surfaces. Rim and upper shoulder lightly burnished. Diagonal ? rouletted pattern on shoulder.

231. RLP (264). Jar in black, soft, coarsely sanded ware.

232. RLP (264). Bowl, originally with hooked flange, in fairly smooth grey ware; buff-black surfaces. Fabric is finely micaceous with a little fine sand. Surfaces burnished to a high gloss — leaving internally a silky finish.

233. RLP (264). Lid ? in soft dark brown grogged ware with buff-pink/dark grey surfaces. Partially burnished exterior.

234. RLP (264). Butt-beaker in very fine smooth

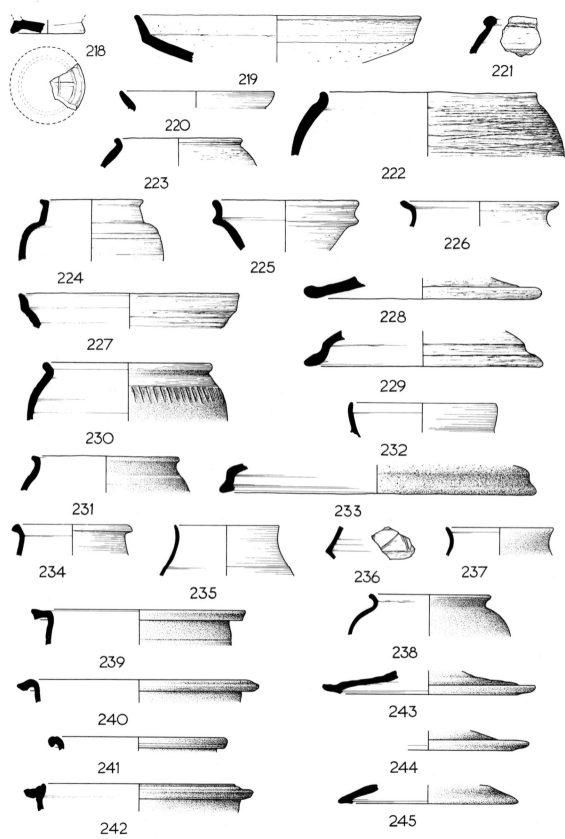

Fig. 73.   Nos. 218-220 : Levels sealing Period I Road.
Nos. 221-245 : Period II Road — Ditch Fills (¼).

235. RLP (264).   light grey ware. Rim and exterior well burnished. Some fine mica. Beaker in smooth buff-brown ware, with thin black core and grey surfaces. Micaceous. Worn exterior burnish.

236. RLP (264).   Sherd from carinated beaker in smooth light grey ware with grey surfaces. Finely micaceous. Exterior burnished. Above carination incised pattern.

237. RLP (303).   Small beaker in brown sandy ware with grey surfaces.

238. RLP (221).   Small jar in lightly sanded brown ware on the exterior streaky buff-grey. The grits are fairly well sorted and mostly of fine rounded milky quartz (up to 0.050 mm.). Well made.

239. RLP (200).   Flanged-bowl in orange-brown sandy ware with grey surfaces.

240. RLP (303).   Flanged bowl in brown sandy ware with light grey surfaces. Fabric contains brown ? grog grains (up to 1 mm.).

241. RLP (200).   Jar/bowl in brown sandy ware, with grey surfaces. Groove in rim top.

242. RLP (303).   Flanged bowl with reeded rim in hard light grey sandy ware.

243. RLP (200).   Lid in hard grey sandy ware.

244. RLP (303).   Lid in fairly soft red-brown sandy ware with dirty grey/pink-brown surfaces. Fabric contains rounded milky quartz grits (up to 0.075 mm.) — fairly dense.

245. RLP (264).   Lid in brown coarsely sanded ware. Soft. Dark grey surfaces. Fabric contains rounded milky quartz grits — ill sorted, (0.025 mm. — 2 mm.); and brown grains of grog/ironstone (up to 2 mm.) and fine black specks.

246. RLP (221).   Small jar in grey finely sanded ware. Occasional rounded milky quartz grits (up to 1 mm.).

247. RLP (264).   Cup/small bowl in soft fine buff ware. Laminated fabric. Decorated horizontally with shallow, oval, near-vertical impressions.

248. RLP (264).   Beaker in pale-buff lightly sanded ware.

249. RLP (303).   Flagon in buff sandy ware, with pale pink surfaces. Fabric contains ill-sorted small ? chalk grits (up to 0.075 mm.).

250. RLP (226).   Flagon in orange sandy ware. Very occasional chalk inclusions (up to 1.025 mm.).

251. RLP (303).   Flagon in ware as 250; without chalk inclusions.

Levels sealing the Period I, II and III Roads. (Fig. 74).

252. RLP (103).   Small pot/beaker in fairly smooth pale-brown micaceous ware, with grey surfaces. Rim and exterior burnished.

253. RLP (103).   Jar in grey sandy ware with rim and neck streak-burnished.

254. RLP (220).   Jar in grey sandy ware.

255. RLP (220).   Jar with flanged and reeded rim in red-brown sandy ware, with grey surfaces.

256. RLP (220).   Flanged bowl in dark grey sandy ware, with grey surfaces. Rim and exterior sooted.

257. RLP (220).   Jar with flanged rim in grey sandy ware. Exterior sooted.

258. RLP (103).   Jar in grey finely sanded ware; fabric very compact. ? Lid recess.

259. RLP (103).   Mica-dusted. Grey sandy ware with orange surfaces.

260. RLP (103).   Jar in coarse light grey ware. Hard; fabric speckled with fine buff grog. Burnished rim, neck and upper shoulder.

261. RLP (103).   Jar in hard coarse buff ware with grey-pink surfaces. Rim and shoulder streak-burnished.

262. RLP (106).   Jar in black sandy ware with brown sandwich to core; dark grey surfaces. Fabric contains profuse milky quartz grains (up to 0.050 mm.), and occasional larger grits of chalk and quartz (2 mm.). Hand-made. BB1.

263-5. RLP (103).   Jars with ware as 262. All hand-made. All BB1.

266. RLP (103).   Flanged bowl in hard, finely sanded light grey ware; grey surfaces. Partially burnished. Fabric contains very occasional black rounded grits (*c*. 2-3 mm.). BB2 ?

267. RLP (103).   Flanged bowl in coarse black

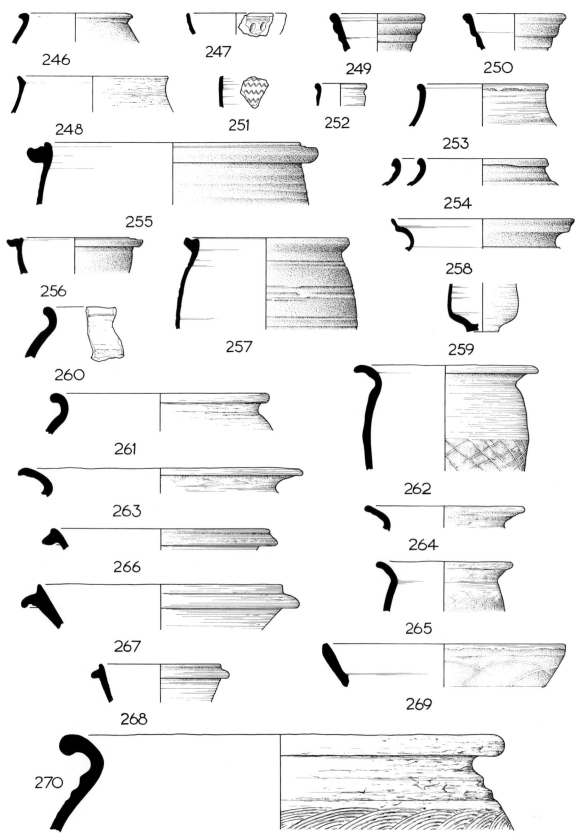

Fig. 74.   Nos. 246-251 : Period II Road — Ditch Fills.
                  Nos. 252-269 : Levels sealing Periods I—IV Roads.
                  No. 270   : Occupation East of Road V (¼).

sandy ware, with brown sandwich to core; dark-grey/black burnished surfaces. Fabric contents as 262-5. Burnished overall, but higher internally. BB1.

268. RLP (106). Small flanged bowl in light grey finely sanded ware; brown sand-

269. RLP (103). wich to core; grey burnished surfaces. BB2.
Dish in coarse black sandy ware. Internal burnish; exterior untreated with tooled arcading. BB1 ?

Discussion

Both Period I Road and the levels sealing it, contain samian dating to the late-first century; the latter, though, have several sherds of Central Gaulish samian, which if not intrusive, could take these layers into the first half of the second century. (Nos. 218-220 are likely to be residual).

The Period II Road and its associated ditch fills sealed the above, and the associated Central Gaulish samian takes the extreme dating of this phase up to c. A.D. 180. However forms such as 240-242, and possibly 250, are unlikely to be so late, and a ceiling-date of c. A.D. 150 or shortly after is suggested. The bulk of the pottery illustrated from this phase is likely to be residual late-first very early-second century.

Periods I, II, and III Roads are sealed and cut by possible ploughsoils. Most of the pottery is post-first century, centring between the mid-second to third centuries. The presence of Oxford, Hadham, Nene Valley and à l'éponge late Roman fine-wares extends the range of this phase well into the fourth century, possibly into the fifth. (Cupped-rim forms, such as 258, increasingly appear in mid-Roman levels from sites in Canterbury, with an unconfirmed date range of c. A.D. 150 - 250).

Sealed by Timber Building Phases:
Occupation East of Road V. (Figs 74–5).

270. RLP (218). Large jar in hard grey coarsely grogged ware with grey surfaces. Cordons and rim lightly burnished. Body comb decorated. Worn.
271. RLP (218). Platter in grey grogged ware.
272. RLP (218). Flanged bowl in grey sandy ware.
273. RLP (218). Flanged bowl in hard grey sandy ware. Reeded rim.
274. RLP (218). Flanged bowl in hard light grey sandy ware, with grey surfaces.
275. RLP (218). Lid in red-brown sandy ware with grey surfaces.

Sealing Road V levels. (Fig. 75).

276. RLP (209). Lid in dark brown-grey grogged ware with black surfaces. Interior and upper body burnished.
277. RLP (209). Bowl in smooth grey ware; fairly micaceous. Burnished surfaces.
278. RLP (209). Jar in smooth light grey ware; slightly micaceous. Rim and exterior burnished.

279. RLP (209). Flanged jar in hard grey sandy ware. Rim and exterior sooted.
280. RLP (209). Flanged jar in brown sandy ware with grey surfaces.
281. RLP (209). Small flanged jar/bowl in buff sandy ware with grey surfaces.
282. RLP (209). Flanged bowl in brown sandy ware with grey surfaces. Rim and exterior sooted.
283. RLP (209). Flanged bowl in dark brown sandy ware with grey surfaces. Exterior sooted.
284. RLP (209). Flanged bowl with ware as 283.
285. RLP (209A). Flanged bowl with ware as 282 — but black surfaces.
286. RLP (209A). Jar in finely sanded grey ware.
287. RLP (209). Flagon in orange sandy ware.
288. RLP (209). Flagon with ware as 287.
289. RLP (209). Bowl in hard, compact, finely sanded grey ware with black surfaces. Burnished exterior tinged pink. Fabric contains occasional rounded black grits and chalk grains (up to 1 mm). BB2.

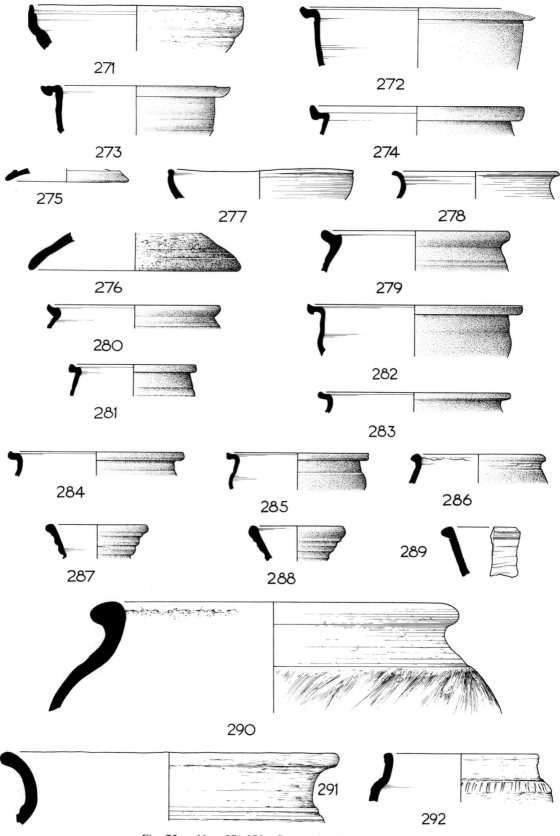

Fig. 75.   Nos. 271-275 : Occupation East of Road V.
Nos. 276-289 : Sealing Road V.
Nos. 290-292 : Area II — Pit (¼).

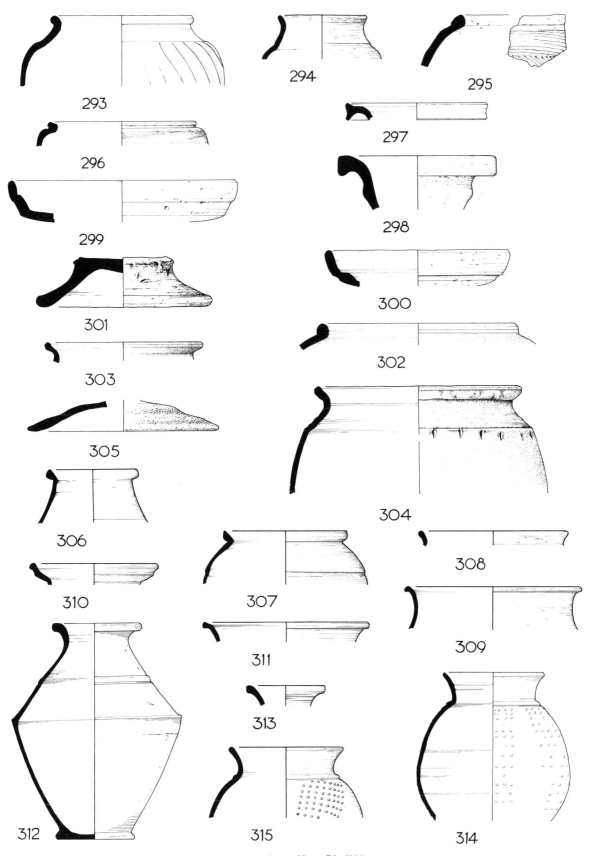

293
294
295
296
297
298
299
300
301
302
303
304
305
306
307
308
309
310
311
312
313
314
315

Fig. 76.   Area II — Pit (¼).

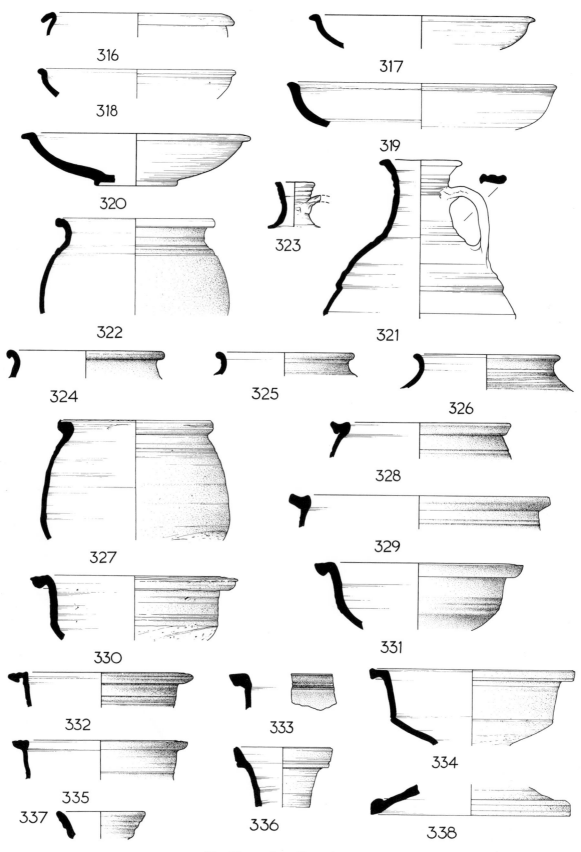

316

317

318

319

320

323

322

321

324

325

326

327

328

329

330

331

332

333

334

335

336

337

338

Fig. 77.   Area II — Pit (¼).

Area II: Pit (Layers 229, 242, 249, 269, 270.). (Figs. 75–8).

290. RLP (270).	Large jar in coarse brown-grey granulated ware. Neck and rim tooled smooth. Body decorated with fine shallow combing.
291. RLP (229).	Jar in fairly hard brown grogged ware with thin brown lining below exterior. Surfaces grey/pale buff-brown. Rim and exterior burnished.
292. RLP (229).	Small jar in dark brown grogged ware; fairly hard. Grey/buff-brown surfaces. Rim-top burnished; neck lightly smoothed. Single row incised decoration on shoulder.
239. RLP (242).	Jar in fairly hard light grey grogged ware. Rim and neck lightly burnished. Body decorated from shoulder with diagonal, spaced, incised grooves. Slightly sooted.
294. RLP (242).	Small jar in dark grey finely grogged ware with grey-buff surfaces. Exterior and rim burnished.
295. RLP (242).	Jar in dark grey grogged ware. Rim and neck burnished. Body combed.
296. RLP (269).	Small jar in coarse pink sandy ware, with buff-orange/black surfaces. Micaceous. Marked burnishing facets on rim and shoulder. Fine horizontal combing on body.
297. RLP (242).	Flagon in hard light grey grogged ware with orange-buff/grey surfaces.
298. RLP (270).	Flagon in grey grogged ware with dirty orange-brown/grey surfaces. Exterior burnished.
299. RLP (242).	Platter in hard light grey grogged ware. Micaceous; voids on all surfaces. Lightly burnished.
300. RLP (242).	Platter in soft buff-grey grogged ware with black burnished surfaces.
301. RLP (270).	Lid in black, fairly hard, coarsely grogged ware. Lip and inside smoothed.
302. RLP (242).	Jar in hard finely sanded grey ware. Micaceous. Rim and shoulder burnished.
303. RLP (270).	Jar in finely sanded dark grey ware.
304. RLP (270).	Jar in hard finely sanded red-brown ware, with thin light grey core and dirty purple-grey surfaces. Fairly heavy mica content. Single row of spaced finger-tip impressions on shoulder.
305. RLP (270).	Lid in light grey grogged ware; hard and grog coarse, giving a pimpled surface. Surfaces orange and black.
306. RLP (242).	Butt-beaker in hard smooth light grey ware. Exterior and rim burnished.
307. RLP (242).	Beaker in hard smooth buff ware with dirty cream/pale grey surfaces. Rim and exterior covered with dirty buff slip.
308. RLP (242).	Jar in hard smooth grey ware with pink-buff surfaces. Fairly thick, worn, red colour-coat on exterior.
309. RLP (242).	Jar in hard, smooth, deep pink ware with pale brown core. Fabric micaceous. Traces of dirty cream slip over pale pink-buff surfaces.
310. RLP (270).	? Flagon in smooth light brown ware; pale buff-brown surfaces. Fine mica. Traces of red colour-coat.
311. RLP (270).	Jar in smooth grey ware. Fairly micaceous.
312. RLP (296).	Carinated beaker in hard smooth grey ware.
313. RLP (270).	Beaker in smooth dark grey ware, with light grey surfaces. Slightly micaceous.
314. RLP (270).	Poppy-head beaker in smooth grey ware; micaceous. Barbotine decoration in vertical panels.
315. RLP (270).	Poppy-head beaker in smooth grey ware. Fabric and surface profusely mottled with dark grey grog/haematite grains. Barbotine decoration in panels.
316. RLP (270).	Hooked-rim bowl in grey, slightly laminated ware. Rim and shoulder lightly burnished.
317. RLP (270).	Bowl in fairly smooth grey ware, with light grey surfaces. Small mica content. Worn.

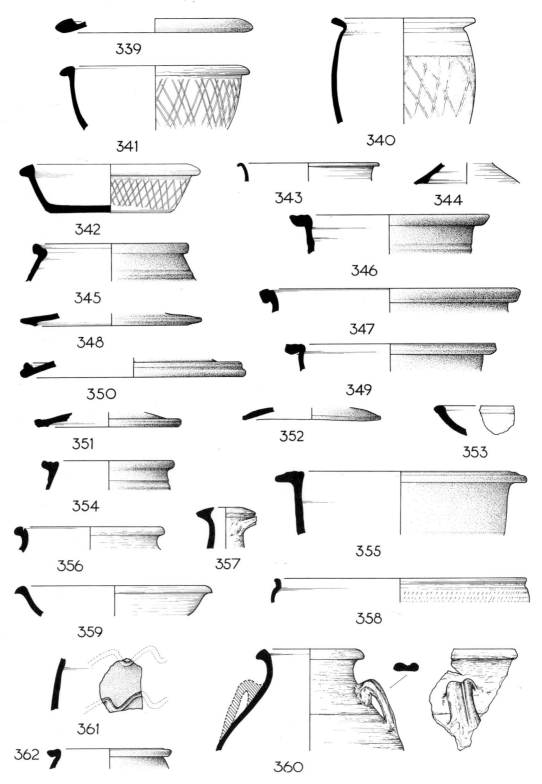

Fig. 78.　Nos. 339-342 : Area II — Pit.
　　　　　Nos. 343-362 : Timber Building : Floor Sequences (¼).

318. RLP (249). Bowl in smooth micaceous grey ware.

319. RLP (269). Bowl in smooth grey, slightly micaceous ware. Worn horizontal ripple burnish on exterior, and one remnant band rouletted decoration inside, near bowl base.

320. RLP (270). Bowl in fairly soft, smooth, black ware; dark grey burnished surfaces. No apparent mica.

321. RLP (270). Flagon in dark grey ware; interior surface purple-grey, exterior light brown-pink. Fabric contains some fine sand, well-sorted and open-spaced, together with an irregular scatter of white angular grits — ? flint (up to 1 mm.). Three-ribbed strap-handle.

322. RLP (242). Jar in dark grey sandy ware. Sooted exterior.

323. RLP (242). Jar in dark grey sandy ware. Sooted exterior.

324. RLP (270). Jar in grey sandy ware.

325. RLP (270). As 324 for ware.

326. RLP (270). Jar in finely sanded light grey ware with dark grey surfaces. Irregular horizontal tooling on shoulder. Rim burnished.

327. RLP (269). Jar in grey sandy ware. Thickened rim with raised outer edge. Faint girth grooves on shoulder. Knife-trimmed base.

328. RLP (270). Flanged jar in hard light grey sandy ware.

329. RLP (270). Flanged jar in hard grey sandy ware.

330. RLP (242). Flanged bowl in grey sandy ware. Fabric includes occasional rounded grit (c. 2 mm.). Body wiped or knife-trimmed below incipient carination.

331. RLP (270). Flanged bowl in hard red-brown sandy ware; thin dark grey core and grey surfaces. Rim and exterior sooted.

332. RLP (270). Flanged bowl in dark grey sandy ware. Reeded rim.

333. RLP (270). Ware as 330. Flat rim.

334. RLP (242). Flanged bowl. Ware as 330.

335. RLP (270). Flanged bowl; dirty brown sandy ware; light grey surfaces. Reeded rim and exterior sooted.

336. RLP (269). Flagon in dirty pink-buff ware, containing occasional small chalk flecks.

337. RLP (270). Flagon in orange-pink sandy ware; paler surfaces.

338. RLP (242). Lid in coarse dark grey sandy ware, with black surfaces.

339. RLP (270). Lid in light grey sandy ware.

340. RLP (269). Jar in light red-brown sandy ware with thin grey core. Drab buff-grey external surface. ?BB2.

341. RLP (270). Bowl in grey sandy ware with double brown and black sandwich to core. Black surfaces; internal burnish giving silver-grey finish; externally pink-grey. BB2.

342. RLP (242). Bowl. BB2.

The Timber Building phases:

Phase I Floor (Fig. 78).

343. RLP (128). Jar/beaker in fairly hard smooth grey ware; slightly micaceous. Rim and exterior burnished.

344. RLP (128). Possible lid ?, in smooth black ware with grey surfaces. Micaceous. Exterior lightly burnished.

345. RLP (128). Flanged jar in dark grey sandy ware; grey surfaces. Lid recess.

346. RLP (128). Flanged bowl in hard dark grey sandy ware; grey surfaces. Reeded rim. Exterior sooted.

347. RLP (128). Flanged bowl/jar; grey sandy ware. Slight lid recess.

348. RLP (128). Lid in dark grey sandy ware; fabric contains occasional rounded chalk grit (c 3 mm.).

Occupation on Phase I Floor. (Fig. 78).

349. RLP (171). Flanged bowl in brown sandy ware with grey surfaces. Rim and exterior sooted. Reeded rim.

350. RLP (171). Lid in dark grey sandy ware with dark grey/buff-pink surfaces. Fabric contains occasional brown ironstone specks (up to 0.025 mm.). and light grey grog grits (2 mm.).

351. RLP (171). Lid in dark grey sandy ware. Rim sooted.

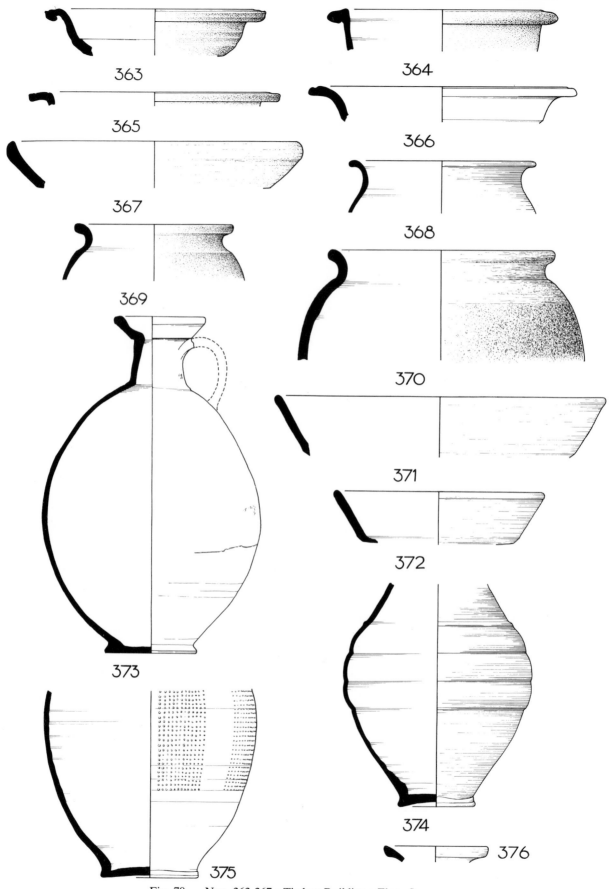

363

364

365

366

367

368

369

370

371

372

373

374

375

376

Fig. 79. Nos. 363-367 : Timber Building : Floor Sequences.
Nos. 373-376 : Well — Construction.
Nos. 373-376 : Well — Basal Fill (¼).

352: RLP (171).   Lid in hard light grey sandy ware. Unusual simple rim.

Levelling prior to Phase II Floor (Fig. 78).

353. RLP (158).   Bowl in hard smooth grey ware; micaceous. Rim and interior with high ripple burnish.

354. RLP (158).   Flanged bowl/jar in brown sandy ware with grey surfaces. Reeded rim. Exterior sooted.

355. RLP (158).   Flanged bowl in hard grey coarsely sanded ware with buff-grey/ black surfaces. Reeded rim.

356. RLP (158).   Mica-dusted. Jar in rather soft orange-brown ware. Fabric contains ill-sorted scatter of milky quartz grains (up to 0.025 mm.).

357. RLP (158).   Flagon in fairly hard smooth cream ware. Fabric contains occasional flecks and streaks of brown-red haematite/grog. Handle missing.

Phase II Floor (Figs 78-9).

358. RLP (127).   Bowl/wide-mouthed beaker in smooth dark grey ware with grey surfaces; slightly micaceous. Rouletted.

359. RLP (127).   Bowl in smooth grey ware; fairly micaceous. Burnished — high on rim and interior.

360. RLP (127).   Flagon in hard finely sanded orange ware with buff-pink surfaces. Cream colour-coat. Fabric contains occasional buff grog (1.050 mm.). ? Two-handled.

361. RLP (127).   Body sherd from decorated jar in buff sandy ware; buff and grey surfaces. Decoration incised.

362. RLP (127).   Flanged jar in grey sandy ware.
363. RLP (127).   Flanged bowl in light grey sandy ware; grey surfaces. Reeded rim.

364. RLP (127).   Flanged bowl in brown sandy ware; dark grey core, dirty grey surfaces. Exterior sooted.

365. RLP (127).   Flanged bowl in dirty grey sandy ware. Reeded rim.

366. RLP (127).   (Not illustrated). Bowl with flaring, everted rim in fairly soft smooth grey ware with pink surfaces. Fabric contains oc-casional ill-sorted vermilion grog/ haematite grains (up to 0.050 mm.). Worn drab buff color-coat.

367. RLP (127).   Mica-dusted. Dish in orange fairly sandy ware with thin buff-grey core and dirty buff surfaces. Fabric contains mixture of occasional black grits (up to 2 mm.) and an ill-sorted scatter of fine milky quartz (0.025 mm.). Lower exterior, horizontally knife-trimmed.

Well: Construction (Fig. 79).

368. RLP (101J).   Jar in smooth hard dark pink ware; grey surfaces. Some mica.

369. RLP (1011/J).   Jar in hard dark grey sandy ware, grey surfaces tinged with mauve-brown.

370. RLP (101J).   Jar in fairly hard light grey ware, with dirty grey surfaces. Fabric contains fairly profuse light/dark grey grog grains, the lighter ones appearing more angular (up to 1.05 mm.).

371. RLP (101J).   Dish in black sandy ware, with brown sandwich to core. Fabric has speckle of milky quartz grains. Probably BB1.

372. RLP (101J).   Dish in dark brown sandy ware; brown lining below interior face. BB2 ?

Well: Basal Fill (Figs 79-80).

373. RLP (101S).   Flagon in buff-pink ware; fabric flecked profusely with brick-red grog/haematite. Handle missing.

374. RLP (101S).   Beaker in smooth light brown ware, with thin black core. Moderate mica. Grey surfaces. Worn exterior burnish, originally giving glossy black surface.

375. RLP (101S).   Jar in smooth dirty mauve ware; thin light grey core and dark grey surfaces. Fairly micaceous. Barbotine decoration.

376. RLP (101S).   Jar in dark grey ware. Slight mica. Worn.

377. RLP (101S).   Base. BB2. Scratched potter's/ batch mark.

378. RLP (101S).   Jar in grey sandy ware; red-brown sandwich to core. Grey surfaces.

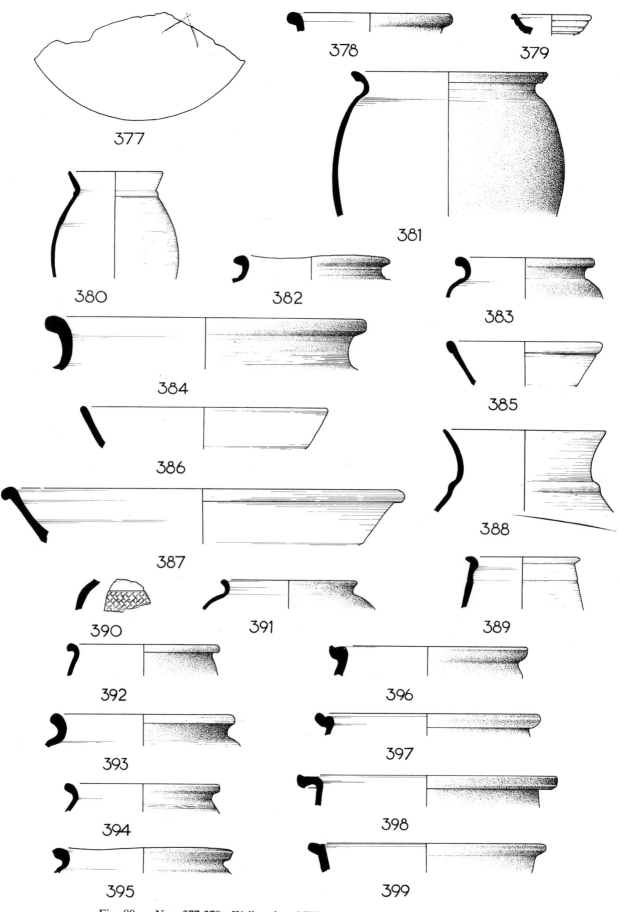

Fig. 80.   Nos. 377-379 : Well — basal Fill.
              Nos. 380-387 : Well — upper Shaft Fill.
              Nos. 388-399 : Timber Buildiing — Floor Sequences seaing Well (¼).

379. RLP (101S).   Flagon in fairly hard dirty brown sandy ware. Close textured.

Well: Upper Shaft Fill (Fig. 80).

380. RLP (101E).   Short-necked poppy-head beaker in smooth light grey ware; grey surfaces. Sparse mica. Cordon at base of neck. Worn exterior burnish.

381. RLP (101E/G). Jar in red-brown sandy ware with black/dirty grey-brown surfaces.

382. RLP (101E).   Second. Jar in brittle, overfired, red-brown sandy ware with blue-grey surfaces.

383. RLP (101G).   Jar in brown sandy ware; black surfaces — grey-brown where burnished on rim and shoulder.

384. RLP (101E).   Jar in hard brown sandy ware with grey surfaces. Partially burnished neck and rim.

385. RLP (101E/H). Small dish in finely sanded grey ware; black surfaces — dirty grey-pink where burnished. Micaceous. BB2.

386. RLP (101E).   Dish in hard finely sanded grey ware. Slightly micaceous. BB2.

387. RLP (101E).   Bowl in dirty grey sandy ware; buff sandwich to core. Surfaces mottled (milky) light grey/dark grey. Burnished. BB2.

Levels sealing Well Shaft and Phase II Floor (Figs. 80-81).

388. RLP (122).   Beaker in smooth dark grey ware; grey surfaces. Slightly micaceous. Lip and exterior gloss-burnished.

389. RLP (101).   Beaker in smooth buff-grey ware. Some mica.

390. RLP (101).   Rouletted sherd in smooth grey ware; hard, overfired.

391. RLP (101).   Jar in brown, rather sparsely sanded ware; buff-grey surfaces.

392. RLP (101).   Jar in brown sandy ware; buff-grey surfaces.

393. RLP (101).   Jar in brown coarsely sanded ware; black surfaces. Rim and shoulder lightly burnished.

394. RLP (122).   Jar in orange sandy ware with thin black core and grey/red-brown surfaces. Tooling on shoulder.

395. RLP (122).   Jar in brown sandy ware; grey

396. RLP (122).   core and surfaces. Exterior sooted. Flanged jar in dark grey sandy ware; grey surfaces.

397. RLP (122).   Flanged jar/bowl in hard grey sandy ware. Rim slightly sooted.

398. RLP (212).   Flanged bowl in brown sandy ware with grey surfaces.

399. RLP (101).   Flanged dish in grey sandy ware.

400. RLP (101).   Bowl in dirty grey sandy ware; flecked with occasional specks of black ? ironstone. Brown sandwich to core. Dark grey burnished surfaces.

401. RLP (101).   Bowl in finely sanded grey ware; buff sandwich to core. Streaked grey surfaces, burnished. BB2.

402. RLP (101).   Bowl in finely sanded grey ware; dark grey burnished surfaces. Rather worn. BB2.

403. RLP (101).   Bowl in black finely sanded ware; brown sandwich to core; black surfaces. Internal ripple burnish. BB2.

404. RLP (101).   Dish in coarsely sanded grey ware; dirty buff-grey surfaces. BB2.

405. RLP (101).   Dish in hard finely sanded grey ware; dirty brown sandwich to core. Grey-buff/black mottled burnished surfaces. Some mica. BB2.

406. RLP (101).   Dish; hard finely sanded grey ware; grey streaked surfaces — burnished. BB2.

407. RLP (101).   Dish in finely sanded grey ware; brown-grey sandwich to core. Grey burnished surfaces. BB2.

408. RLP (101).   Dish in black finely sanded ware; buff-brown sandwich to core. Black burnished surfaces — 'rippled' interior face. Very slightly micaceous. Exterior covered with ? worn dirty brown-buff slip. BB2.

409. RLP (101).   Dish in finely sanded grey ware; brown sandwich to core. Black, burnished surfaces, worn.

Phase III Floor: overlying Well Seal and Phase II Floor (Fig. 81).

410. RLP (110).   Carinated beaker in smooth brown-red ware; light grey core

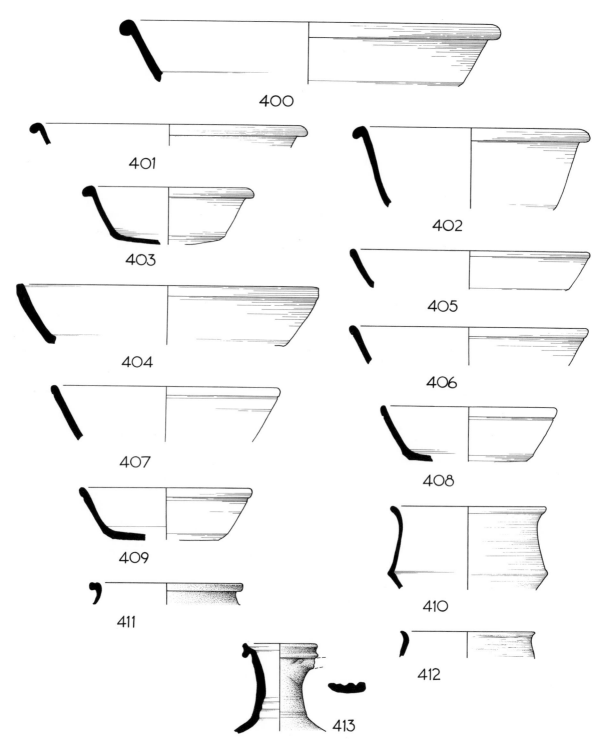

Fig. 81.   Timber Buildings — Floor Sequences sealing Well (¼).

and grey/red-brown surfaces. Micaceous: internal voids (up to 2 mm.). Burnished exterior 'skin', almost completely flaked off.

411. RLP (110).   Jar in dirty brown sandy ware; dark grey surfaces.

412. RLP (110).   Jar/beaker in black sandy ware. Fabric contains ill-sorted milky quartz grits. Rim and exterior burnished.

413. RLP (110).   Flagon in pink-buff sandy ware. Colour-coated. The sand is mostly black, with milky quartz grits (up to 0.050 mm.); the occasional chalk grain (*c.* 1.025 mm.).

Discussion

The dating of the Timber Building and the features sealed by its Phase I floor is entirely dependent on the construction date of the well, and it is felt that further detailed study is needed before any firm dating can be put forward for the above features and their related pottery. For the present, only one point can be made: the combined evidence of the pottery from the well construction, the primary well fill and the levels sealing the backfill of the well, places the whole 'event' between the mid-second and the early-third centuries, with a probable emphasis on the later-second.

A small quantity of pottery from late and post-Roman levels was examined by Miss A. Mainman, at Sheffield University, using the thin-section method. Her results confirmed the already anticipated return, in the late-Roman period, to the local hand-made production of heavily grog-tempered wares with forms confined almost exclusively to jars, flanged-bowls and straight-sided dishes. However, the sample was too small to provide a useful statistical analysis and the results will be integrated into a study of the late-Roman coarse-wares from Canterbury.

D. GAS LANE SITE

The lack of a reliable stratigraphic sequence precluded the publication of the coarse wares from this site. With the exception below, the small quantities of samian and imported fine wares have also been excluded. Context-related lists of all the wares have been placed with the site records in the Royal Museum, Canterbury.

X. *Imported German Coarse Ware* (M.R.)

Layer 7:
(Fig. 82, no. 2).   Disturbed Roman foundation. Base sherd; reduced exterior, dark grey (Munsell 10YR 4/1), cream interior (10YR 8/1).

Layer 10:
(Fig. 82, no. 3)   Possible medieval ploughsoil. Base sherd, reduced exterior (Munsell 7.5YR 3/0), light brown interior (7.5YR 6/4).

Layer 16:
(Fig. 82, nos. 4-6)   Disturbed Roman foundations. Handle, possibly from *Alzei* type 30, (Unversagt, 1916, 35). Pale yellow to light blue-grey (Munsell 2.5Y 7/4 — 2.5Y 6/2). Lid-seated jar (*Alzei* type 27: see Unversagt 1916, Taf. II). Yellow to greyish-brown (Munsell 2.5Y 7/6 — 2.5Y 5/2). Lid sherd (cf. Gose 1950, Taf. 57). (Munsell 10YR 5/1 — 2.5Y 7/4).

The surfaces and fresh fractures of the above sherds were visually examined 'life size' and under a 10x hand-held lens, and polished sections under a 20x (area) binocular microscope. The fabrics displayed a wide colour range from yellow to blue-grey but all the fabrics were very

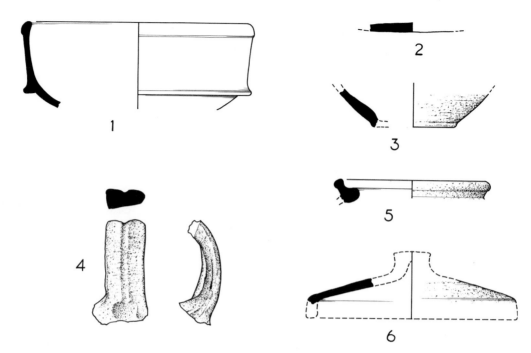

Fig. 82.   Gas Lane : No. 1 Argonne Ware;
: nos. 2-6 Mayen Ware (¼).

hard and rough, with hackly laminated fracture (smooth between inclusions), and contained volcanic, quartz and ironstone inclusions closely comparable with sherds of Mayen ware from the Eifel region of the mid-Rhine, which appear in Great Britain in the fourth century (Fulford and Bird, 1975, 171f.). The concentration of *Eifelkeramik* to the south-east of the country is given added emphasis by the relatively high proportion from the Canterbury excavations in Burgate Street (Jenkins, 1951, 110; fig. 15, 95); and at the Cakebread Robey site (1976 forthcoming), and the Gas Lane site (present report).

E. THE MORTARIA. (K.H.)

The material published here is selective; a full context-related catalogue is placed with the site records.

Notes:

BS: Body sherds.

All drawings of stamps have been completed as far as it is possible.

Fabric 2 — always means made in Kent.

All the mortarium fabrics are described as they appear under x10 magnification.

*Fabric 1*A-D.

Many of the mortaria found in Canterbury are in relatively iron-free fabrics; several of these are grouped under Fabric 1 which, therefore, covers products from a number of workshops in Gaul, Colchester, Canterbury and elsewhere (probably including one Rhineland fabric). Some distinctions can be made and the terms Fabric 1A, 1B etc. are then used though it should be remembered that Fabrics 1A, 1B and 1C can contain fabrics made in widely separated potteries; such potteries often produce rim-forms which are distinguishable and used equally with the fabric evidence in attributing a vessel to its probable origin. Occasionally, the fabric is a borderline one which cannot easily be placed in the A-D categories although it is clearly within the general range of Fabric 1; it is then described as Fabric 1, or 1 C/D, etc.; such difficulties arise most often with body sherds and fragments which are discoloured or excessively weathered.

Where iron-free fabrics can always be distinguished and attributed to a region they are listed separately (see Fabrics 5-7).

Fabric 1A. North-east Gaul or Kent; south-east England.
A self-coloured, fine-textured cream fabric, sometimes with pink core, and with no visible tempering; mainly flint with a little quartz trituration grit. At least two and probably more potteries in Gaul and perhaps south-eastern England produced fabrics in this range; they cannot be distinguished from each other visually and they include some of the mortaria in Groups I and II (Hartley 1977, 5-17), and some of Bushe-Fox type 26-30 (Bushe-Fox 1913, fig. 19), and others.

Fabric 1B. Colchester; other parts of south-eastern England, probably Gaul; the Rhineland. A self-coloured, fine-textured, yellowish cream fabric, often softish and usually tempered with a little flint and quartz; the trituration grit is largely composed of flint with a little quartz and occasionally red-brown fragments. This fabric was produced at Colchester (Hull 1963) and probably elsewhere in East Anglia but some mortaria, which were almost certainly imported, are in a similar fabric, including mortaria of Group I and II and Bushe-Fox type 26-30 and others.

Fabric 1C. North-east Gaul ?, south-eastern England.
Fine-textured, brownish cream or very pale brown fabric often with pink core and little if any tempering visible; flint and quartz trituration grit. Workshops in Gaul and southern and south-eastern England (including East Anglia) produced mortaria in Fabric C. It can be superficially similar to Fabric D but it includes mortaria of the types mentioned under Fabrics A and B.

Fabric 1D. Canterbury.
A fine-textured, cream, brownish cream or buff-brown fabric with very little tempering; it may have a pink core and may in fact have fired to cream only at the surface. The trituration grit consists of flint, quartz and red-brown material; very occasionally a chalk fragment may occur either in the fabric or amongst the trituration grit. This fabric is typical for material made at one workshop in Canterbury (Kirkman 1940; Webster 1940), though the variations in fabric may indicate that there were other local workshops involved. Some of the variations possible in this fabric cannot easily be distinguished from Fabrics 1A-C; it is especially useful to have the rim-profile or a substantial amount of trituration grit.

Fabric 2A-E Kent.
The iron-bearing clays listed under Fabric 2 (A-E), were oxidised to various shades of orange- and pink-brown. It is difficult to assess the importance of the differences in colour of Fabrics 2A and 2B, and also the differences between 2C and 2D. IVVENALIS produced both 2A and 2B and VALENTINVS also, but the latter had a far more complex career. However, the distribution of Fabrics 2A-E makes it clear that they were produced at small work-shops in Kent which, with one possible exception, served only a local market. Borderline fabrics which

do not fit exactly into any category but which were probably made in Kent are listed as Fabric 2. All the fabrics have similar trituration grit.

Fabric 2A

A hard, orange-brown fabric with paler surface and sometimes with a grey or greyish-pink core. The fabric is made slightly abrasive by being packed with fine grit, mostly quartz; the trituration grit consists of flint, quartz, red-brown material and sometimes a little chalk. The fabric may be self-coloured or have a white or cream slip.

Fabric 2B

A hard, pink-buff fabric with paler surface and sometimes with grey core; the temper is quartz. The mortaria may be self-coloured or with white or cream slip; trituration grit as 2A.

Fabric 2C.

Very fine-textured, orange-brown fabric with dark grey core and cream slip; no tempering is visible at x10 magnification; trituration grit mostly flint, quartz and red-brown material.

Fabric 2D.

A muddy, brownish-pink fabric with cream slip; the texture is similar to 2C but with a little sporadic tempering; trituration grit as 2A.

Fabric 2E

Basically fine-textured, bright orange fabric containing a moderate amount of tempering; trituration grit as 2A. This fabric can be self-coloured.

Fabric 3. Oxford, (Young 1977).

A slightly sandy, cream fabric, occasionally fired to buff and sometimes with a brownish-pink slip; normally abundant, very distinctive, pink, brownish and transparent quartz grit. Workshops are known at Cowley, Headington, Sandford and several other locations in the vicinity of Oxford (Young 1977). The potteries were active from early in the second century until the end of the Roman occupation, but distribution was very thin in the second century outside the area of production; in the second half of the third century and in the fourth century, they enjoyed very wide markets throughout the whole of southern England and in many parts of the Midlands. Their products are unlikely to have reached Kent before A.D. 170 at the earliest.

Fabric 4A. Oxford (*ibid.*)

A fine-textured, slightly micaceous, orange-brown fabric sometimes with grey core and white or cream slip; the trituration grit is identical with Fabric 3. This fabric was produced in workshops at Dorchester, Cowley, Sandford, Baldon and probably elsewhere in the vicinity of Oxford during the period *c.* A.D. 240 - 400 plus.

Fabric 4B.

This fabric is identical with Fabric 4A except that it has a red-brown slip reminiscent of samian ware. It was produced in the same workshops during the same period, but was probably more popular in the fourth century.

Fabric 5.

Castor-Stibbington area of the lower Nene Valley.

A hard, off-white fabric occasionally with pink or grey core; the clay is usually tempered with a relatively small amount of tiny red-brown and quartz particles and there is often a brownish buff slip. The trituration grit is composed of grey-black ironstone with occasional haematite. A few mortaria, apparently in this fabric, have sandwich cores or are slightly sandier than the norm; these differences may indicate different firing techniques but there could also be minor differences in the clays available.

The potteries in this region had a very wide market in Britain in the third and fourth centuries, but their mortaria are never found in large numbers away from the area of production.

Fabric 6. The Rhineland.
A very hard, fine-textured, cream-buff fabric with abundant quartz tempering; often with brownish-buff slip. Widely and evenly dispersed quartz trituration grits are often evident. Mortaria in this fabric are known to have been made at Soller, Kreis Düren, in Lower Germany (publication of this workshop forthcoming, by Frau Dr. Dorothea Haupt of the Rheinisches Landesmuseum, Bonn). Similar fabrics may well have been produced elsewhere in the Rhineland.

Fabric 7. The Rhineland.
A very hard, off-white fabric occasionally with pink core and with abundant quartz tempering; often with buff slip. It often has an overall trituration surface composed of tiny quartz particles. This fabric is certainly an import from the Rhineland and may have been produced at Soller.

Fabric 8. Verulamium region.
A granular fabric, mostly greyish cream, sometimes with pink core, occasionally with black core; less commonly the fabric can be buff- or reddish-brown throughout. The fabric is heavily tempered with quartz; the trituration grit is composed of flint, quartz and red-brown material. Extensive potteries existed in the area south of Verulamium and near Watling Street; kilns are known at Brockley Hill, Bricket Wood, Radlett and Verulamium, but unless the precise pottery is known or suspected the term 'Verulamium region' is used for convenience.

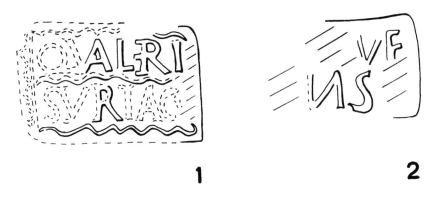

Fig. 83.   The Mortarium Stamps (1:1).

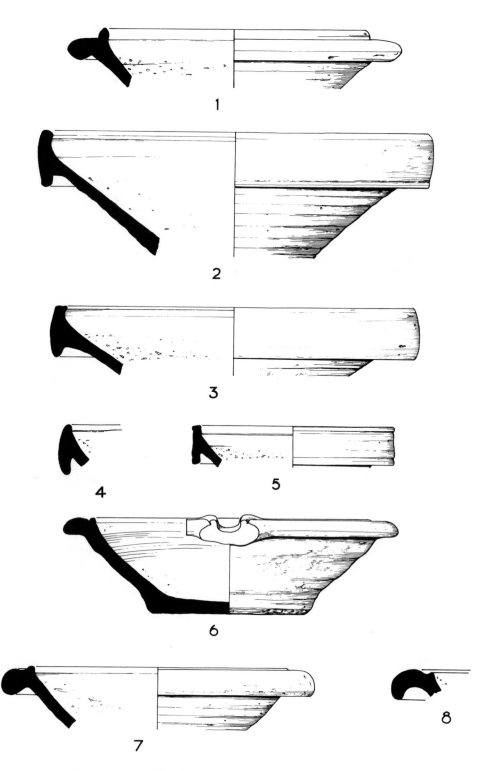

Fig. 84.   The Mortaria (¼).

Stamped Mortaria

Layers 142, 143, 101 joining: Fig. 88, no. 1

At least a quarter of the rim survives of a mortarium in Fabric 1A. The faint potter's name is from one of the two dies of Q. Valerius Suriacus. Other mortaria of his are known from Caerleon (2), Richborough (2) and York in Britain, and from Bavai and Evreux in France. He is one of a number of potters who had workshops either in north-east France or Kent, or who may have had a subsidiary workshop in Kent (Hartley 1977, Group II).

Layers 278, 279 joining: Fig. 83, no. 2 and Fig. 84, no. 8

A mortarium in Fabric 2. The very poorly impressed two-line stamp cannot be identified with certainty, but it seems likely to be from an unknown die of Iuvenalis, who certainly worked in Kent in the early second century, possibly beginning in the late first century.

Unstamped Mortaria

Layer 1:

Early Roman ditch: Area I: Disturbed fill.
i. Two fragments, not joining but probably from the same vessel in a fabric generally similar to Fabric 1, with concentric scoring on the inside only. This type was never stamped and was probably imported *c.* A.D. 55-80 (Bushe-Fox 1932, no. 350 in pit 57 and an unpublished one in pit 195 are close parallels).
ii. A broken rim-fragment from a different mortarium of similar fabric and date.
iii. BS burnt. Possibly from one of the two vessels above.

Layer 2:

Pit : Area 1.
Three BS from a burnt mortarium in fairly fine-textured pink fabric with transparent, pinkish, and brownish crystalline grit; probably made in the Oxford kilns and a variation on Fabric 3. Mortaria were made here from the early second century, but distribution was limited in the second century and I do not know of any in Kent which could be earlier than A.D. 170.

Layer 9:

Pit : Area I : Pit Group I.
A mortarium in a variant of Fabric 3, fired almost to brownish-buff. Either made at one of the kilns in the vicinity of Oxford or possibly in a workshop imitating their products, (Young 1977, Type M22). A.D. 240-400+.

Layer 10:

Early Roman ditch : Area I : Disturbed fill.
i. BS Fabric 1A, worn. Probably first century. Joins 57A i BS.
ii. BS. Probably Fabric 1B. First or second century.

Layer 57:

Early Roman ditch : Area I : Later backfill.
3 BS probably from two different vessels in Fabric 2; some burning on one fragment. Not closely datable, but I would not expect them to be earlier than the second century. See comments for Fabric 2.

Layer 57A:

Description as Layer 57.
i. BS worn, joins 10i. Fabric 1A. Probably first century.
ii & iii joining. BS worn and burnt. Fabric 1A. Similar to i. but probably different vessel. Probably first century.
iv & v. 2 BS, Fabric 1. Indeterminate but probably first or second century.

Layer 70:

Description as Layer 57 and 57A.
ii. BS Fabric 1B. Indeterminate.

Layer 71:

Description as Layers 57, 57A and 70.
i. BS Fabric 1B. First or second century.
ii. BS. Near to Fabric 1A. Could well be first century.

Layer 72:

Early Roman ditch: Area I: Occupation backfill.
An incomplete rim-fragment from a mortarium of unstamped

type, related in form to 1(i). Probably imported in the Neronian-Flavian period.

Layer 101:
(Fig. 84, no. 1)

Timber well: General fill.
i. Diameter 32 cm. Four large fragments, three joining; making up more than half of the rim of a worn, wall-sided mortarium in Fabric 2. The fabric is tempered mostly with quartz, with some black, red-brown and chalk grits; it had little if any trituration grit. This mortarium was almost certainly made in Kent, but it is an imitation of a Rhineland form, popular within the period A.D. 150-250. Many mortaria of this type in the Rhineland had no trituration grit but it is unusual to find them without grit in Britain.

(Fig. 84, no. 2)

ii. A mortarium of unusual form in hard, brownish-buff fabric with paler core; flint and quartz tempering and trituration grit. Mortaria of this type were made on a small scale at Colchester possibly in the third century although Hull dated them to the fourth century (Hull 1963, Fig. 89, no. 20).
iii. Joins 143ii, Gillam 238. Fabric 1A with concentric scoring inside and on top of flange. A.D. 70-100. Made in Kent or imported from north-east France (Hartley 1977, Group 11). Residual.
iv & v. 2 BS Fabric 1. Indeterminate.

Layer 101C:

Layer sealing timber well.
i. A rim-fragment from a mortarium in Fabric 1B. This type made at Colchester (Hull 1963, Figs. 64 and 65) but similar forms in fairly similar fabric may also have been made in Kent. c. A.D. 180-250.
ii. BS. Burnt. Fabric 2.

Layer 101E:
(Fig. 84, no. 3)

Latest well backfill.
A wall-sided mortarium probably from the same workshop as 101i.

The form is similar to many produced at Colchester (*ibid.*, Fig. 89, no. 90 and Fig. 64, no. 1). c. A.D. 170-250.

Layer 101F:

Description as Layer 101E. BS. Fabric 1B.

Layer 101I:

Well construction. BS. Fabric 2.

Layer 103:

Ploughsoil west of Roads I - III.
i & ii. Body and bead fragments possibly from different mortaria made in the Castor-Stibbington area of the lower Nene Valley; off-white fabric with pinkish-brown slip and ironstone trituration grit. A.D. 230-400+.
iii. BS. Fabric 2.

Layer 106:

Ploughsoil west of Roads I-III.
A partly burnt mortarium in Fabric 2. Probably third century, though a date in the late-second century is not impossible.

Layer 122:

Timber building: deposit sealing Phase II floor.
Probably from a pottery in the Brockley Hill complex south of Verulamium: a flange fragment in granular, cream fabric with an orange-brown core. Flavian-Trajanic. ? Residual.

Layer 127:

Timber building — Phase II floor.
i. Flange fragment from a Gillam 238 in fine pink-brown fabric. A.D. 70-100. See 101i for comments. Residual.
ii. BS Fabric 1.

Layer 140:

Post-Roman level — sealing Timber building.
A slightly burnt fragment from an imitation Dr 45, with rosette decoration, in Fabric 4B, made in some workshop such as that at Baldon, Oxon. (Young 1977, C99.1). Probably made only in the fourth century, possibly only A.D. 360-400+.

Layer 151:

Timber building — Phase II floor.
Small fragment with bluish-green

stained surface, in granular, cream fabric. Probably made in the Brockley Hill area, Herts/Middx., in the Flavian or Flavian-Trajanic period.

Layer 158:
Timber building — levelling prior to Phase II floor.
A mortarium with deep hook, in Fabric 2. Probably made in the Flavian period in Kent. Probably residual.

Layer 165:
(Fig. 84, no. 4)
Period VI road matrix.
i. A worn, wall-sided mortarium is off-white fabric with pink core, packed with trituration grit, mostly quartz, below the bead. It was probably imported from the Rhineland where this is a very common form, though some imitations were made in Britain. A.D. 150-250 (Hartley 1978, 251, nos. 40-41).
ii. 2 BS. Probably Fabric 1B. Indeterminate.

Layer 173:
(Fig. 84, no. 5)
Pit, Area II.
Diameter c. 19 cm. A burnt mortarium of unusual wall-sided form, in hard, brown fabric with greyish-brown core and quartz and flint trituration grit. This neat little form is more reminiscent of a bowl but the trituration grit leaves no doubt of its purpose. Two other closely similar mortaria are known to me, from Brancaster and Colchester (Hull 1963, Fig. 94, no. 50). They may well have been made at Colchester, but some production in Kent cannot be ruled out. They are almost certainly not earlier than the third century.

Layer 179:
Period II road ditch fill.
A slightly burnt, wall-sided mortarium in Fabric 1. This is typical of most of the mortaria used in Britain during the Claudian period. Many of these survived in use into the Neronian period, but they are unlikely to have been made later than A.D. 55-60

(Detsicas 1977, 26 and 28). Made in south-eastern England or imported. Residual.

Layer 185:
Timber building — post-hole.
A mortarium in Fabric 1B. This is a difficult mortarium to date, but it is more likely to have been made in Colchester in the Antonine period than in the first century.

Layer 198:
Disturbed road metalling.
i. Two joining fragments in Fabric 1A from a mortarium of fairly similar type to those made by Q. Valerius Se-- (Hartley 1977, Group I), but which is never stamped. They are almost certainly imports and are dated c. A.D. 50-80. (See Bushe-Fox 1932, pl. XLI, no. 350 for a close parallel).
ii. Flange fragment in fine, brownish-cream fabric containing chalk and quartz; made in Kent in the second century and later than A.D. 120 at the earliest.

Layer 226:
Rim-fragment, probably from the rim of a wall-sided mortarium of the Claudian period.

Layers 229 & 242 joining:
(Fig. 84, no. 6)
Area II pit.
A worn mortarium in fine-textured grey fabric tempered with a fair amount of quartz grit. It has fine concentric scoring on the inside instead of the trituration grit. This is undoubtedly pre-Flavian, probably Neronian. Place of manufacture unknown.

Layer 233:
Occupation east of Road V.
Fragment in Fabric 1. First or second century.

Layer 263B:
Early Roman ditch: Area II: recut ditch.
Indeterminate fragment in Fabric 1B.

Layer 264:
Period II road ditch fill.
BS burnt. Fabric 4B. Oxford. A.D. 240-400+.

Layer 270:   Area II pit.
(Fig. 84, no. 7) A mortarium in Fabric 1A, probably imported from Gaul in the late first or early second century.

Layer 303:   Period II road ditch fill. Fragment from a mortarium. Not drawable. In Fabric 1A; probably imported in the late-first or early-second century.

TABLE I : MORTARIA FROM CANTERBURY CASTLE EXCAVATIONS, 1975-7.
(Quantified by rim count).

Origin	Fabrics	Date	Total
Gaul or South-East England.	1A; 1C	A.D. 43-150	14
Kent.	1D; 2A; 2B;	A.D. 70-250	9
Colchester or Kent.	1B; 2B;	A.D. 140-250 plus	2
Colchester.	1B	A.D. 140-180	3
South-East England.	1B	A.D. 50-65	2
Verulamium Region.	8	A.D. 70-120	2
Oxford.	3; 4B; 4A;	A.D. 240-400 plus	6
Lower Nene Valley.	5	A.D. 230-400 plus	2
Rhineland	7	A.D. 150-250	1
Unknown	9	A.D. 50-65	1
Indeterminate	1	First or second Century	3
		Rim-Fragments :	45

F. OVERALL SUMMARIES

XI. *The Samian Ware* (J.B.)

The samian pottery from the Rosemary Lane and Gas Lane sites was in sufficient quantity to allow some summary to be made of the dating evidence obtained. A possible maximum of 898 vessels was identified: these included 81 decorated bowls and 47 stamped by potters. The graph (Fig. 85) is based only on the decorated and stamped vessels, as with these it is possible to know the exact number of pots involved.

The general outline of the graph follows a pattern which now seems to be fairly standard on Romano-British urban sites[1] and may be as much a reflection of samian supply as of the occupation of individual sites. However, here the high peak in the Neronian period can be partly explained by the large group of material from the early ditch. Stamps of this period included 6 of PASSIENVS, 4 of MODESTVS, 3 of LICINVS and 2 each of MVRRANVS and NIGER. Trajanic pottery from Les Martres was rare: only one, unidentified, stamp, and 4 attributed bowls, to DRVSVS I, the Rosette Potter, IOENALIS/X-12 and MEDETVS-

[1] Bird and Marsh 1978, and various forthcoming reports; additional information from S.J. Greep, University of Cardiff.

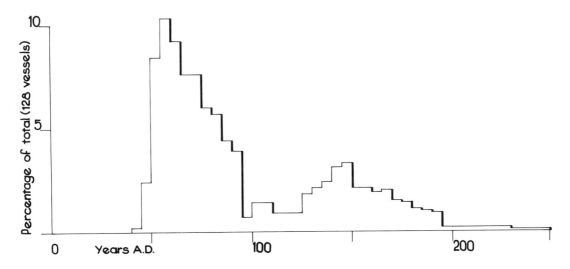

Fig. 85.   Percentage Graph of decorated and stamped samian Ware.

RANTO/X-9. Hadrianic to early Antonine pottery from Lezoux, however, was well represented, and included a signed bowl of ATTIANVS, 3 others of the SACER-ATTIANVS group, and bowls attributed to QVINTILIANVS and Potter X-6, as well as several stamps. Several mid-Antonine stamps were also recovered, and 3 bowls in the style of the CINNAMVS group, but late Lezoux wares were scarce: a stamp of DOECCVS and 2 bowls in his style.

Only 2 decorated East Gaulish sherds — one from Rheinzabern, one probably from Trier — were found, and an illiterate stamp of Central or East Gaulish origin.

The evidence of the plain wares supports that of the stamped and decorated pots. Although early forms were rare (Dr 15 1 example), Dr 16 (1), Ritt 8 (1), Ritt 9 (8), Ritt 12 (3)), there were large quantities of Dr 15/17 (with a possible maximum of 64), Dr 18 (158) and Dr 27 (144), mainly of pre- to mid-Flavian date. In the second century, the commonest plain forms were Dr 18/31 (poss. max. 53), Dr 31 (35) and Dr 33 (39), while the latest forms were relatively scarce (Walters 79 (poss. max. 11), Walters 80 (2), Dr 45 (14), Lud Tg (1)). The overall proportions of fabrics, plain and decorated:

South Gaul	Central Gaul	Central/East Gaul	East Gaul
65%	31%	1%	3%

The scarcity of East Gaulish wares, when taken with the fall in Central Gaulish products towards the end of the second century, may indicate a break or change in the use of the site during the later second century and the first half of the third. A site in Canterbury, lying close to the main south-eastern trade routes, might be expected to produce more late samian, if occupation had continued on the scale of the preceding decades.

XII. *The Late Roman Fine Wares — Summary* (C.J.Y. and J.B.)

This report includes all the late Roman fine wares from excavations at Gas Lane in 1975 and at the Rosemary Lane Car Park in 1976-7, with the exception of the white-ware mortaria which are reported on elsewhere. The imported wares have been identified and reported on by

Joanna Bird. Mrs. K. Hartley identified the colour-coated mortaria which are included here for comparison only (see also Mrs. Hartley's report, pp. 150-8).

A full context catalogue has been prepared and is deposited with the site records. Publication of the complete catalogue here was not considered necessary since little of the material came from Roman contexts and its primary value to the archaeologist lies in the light that it can shed on late-Roman ceramic trading patterns. The pottery is therefore described in a type series, quantified by sherd count. This was felt to be the most representative of actual proportions of vessel types and wares present, since the quantities found were relatively small. Little pottery has been illustrated since all the publishable sherds come from recognisable types drawn in easily available *corpora* and other publications.

The type series is classified first by ware and then by type proceeding from closed to open types:

CORPUS OF LATE ROMAN FINE WARES

Argonne Ware
Five sherds of Argonne ware were found.

Gas Lane

One sherd from bowl as Chenet 1941, form 324d. This type is not common in Britain (Fig. 82, no. 1).

Rosemary Lane

One closed beaker as Chenet 1941, forms 333-341, later 3rd-4th century.
One mortarium copying Dr 45, as Chenet 338 probably, later 2nd-4th century.
One body sherd.

'À L'Éponge' Ware
The most distinctive characteristic of this ware is its blotchy yellow-orange colour-coat which has given rise to its name. The fabric is a pale yellow in colour and fine in texture (Fulford 1977, 45). The ware was made in the Loire valley and a wide range of forms is known there. Only one form, a bowl with a very deep flange, has so far been identified in Britain. Its presence in Britain has recently been discussed by Dr Fulford who has postulated a distribution based on entry via the Solent (Fulford 1977, 45-7). The ware is normally dated to the 4th century.

Rosemary Lane

Three body sherds and one base sherd, all probably of the same deep-flanged bowl form (as Fulford 1977, Fig 3).

North African Red Slip Ware
Two sherds of this ware were found at Rosemary Lane (see Bird 1977, for general discussion).
One base sherd of dish or platter as Hayes 1972, forms 48-50, 3rd-4th century.
One body sherd of a small bowl (cf. Hayes 1972, form 52); probably African Red Slip Ware; 4th century.

Hadham Ware
This is a hard, orange sandy ware with a burnished orange surface. It was apparently made at kiln sites around Much Hadham on the Essex/Hertfordshire border and is widely distributed

throughout East Anglia and the home counties north of the Thames (e.g. Frere 1972, Fig. 136, 1204; Orton 1977, 37). Others have been found as far away as Wroxeter. The most common forms appear to have been bowls copying samian forms such as Dr 36, or 38, large face-mask jars and flagons, and necked bowls copying the Oxford form C75, often with 'Romano-Saxon' decoration. One sherd was found at Rosemary Lane.

TABLE II. LATE-ROMAN FINE WARES FROM CANTERBURY CASTLE EXCAVATIONS, 1975-7. (Quantified by sherd count; figures in parenthesis are percentages; X = less than one per cent).

WARE	Closed forms	Tableware	Other bowls	c/c mortaria	TOTALS
Argonne	1(1)	2(1)	—	1(1)	4(3)
A l'|Éponge	—	4(3)	—	—	4(3)
N. African Red Slip Ware	—	2(1)	—	—	2(1)
Hadham	—	1(1)	—	—	1(1)
Nene Valley	3(2)	3(2)	1(1)	—	7(5)
Oxon p.w.	2(1)	1(1)	—	—	3(2)
Oxon c/c	38(27)	70(49)	—	11(8)	119(84)
German	2(1)	—	—	—	2(1)
TOTALS	46(32)	83(58)	1(1)	12(9)	142(100)

Rosemary Lane

One body sherd from a bowl.

Nene Valley

The most distinctive colour-coat ware from the Nene Valley kilns around Durobrivae has a fine white, sandy fabric containing small fragments of grog. The colour-coat varies from red-orange to black. Less common varieties of the ware can be orange or reddish in colour (Hartley 1960). Seven sherds were found at Gas Street and Rosemary Lane.

Gas Street

Flange-rim pie dish (cf. Hartley 1960, Fig. 4, 16).
Bowl base with footring, probably from some form copying a samian or similar form.
Rouletted bowl body sherd, probably from same bowl as last.

Rosemary Lane

Lid of 'Castor Box' (cf. Hartley 1960, Fig. 4, 18).
Three body sherds of enclosed vessels.

Oxfordshire Wares

The vast bulk of the late-Roman fine wares from the two sites were from the Oxfordshire kilns. Type references here are to the recently published survey of the industry where full discussions of the wares and their dating will be found (Young 1977).

a. Parchment Ware

This fine white ware with red-painted decoration is the least common of the widely traded Oxfordshire wares. Only three sherds were found.

Rosemary Lane

Two body sherds of enclosed vessels, probably either P8 or P9. *c* A.D. 240-400+.
P24, carinated bowl. This was the most common parchment-ware form *c*. A.D. 240-400+.

b. Colour-coated ware

This ware was well represented, over 100 sherds being found on the two sites. The following types were found:

Gas Street

C22, bulbous beaker, undecorated or decoration not known, *c*. A.D. 240-400+
C51, flanged bowl copying Dr 38; 4 examples, *c*. A.D. 240-400+
C77, necked bowl with painted decoration; one example, *c*. A.D. 340-400+
C81, wall-sided bead-rim bowl, one only, *c*. A.D. 300-400+
C97, mortarium copying Dr 45, 2 examples, *c*. A.D. 240-400+

Also 3 body sherds of beakers, flagons or jars, 12 body and base sherds of bowls, 3 body sherds of mortaria.

Rosemary Lane

C22, bulbous beaker, undecorated or decoration not known; 4 examples, *c*. A.D. 240-400+
C23, as last but with broad rouletted band on shoulder and upper body; 3 examples *c*. A.D. 240-400+
C28, as C22 but with applied barbotine scales on the body, one only, *c*. A.D. 270-400+
C31, as C22 but with round indentations on body, one only; *c*. A.D. 300-400+
C46, bowl copying Dr 31R with very fat bead rim; one only *c*. A.D. 340-400+
C51, bowl copying Dr 38; 6 examples, *c*. A.D. 240-400+
C52, as last but with painted decoration on flange; one only *c*. A.D. 350-400+
C68, full-bellied bead-rim bowl; one only *c*. A.D. 300-400+
C69, as last but with painted decoration; one only *c*. A.D. 325-400+

C71, full-bellied bowl with double bead-rim; one only *c.* A.D. 300-400+

C75, necked bowl; 6 examples, *c.* A.D. 325-400+

C78, as last but with impressed decoration, 2 examples, *c.* A.D. 340-400+

C79, as last plus dimples; one only *c.* A.D. 340-400+

C82, wall-sided bead-rim bowl with painted decoration, *c.* A.D. 325-400+

C97, mortarium copying Dr 45; one only *c.* A.D. 240-400+

C99, mortarium copying Dr 45; one only *c.* A.D. 360-400+ (see pp. 164-5 below).

Also 25 body sherds of beakers, flagons or jars, 29 body or base sherds of bowls, 4 body sherds of mortaria.

German Imports
Several sherds of 2 colour-coat pitchers, probably from the Mosel valley, were found. They are reported on elsewhere by Joanna Bird. (See p. 133).

Discussion.

Table II summarises the information given above. The vessels of each ware represented have been categorised into closed vessels such as flagons, beakers or jars, bowl forms copying or derivative from samian and intended for fine tableware, bowl or dish forms derived from utilitarian forms more common in reduced-fired wares, and colour-coated mortaria. The widespread use of this type of approach will eventually produce the quantified evidence necessary for the proper discussion of the trade and distribution of pottery (cf. Fulford 1975, Fulford and Young 1978).

The total sample discussed here is quite small (142 sherds only) and is not particularly suitable for statistical analysis. However, certain points can be made. The major source of supply was clearly the Oxford industry, providing nearly 90 of the sample. Five per cent came from the Nene Valley industry. Of particular interest is the appearance of one sherd from the Hadham industry on the Essex/Hertfordshire border. This is not perhaps surprising since the ware is strongly distributed along the north side of the Thames estuary, but it must be noted that this is the first *recorded* find in Kent.

About eight per cent of the late Roman fine wares from the two sites were imports from the Continent. The presence of such wares from the Rhineland and north-east France should not cause surprise in view of the known distribution of Argonne ware (Fulford 1977, Fig. 1) and of coarse wares from the Eifel region (Fulford, Bird 1975). Of particular note is the occurrence of pottery 'à l'éponge' made in the Loire valley and thought to be imported through the Solent (Fulford 1977, 45-7), as this indicates that it may well be more common in the south-east than might have been thought. The two sherds of African Red Slip Ware are further evidence of its sporadic occurrence on sites in south-east England throughout the Roman period (cf. Bird 1977). It will be most interesting to see if other groups of late-Roman fine wares from Canterbury or the south-east confirm or substantially alter the pattern suggested here.

XIII. *Overall List of Roman and Late Roman imported Wares*

A summary list (Table III) of the imported wares from both sites was considered necessary in order to emphasize the unusual range and quantity of imports from these excavations (samian excluded). It should be noted that many of these wares are as yet imperfectly known and the sources are in some cases unconfirmed.

TABLE III: LIST OF ROMAN AND LATE ROMAN IMPORTED WARES FROM CANTERBURY CASTLE EXCAVATIONS, 1975-7. (Quantified by sherd count. RLP — Rosemary Lane; GL — Gas Lane. RLP 1 — Early Roman Ditches: RLP 2 — Other Roman Levels)

TYPE	FABRIC SOURCES	RLP 1	RLP 2	GL	TOTALS
Gallo-Belgic	Terra Nigra	6	7		13
	Terra Rubra	3	3		6
	Rhineland/Bavay	5			5
Roman Fws	Lyons c/c	12	2		14
	White Ware ? SE England	2	1		3
	? Colchester	2	20		22
	CG Lead-Glazed	1	1		2
	Lamps ? Italian	1			1
	? c. A.D. 70-150 Cologne area		24		24
	? Early Nene Valley		1		1
	? Cologne/Early Nene Valley	2			2
	? Pompeian Red Ware		1		1
	African Red Slip Ware		2		2
	CG product		1		1
	CG 'Rhenish' Ware		9		9
	Trier 'Rhenish' Ware		12		12
	Nene Valley	2	4	3	9
	? Nene Valley		6		6
	Oxford p.w.		3		3
	Oxford c/c	3	94	22	119
	Hadham		1		1
	Argonne		3	1	4
	A l'Eponge		4		4
	German		2		2
	Unknown source		3		3
	Unknown source ? import	2	8		10
Roman Cws	German Eifel Region			5	5
Mortaria	Fabric 1 ? source	4	12		16
	NE France/Kent	7	14		21
	Colchester/Kent 2nd century	4	18		23
	Kent	5	24		29
	Oxford		15		15

TYPE	FABRIC SOURCES	RLP 1	RLP 2	GL	TOTALS
Mortaria	Nene Valley		3		3
	Rhineland		2		2
	Colchester 3rd-4th century		1		1
	Brockley Hill		2		2
	Other Kentish		2		2
	Unknown source		10		10

The table also summarises the information contained in a full context-related catalogue of the early Roman colour-coat wares found — compiled jointly by Mrs. Bird and Dr. Young. As above, the catalogue has been placed with the archive material. However, three of the ware types identified by them are unconfirmed, and as such warrant extraction and mention here:

? Cologne fine white ware — hard, fine white ware with no visible inclusions, often rough-cast, with a dark grey colour-coat. This ware was probably made in the Cologne area *c.* A.D. 70-150.

? Nene Valley — fine ware, with some rounded red and white inclusions; normally the fabric is creamy-white but can be pinkish or yellow. The colour-coat is normally dark. This ware probably comes from the Nene Valley and little of it is likely to date earlier than the mid-second century.

? Colchester — fine, hard orange ware often with a grey core, and a variety of small white inclusions, with matt-brown or black colour-coat. Most vessels in this ware will date to the second half of the second century.

G. THE SAXO-NORMAN FEATURES

XVI. *The Coarse Wares* (N.C. M-G.)

Area I : Pits. (Figs. 86–7)

414. RLP (3). Bowl/wide mouthed cooking-pot, in fairly hard light grey sandy ware with grey/dirty buff-brown surfaces. Fabric contains sparse scatter of brown-red grog (up to 1 mm.). Hand-made. Internal finger pulls only roughly smoothed over. Marked knife-trimming leaving external body faceted.

415. RLP (56). Large cooking-pot in hard light grey sandy ware.

416. RLP (56). Large cooking-pot in light grey sandy ware with orange-grey surfaces. Small grog inclusions. Outer surface lumpy below neck.

417-9. RLP (56). As 415-6 for ware.

420. RLP (56). Import. Strap-handle from spouted pitcher, with red paint; probably Pingsdorf-type ware.

Examined and commented upon by Miss A. Mainman, Sheffield University:

Recent research has emphasized the extent of the Pingsdorf-type production. As a result, besides the famous centres in the Vorge-birge, other kilns producing macro-scopically and typologically identical wares have been found near Hanover and Aachen. There still remains the problem of distinguishing between the Limburg wares, of similar form, and the authentic Pingsdorf types.

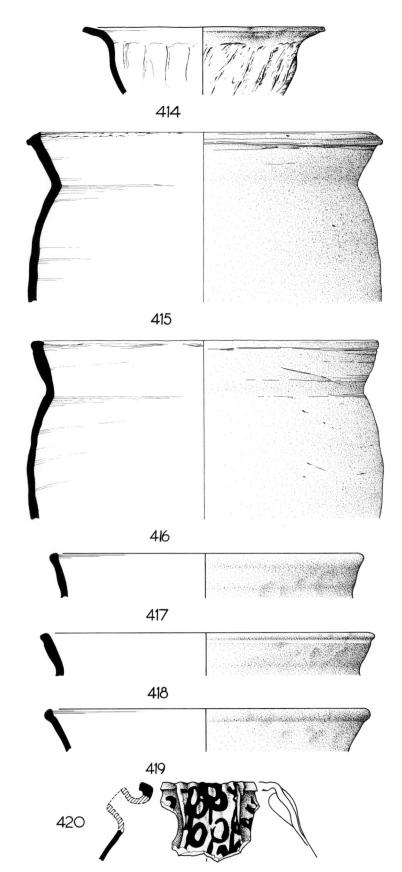

414

415

416

417

418

419

420

Fig. 86.   The Saxon-Norman Features : No. 420 Pingsdorf-type Ware (¼).

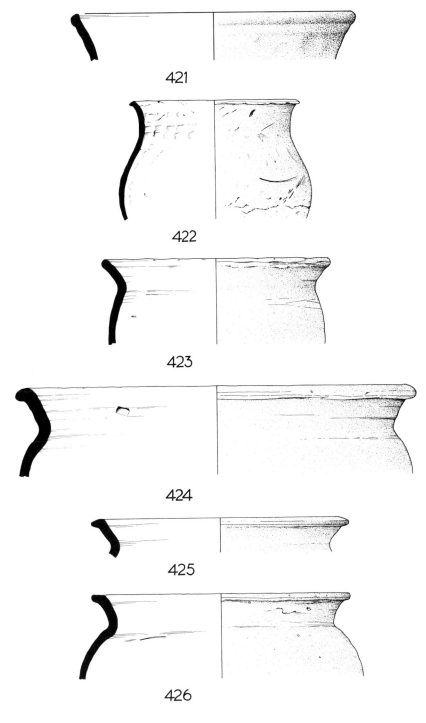

421

422

423

424

425

426

Fig. 87.   The Saxon-Norman Features (¼).

Pingsdorf-type production was in operation in the Rhineland after 900 A.D. and the red-painted 'comma' decoration of this type is often attributed to the early phases of the industry. It seems to have been replaced in the 12th (or early 13th) century by straight-line decoration.

421. RLP (59).   Large cooking-pot in fairly soft grey-pink coarsely sanded ware; dirty grey-brown/orange-grey sur-faces. Occasional small brown-red grog.

Area II : Barrel-lined well. (Fig. 87).

422. RLP (152A).   Small cooking-pot in grey sandy ware with chocolate-brown sur-faces, sooted black outside and over the lip. The fabric includes a rather coarse sand, small specks of a shiny black substance (? coal), grains of brown and vermilion grog (up to 0.07 mm.), and grits of dark grey and buff clay. Several

voids. Hand-made.

423. RLP (159).   Cooking-pot in hard dark grey. Structure very slightly laminated where the thin, and harder, dark grey core is present. Occasional large grits (0.05 mm.) of chalk or stone.

424. RLP (159).   Large cooking-pot in hard grey sandy ware; surfaces light grey. Structure very slightly laminated where the thin, and harder, dark grey core is present. Occasional large grits (0.05 mm.) of chalk or stone.

425. RLP (159).   Cooking-pot in soft red-brown sandy ware, with thin grey core. Several grits of buff clay.

Pit: Layer 163. (Fig. 87).

426. RLP (163).   Cooking-pot in dark grey sandy ware with grey surfaces. Rather coarse with several large grits of brick-red grog (0.03 mm.). Sooted.

Discussion

Although a moderate quantity of medieval and post-medieval wares came from the excavation, only the Saxo-Norman pottery is presented here — the material coming from features outside the Castle ditch which are either prior to, or contemporary with, the construction of the Castle.

The knife-trimmed bowl, No. 414, is certainly the earliest of the illustrated pottery, and tentatively dated to the tenth century.

The pottery from Pit 59 is the most useful. The pit was cut by the Castle ditch which pre-sumably, as with the Castle construction, can be dated to the 1080s. Cooking-pot 421, from this pit, falls into Professor Frere's Group II (*Arch. Cant.* lxviii (1954), 128 ff., and present report p. 68, fig. 35, no. 28) which was then (1954) provisionally dated to *c.* 1050–1100. The presence of 421 in this context considerably substantiates the original estimate. The material from Pit 56 (nos. 415-420) is also in Group II and dated as 421; the Pingsdorf handle, with a relatively long stylistic life, fits reasonably well here.

The pottery from the Area II Barrel Well is more difficult to place since it contains elements from Group II (424 certainly), and possibly Group III (425); nos. 422 and 423 are both probably Group I, though the latter could be transitional I/II. If none of the material is intrusive, this gives the well a potential use range from *c.* 1000–1150, though the original date is likely to have been narrower.

A small selection of Saxo-Norman and medieval pottery was examined petrologically by Miss A. Mainman at Sheffield University. The results will be included in a future report.

PART III

THE FINDS

Mrs. I.P. Garrard

(with contributions by D.F. Mackreth, G. Webster, J. Watson, J. Anstee, L. Biek,
R.M. Reece and Miss M. Archibald).

For brevity, in the individual reports the first number in brackets e.g. RLP (33, 45) equals the layer number, and the second the small find number. Except where the individual find is of great importance, no attempt has been made to quote all the parallels. (RLP is the Rosemary Lane site and GS the Gas Street site).

We are most grateful to Gill Brown, for drawing the small finds, to Dave Gilbert, for the quernstones, to John Bowen, for the architectural stone, and to Margaret Tremayne, for drawing the swords and their associated small finds.

A. THE BROOCHES D.F. Mackreth.
   (Fig. 88)

Colchester

1. RLP (277, 114). The spring has ten coils. The hook is attenuated and is carefully tapered to a point. Each wing has two vertical flutes lying between grooves and divided by another. The bow is broad, has a sharp bend at the head, a groove down the centre, and tapers to a narrow foot with two cross-cuts. On either side of the head is a step made by cutting into the edge of the expanding bow. Down the front, and lying across the groove, is what appears to be a line of rocker-arm ornament. Both sides of the catch-plate are outlined by lightly marked and close-set rocker-arm decoration. The return has a groove at the top and four sets of grooves arranged to form a chevron down its length. There are seven holes which were punched through the catch-plate and arranged as a *quincunx* with a vertical pair below. The brooch is carefully finished.

It is the manner in which the spring and hook for the chord grow out of the body of the brooch which demonstrates that it is a Colchester type, otherwise it is a development from the proper type which is hardly ever decorated on both wings and bow. The ornament on the former would normally consist of simple fluting, while on the latter, the common form is a raised chevron lying in a hollow. The foot is, except for significant examples, always plain. While rocker-arm ornament is often to be found on the Colchester's catch-plate, it is not supplemented with extra decoration on its return. In the case of the present example, the general proportions, the more elaborate decoration, including the steps on either side of the

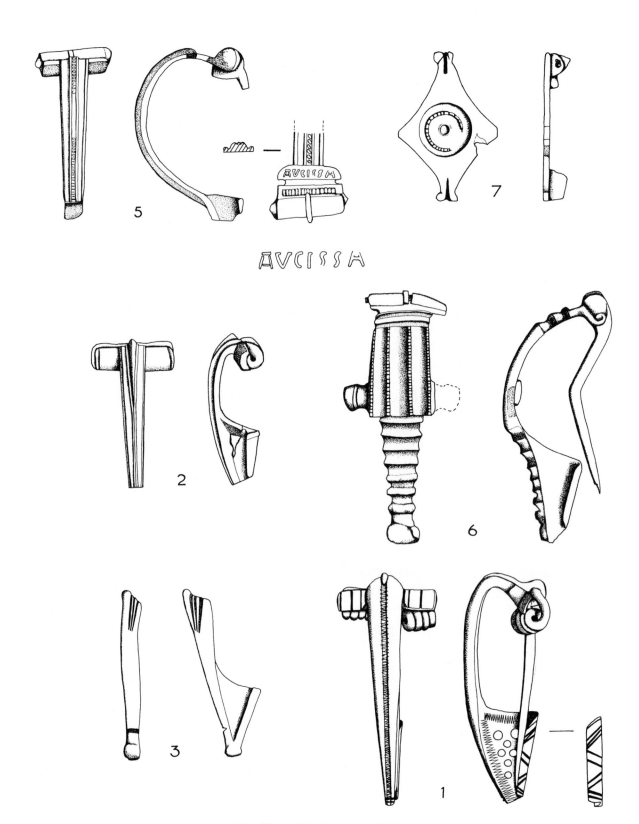

AVCISSA

Fig. 88.   The Brooches (1:1).

head, make it more of a Derivative than of the parent type itself. Which particular variety of Derivative is foreshadowed is unclear, and it is almost certainly a fruitless task to try and determine the matter. However, the steps on either side of the head might be related to those of the progeny which have prominent mouldings in this position (cf., Frere 1972, 114, fig. 29, 9; Curle 1911, 318, pl. LXXXV, 4).

The date is difficult to determine in that the Colchester's main *floruit* was before the Roman Conquest, but metal finds on pre-Conquest sites are at a premium when compared with those from Roman deposits. The result is that, although it is fairly clear that the Colchester had developed some late characteristics before the Conquest, it is less certain that any Derivatives had come into being then. The only type of Derivative from Skeleton Green, Puckeridge, Herts. (excavations, C. Partridge, forthcoming), akin to 47 (80) below, does not have a secure context, but even if it is assigned to the latest period on that site, it is probable that it was made before the Conquest. Similarly, in the King Harry's Lane cemetery at St. Albans, the same type is the only Derivative present and it occurred in the latest stages of the site's development (I am grateful to Dr. I.M. Stead and Miss V. Rigby, for the information prior to publication). The same type occurs in the collection from Holbrooks, Old Harlow, Herts., where one specimen has a Colchester spring arrangement. Even if at a conservative estimate the Colchester's family had already begun to come into being by A.D. 40, there can be no guarantee that the parent type displaying late decorative traits could not have continued in manufacture until as late as A.D. 50 or 60, although the latter date may be a little late. A date range of A.D. 35-55 might be suggested for the present example.

Colchester Derivatives

2. RLP (80, 47). The nine-coil spring is held in position by an axis bar which passes both through the coils of the spring and the lower hole in a plate which projects behind the head of the brooch. The upper hole holds the chord. Each wing is curved in section to fit the curve of the spring and has at the end a pair of vertical grooves. The bow has a concave surface on each side with a groove down the central face except at the top where there is a skeuomorph of the hook to be found on brooch 1. Along both sides of the top of the catch-plate is a prominent ridge with a cut-out for the pin. The catch-plate also has a three-sided piercing one side of which is curved.

The brooch is a minor variant of a well established type (cf., Down 1978, 279, fig. 10.26, 7) in which there are grooves on the wings and another down the bow: the main type has plain wings and a line of rocker-arm ornament down the flat face of the central ridge. There is no reason to suppose that the dates of the two should differ and the possibility that the main type had come into existence before the Roman Conquest has been rehearsed under brooch 1. The determination of an end-date for manufacture is more difficult as a brooch can continue in use for a long time after the type was no longer being made. One from Verulamium appears to have been lost during the Boudican Revolt (Wheeler and Wheeler 1936, 91, fig. 4, 3). Two come from Period VI at Camulodunum and may be regarded as having been derived from an earlier period on the site (Hawkes and Hull 1947, 311, pl. XCI, 38, 39), the second one belonging to the same variant type as the present example. That both the main type and the variant were established before A.D. 60 is shown not only by those referred to under brooch 1, but also by several stratified examples (Frere 1972, 114, fig 29, 6; Hawkes and Hull 1947, 311, pl. XCI, 36, 37; Wheeler and Wheeler 1936, 207, fig. 44, 22). There are no good indications of the date of the end of the main period of use. The date range is probably *c.* 40-65.

3. RLP (56, 94). The head of the bow is missing. At the top of the surviving fragment are three grooves which all but meet at a point. The foot is finished off with a knob above which is a cross-cut and from which rises the plain catch-plate.

As the top of the brooch is absent, there is little to help determine a date. The foot-knob, as well as the grooves at the upper end of the surviving piece might indicate that the original brooch type was the Dolphin (cf., Gould 1967, 17, fig. 7, 7; Down 1978, 279, fig. 10, 26, 9), which has a date range from the late-first century into the second, but the equation cannot be pressed.

4. RLP (101, 83) (not illustrated). A tiny fragment with a tight curve ending in a thin cross-piece, which may be part of an exceptionally small brooch. The piece is badly corroded and there is no visible decoration. No comment.

Aucissa

5. RLP (57 A-D, 3). The bow has the usual cross-section of a ridge down each side with a buried bead-row down the centre of the swelled front. The head is made up of three elements with the name AVCISSA in raised lettering nearest the bow — the tops of the letters A, V and I appear to have marked serifs. The central section is a flute with a cut-out at each end. The third section, next to the rolled-over head, has a sunken bead-row. Most of the foot is missing, but a small moulding survives at its top beneath which the foot is chamfered on each side.

At the time of the Conquest the Aucissa was at the end of its manufacturing period. Its descendant, the Hod Hill, had been fully developed, and it may be that the Aucissa should be considered to have finished being made some years before. The name is given to several varieties, but only those like the present one bear this particular maker's name, although the same design was used by other makers — TARRA and ATGIVIOS, both from Wroxeter. No example of Aucissa's work is published as having come from a pre-Conquest context and for the moment it seems best to consider that it was introduced at the Conquest and the large numbers lost here is probably a reflection of the type's popularity, itself probably based upon its cheapness, to judge from the mass-production methods used which a close examination reveals. The date range in this country is from the Conquest to *c.* A.D. 60 when it was becoming rare.

Hod Hill

6. RLP (226, 70). The upper part of the bow has three wide, shallow vertical flutes with beading on the ridges and is finished off at the top by two marked cross-mouldings. At the lower end of the main panel were two wings of which one is present and has a flute next to the bow and a knob divided from the flute by a ridge. The lower bow has six cross-mouldings below a step and is finished off with a single elongated foot-knob.

Study so far has failed to suggest that there is much if any real chronological significance between one group and another of the many varieties of Hod Hill brooches, except for those which have a separately made foot-knob which is then sweated on as in the parent Aucissa. The type arrives fully developed at the time of the Conquest and has largely passed out of use by A.D. 70 as the few examples in the land taken over by Cerialis demonstrate.

Plate

7. RLP (76, 15). A flat lozenge with concave sides the extremities of which are bifurcated by a

groove and finished off with small out-turned circular projections. In the centre of the plate is a sunken circle in which lies a crudely made raised circular bead-row and which once had a separately made boss riveted through the middle. Traces of tinning or silvering survive on the front.

The main feature which marks the family to which this brooch belongs is the sunken circle in the centre with its bead-row and the remains of a riveted boss. Some of the other varieties have the bifurcated terminals while others do not (e.g., Clifford 1961, 184, fig. 36, 6; Hawkes and Hull 1947, 325, pl. XCVIII, 170, and 326, pl. XCVIII, 179; Bushe-Fox 1949, 109, pl. XXV, 6; Brailsford 1962, 13, fig. 11, F2 and F5). The examples from Hod Hill (Brailsford 1962 above) show that the type had arrived with the Conquest as that site had come to an end *c.* A.D. 50 (Richmond 1968, 117-9). One from Wroxeter (unpublished) shows that some survived to at least A.D. 55-60, but in general it seems reasonably clear that none should be regarded as still being in use after the latter date.

Fragment (not illustrated)
8. RLP (203, 82). A piece of wire with a slight taper from a sub-rectangular section down to a rounded section. There is a curve at the former end which looks as if it might be from the end of spring coil. It is not possible to tell from which kind of brooch this possible pin might have come.

B. OBJECTS OF BRONZE
   (Figs. 89-90)

9. RLP (57 A-D, 8)	Needle, incomplete; part of eye and shank survive. Length 9.10 cm. (Not illustrated).	17. RLP (115, 52)	Possible lock fitting length 5.70 cm. and 0.70 cm. thick. (See also no. 34).
10. RLP (57 A, 11)	Needle, incomplete; stoutly made, with two eyes pierced alternately on different planes of the shaft: point and head missing. cf. Down and Rule 1978, 302, no. 95 and 303, fig. 10, 37.	18. RLP (200, 64)	Shaft with baluster-type moulding, probably probe and spatula.
		19. RLP (226, 66)	Spatula with damaged blade, three cordon moulding; probe end is missing.
11. RLP (57 A, 12)	Finial with grooved decoration.	20. RLP (167 A, 78)	Tube of twisted sheet strip. (Not illustrated).
12. RLP (103, 45)	Two strips 0.80 cm. wide with rivet holes in each strip. (Not illustrated).	21. RLP (203, 79)	Strip, 0.30 cm. wide. (Not illustrated).
13. RLP (106, 46)	Ring fitting, 2 cm. diameter; and sheet fragment. (Not illustrated).	22. RLP (101 N, 80)	Hook with broken end.
		23. RLP (101 G, 81)	Wedge-shaped fragment with two prongs, possibly needle head and part of eye. cf. Kenyon 1948, 262 fig. 89, no. 19.
14. RLP (140, 48)	Nail cleaner, surviving length 5.50 cm. with broken ring loop on the same plane as the blade, hatched decoration. cf. for example Cunliffe 1971, 110, no. 67, and 109, fig. 42.	24. RLP (101, 83)	Two dome-headed studs, 080 cm. diameter. (Not illustrated).
		25. RLP (242), 88)	Speculum fragments, probably of a mirror. (Not illustrated).
15. RLP (100, 50)	Twisted sheet strip fragment with torn rivet hole, possible scrap. (Not illustrated).	26. RLP (218, 89)	Pin shank fragment. (Not illustrated).
		27. RLP (278, 91)	Pin shank fragment. (Not illustrated).
		28. RLP (263, 92)	Small fragment. (Not illustrated).
16. RLP (+, 51)	Wire fragment. (Not illustrated).	29. RLP (244, 95)	Wire fragment. (Not illustrated).

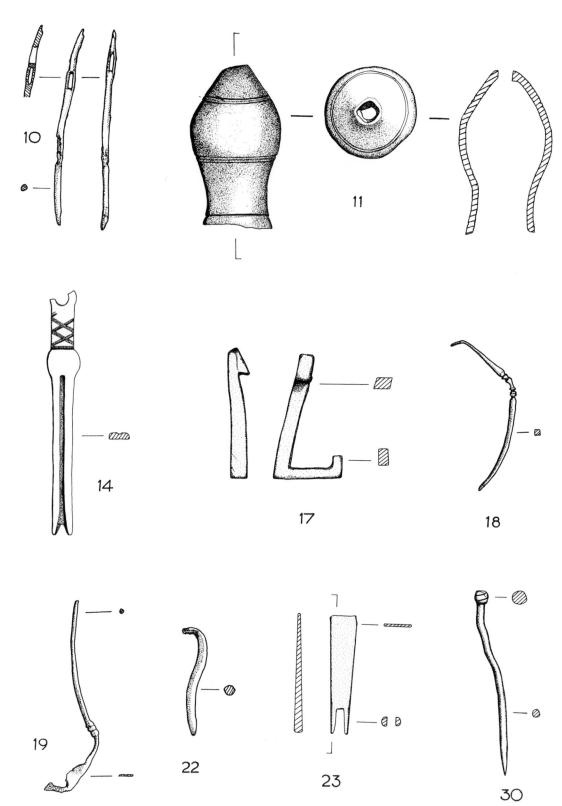

Fig. 89.   Objects of Bronze : 10, 17-19, 22, 23, (½); 11, 14 and 30 (1:1).

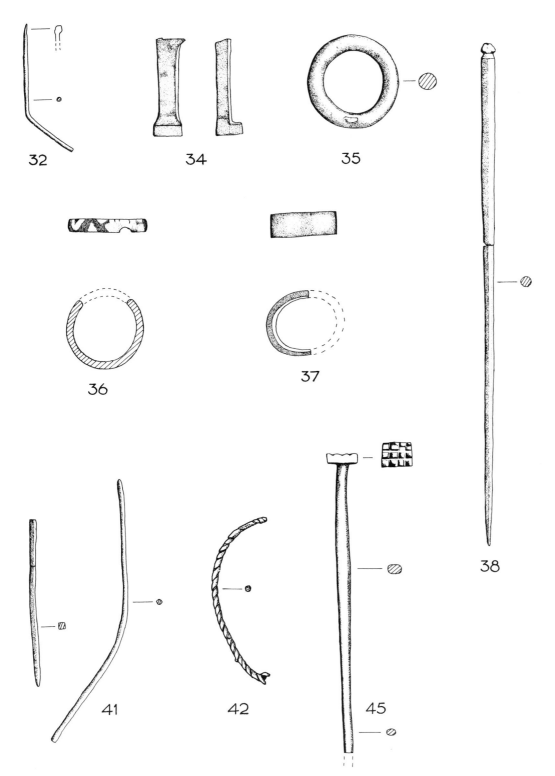

Fig. 90. Objects of Bronze : 32, 34, 35, 41, 42 (½); 36, 37 and 45 (1:1).

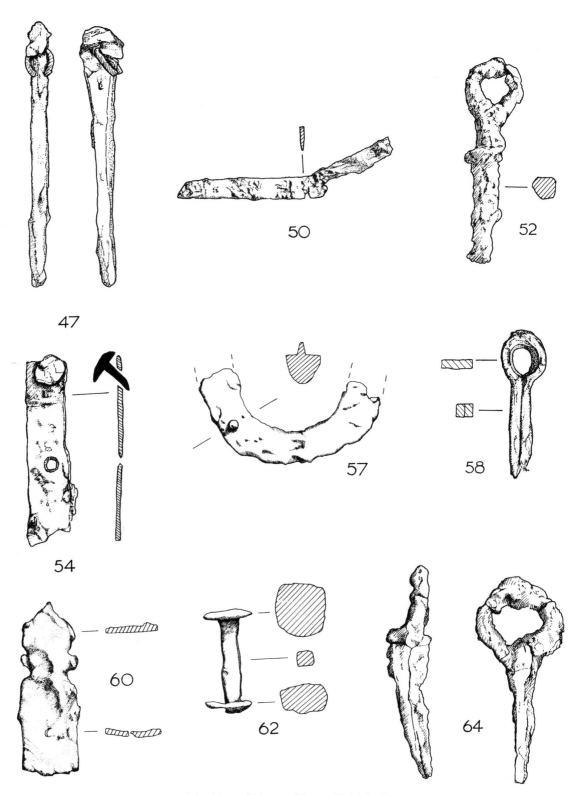

Fig. 91.   Objects of Iron : 47-64 (1:1).

30. RLP (244, 96)   Small silvered pin with twisted wire head; 4.10 cm. long, head diameter 0.25 cm.

31. RLP (262, 97)   A length of twisted wire. (Not illustrated).

32. RLP (78, 98)   Ligula fragment.

33. RLP (277, 99)   Wire fragment. (Not illustrated).

34. RLP (263 B, 106)   Possible lock fitting, broken end. (See no. 17).

35. RLP (262, 109)   Large ring fitting, diameter 4.30 cm., 0.70 cm. thick.

36. RLP (103, 115)   Finger ring fragment. 0.25 cm. wide.

37. RLP (204, 116)   Finger ring fragment, no decoration. 0.40 cm. wide.

38. RLP (279, 118)   Pin, (broken) with cone-shaped head. 11.30 cm. long.

39. RLP (256, 119)   Sheet fragments. (Not illustrated).

40. RLP (278, 121)   Pin-shaft fragments. (Not illustrated).

41. RLP (282, 122)   Two needles, stoutly made, both with missing heads, but eye-notch just discernible; lengths 13 cm. and 7.50 cm. Perhaps netting needles. cf. Cunliffe, 1975 214, no. 66, and 213, fig. 114.

42. GS (16, 6)   Two-strand wire bracelet, incomplete. cf. Cunliffe 1968 98, no. 154 and Pl. XL.

43. RLP (16, 7)   Three fragments: a strip, a sheet with rivet, and a fragment of thick wire. (Not illustrated).

44. RLP (16, 9)   A crumpled sheet fragment riveted to an iron fragment. (Not illustrated).

45. RLP (16, 12)   Pin, (point missing), flat oblong head with deep criss-cross line decoration.

46. RLP (16, 13)   Possible box binding fragments. (Not illustrated).

C. OBJECTS OF IRON

   (Figs. 91-2)

47. RLP (57 A, 9)   Pin-staple with broken bronze ring inserted through hole at upper end.

48. RLP (3, 10)   Possible knife blade fragments. (Not illustrated).

49. RLP (57 A-D, 13)   Wedge-shaped fragment. (Not illustrated).

50. RLP (56, 14)   Knife and handle, incomplete.

51. RLP (1, 18)   Ring fitting, 1.80 cm. deep. (Not illustrated).

52. RLP (57 A-D, 19)   Possible linch-pin with collar.

53. RLP (57 A, 27)   Binding fragment, possibly a box fitting. (Not illustrated).

54. RLP (59, 28)   Binding fragment with two nail holes and a nail *in situ*.

55. RLP (80, 29)   Three thin sheet fragments. (Not illustrated).

56. RLP (100, 43)   Bar wrapped with lead strips. (Not illustrated).

57. RLP (4 D, 44)   Flat ring binding with nail, or possible horse-shoe fragment. cf. for example Cunliffe 244, no. 241, and 245, fig. 130.

58. RLP (101, 54)   Split spike loop with straight arms. cf. Porchester I, 242, no. 224 and 243, fig. 129.

59. RLP (103, 57)   Slightly curved fragment, perhaps part of a flat ring binding. (Not illustrated).

60. RLP (122, 58)   Box binding fragment.

61. RLP (106, 59)   Fragment, pointed at one end and a mid-rib on one surface. (Not illustrated).

62. RLP (103, 60)   A tie for carpentry, consisting of a shaft, one round end and one chipped lozenge-shaped end. cf. Cunliffe 1975, 242, no. 228, and fig. 129.

63. RLP (136, 61)   Fragment, possibly scraper head of stylus. (Not illustrated).

64. RLP (164/5, 69)   Ring-spike.

65. RLP (220, 72)   Incomplete object, possibly knife and handle or part of a hinge.

66. RLP (110, 73)   Two binding fragments. (Not illustrated).

67. RLP (71, 74)   Group of hobnails from boot fragment. (Not illustrated).

68. RLP (228, 75)   Eyelet spike. cf. for example Chichester III, 310, no. 172, and 311, fig. 10, 42.

69. RLP (101 P, 76)   Sheet fragment with parallel sides and rounded corners. (Not illustrated).

70. RLP (101, 87)   Nail with large flat head, 4 cm. diameter, square-sectioned shaft. (Not illustrated).

71. RLP (251, 108)   Complete knife with silver mounting on handle.

72. RLP (78, 110)   Knife blade.

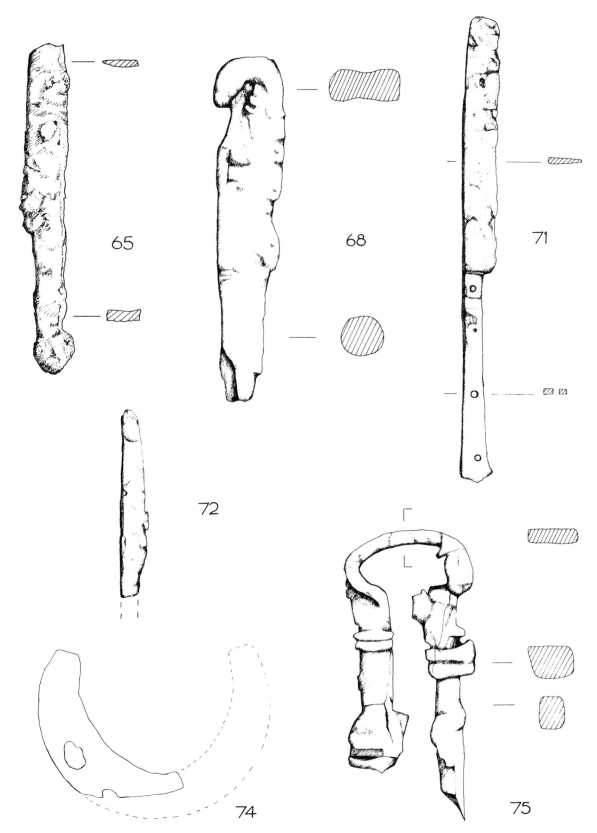

Fig. 92.   Objects of Iron : 65, 71, 72, 74 (½); 68 and 75 (1:1).

73. RLP (57, 111)   Wire fragment. (Not illustrated).

74. RLP (253, 113)   Horseshoe fragment. (Drawn from X-Ray photograph).

75. RLP (56, 90)   A pair of small tongs, incomplete, with a curved sheet iron spring and adjoining arms. The ends are missing.

D. OBJECTS OF LEAD

(Fig. 93)

76. RLP (101 S, 124) Steelyard weight with broken attachment at the top for suspension. The weight is pear-shaped with a flat band round the widest part. It is damaged on one side. The weight is 2 *lb.* 1 *oz.* (925 *gm*). cf. Cunliffe, 1975, 232, fig. 123, no. 166.

77. RLP (305, 93)   Rivet with domed head, (diameter 0.80 cm.) and flattened beaten end.

Gas Lane

GS (2, 14) Miss Marion Archibald writes:

Elizabethan counter, threepenny size

Obverse:+HONI SOIT (QUI covered by crown) MAL.Y.PENS in garter within which is a crowned lion rampant. (NS reversed in the inscription).

Reverse:Crowned shield of France modern between two crowned pillars, a floral spray at either side with — illegible on this specimen — two stylized cornucopiae below.

Wt.: 2.9gm = 44.7gr Technique: cast pewter Die axis:

Diameter: 22mm

Reference: E. Hawkins, *Medallic illustrations of the history of Great Britain and Ireland to the death of George II*, I, 121, No. 60.

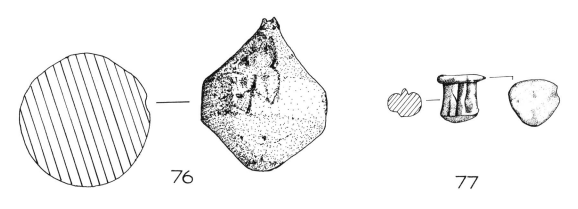

Fig. 93.   Objects of Lead : 76 (½); 77 (1:1).

This piece belongs to a series of pewter counters with various closely-related, regally-associated types. One group of them is dated, 1574, and another bears the royal cipher ER and the legend GOD SAVE THE QVENE. One sub-group has the inscription CAMERE CO REGIORVM, which would suggest that these particular pieces at least were used for Exchequer accounting purposes. Several of the basic designs are found on counters of different sizes which approximate to those of the currency denominations. This would support the hypothesis that they were used as counters. While their type would suggest that they were official issues, some groups are of very poor style, and it is not yet possible to be certain that these are not unofficial copies. On the whole, most of the counters, like the Canterbury example, are of good style and likely to have been issued for official purposes. The British Museum collection includes several examples from the Roach Smith collection, which were found in the Thames at London, and the Museum also has a note of two other provenances, at Lydiard Tregore (Wilts.) and Lincoln.

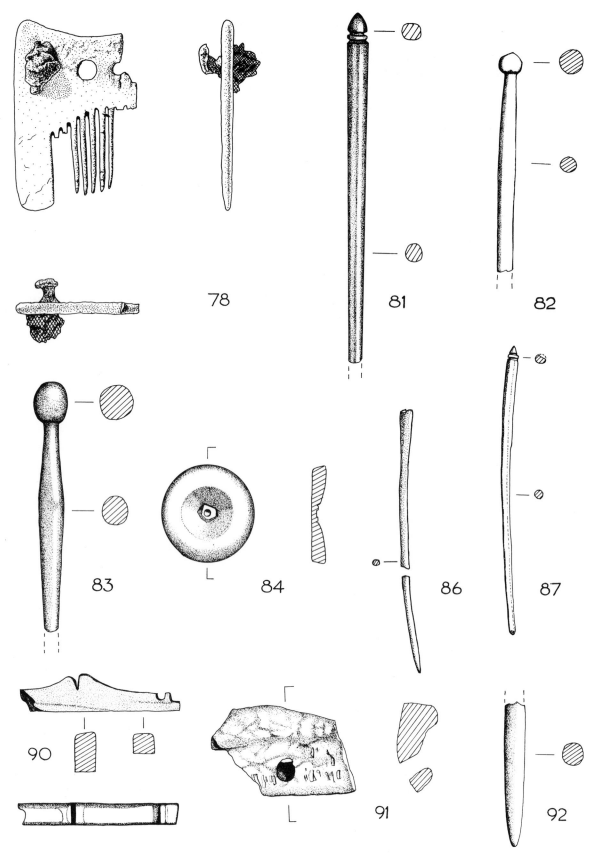

Fig. 94.   Objects of Bone : 86, 87, 91, 92 (½); the Remainder (1:1).

This would suggest that the counters were official issue for royal accounts whether in the Exchequer, or perhaps in tax or customs calculations and for use on royal estates. The names of the French kings Charles and Henry appear on one group, which was perhaps used for denoting sums in French coin or currency in these calculations.

It is unlikely that these counters were around in any quantity after *c.* 1600.

E. OBJECTS OF BONE
(Fig. 94)

78. RLP (103, 35)   Fragment of single-sided comb, with iron rivet and hole with rust stain for another rivet, now missing. Another larger hole perhaps for decoration.

79. RLP (104, 36)   Pin or needle, upper half missing. (Not illustrated).

80. RLP (103, 38)   Pin fragment. (Not illustrated).

81. RLP (112 A, 39)   Pin with lathe-turned cone head and collar moulding; regular tapered shaft, the point is missing.

82. RLP (100, 40)   Pin with hand-cut round head, mid-shaft swelling. The point is missing.

83. RLP (228, 65)   Pin with hand-cut ovoid head, shaft swells below neck of pin; the lower part is missing.

84. RLP (101 S, 67)   Counter with bevelled edge, flat underside, flat rim and scooped centre and ring and dot decoration. Diameter 2 cm.

85. RLP (101, 77)   Fragment of large thin bone ring, oval in section. (Not illustrated).

86. RLP (278, 101)   Needle (broken in half), part of the eye and head are missing. 11.30 cm. long.

87. RLP (278, 102)   Pin with lathe-turned cone head and single moulded collar.

88. RLP (262, 103)   Button with four holes. Possible intrusion. (Not illustrated).

89. RLP (262, 104)   Pin fragment. (Not illustrated).

90. RLP (249, 130)   Polished moulded fragment, burnt at one end.

91. RLP (101, 135)   Fragment of antler tine with drilled hole.

Gas Lane

92. GS (16, 18)   Pin beater, one point missing.

F. MISCELLANEOUS OBJECTS
(Fig. 95)

93. RLP (57 A-D, 4) Annular, pale green glass bead, damaged by corrosion. Diameter 1.40 cm.

94. RLP (262, 129)   Annular green glass bead, incomplete. Diameter 1.50 cm.

95. RLP (7, 16)   Two fragments of shale bracelet, very worn; grooved decoration on exterior surface.

96. RLP (101 E, 71)   Shale bracelet fragment, with three-grooved decoration on exterior surface.

97. RLP (272, 127)   Piece of worked shale, possible fragment of a plate.

98. RLP (106, 43)   Possible spindle-whorl, made from an early Roman coarse ware base. Diameter 3.50 cm. (Not illustrated).

99. RLP (1/10, 131)   Half spindle-whorl of Belgic coarse ware body sherd.

100. RLP (264, 133)   Possibly unfinished spindle-whorl of early Roman coarse ware body sherd. Unfinished central perforation on both sides. Diameter 7 cm. (Not illustrated).

101. RLP (242, 134)   Perhaps unfinished spindle-whorl or counter, of Roman coarse ware body sherd. Diameter 3.50 cm. (Not illustrated).

102. GS (10, 8)   Fragment of 'bun'-shaped late Saxon clay loom-weight, worn and burnt.

G. OBJECTS OF STONE (including architectural fragments)
(Fig. 96)

103. RLP (4 C, 1)   Purbeck marble engaged column base for a detached column, part of an internal wall arcade. Its deep curvetto, round base and rather deep pillar bed are unusual. The block has certainly been reworked. A date of 1170 — 1180 is possible, but it could be as late as 1250. (I am indebted to the late Mr. S.E. Rigold for the above comments).

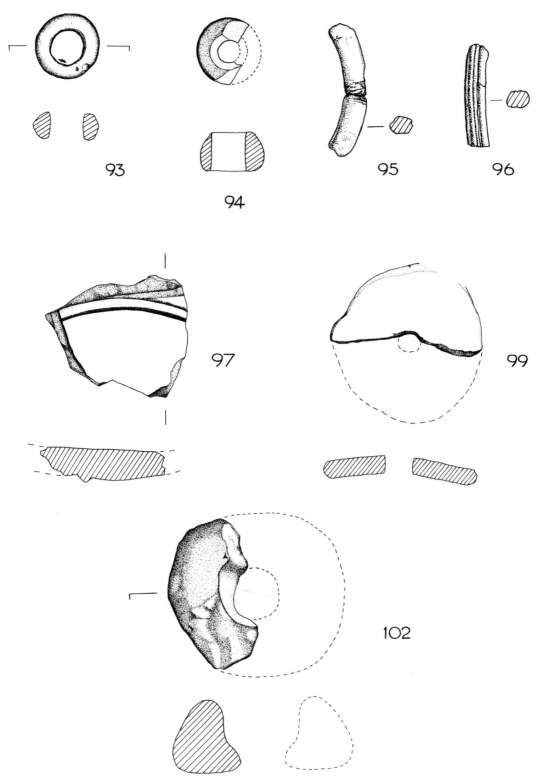

Fig. 95.   Miscellaneous Objects : 93, 94 (1:1); the Remainder (½).

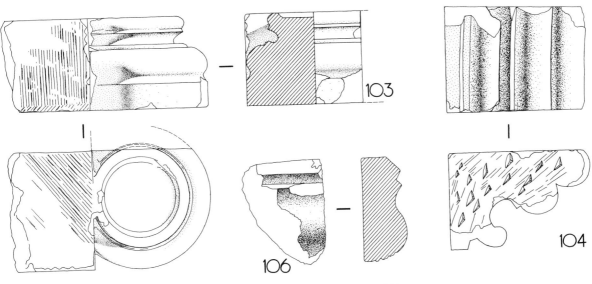

Fig. 96.   Architectural Fragments (¼).

104. RLP (4 C, 137) Block of worked Caen-stone, possibly a voussoir. It has the classical curves of the twelfth century and could be contemporary with the Purbeck marble column-base.

105. RLP (4) Block of worn Caen-stone. (Not illustrated).

106. RLP (45) Block of Caen-stone.

107. RLP (+, 6) Die of white crystaline marble. (Not illustrated).

108. RLP (100, 31) Fragment of white crystaline marble. (Not illustrated).

109. RLP (110, 34) Veneer fragment, possibly Perfido Verde Antico. (Not illustrated).

110. RLP (159, 86) Veneer fragment of white crystaline marble, possibly Carrara. (Not illustrated).

111. RLP (140, 49) Chalk counter, diameter 2.40 cm., 0.90 cm. thick. (Not illustrated).

112. RLP (262, 105) None stone of sandstone, worn. (Not illustrated).

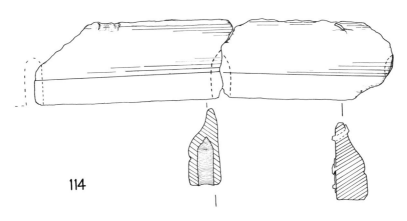

Fig. 97.   Objects of Wood (⅓).

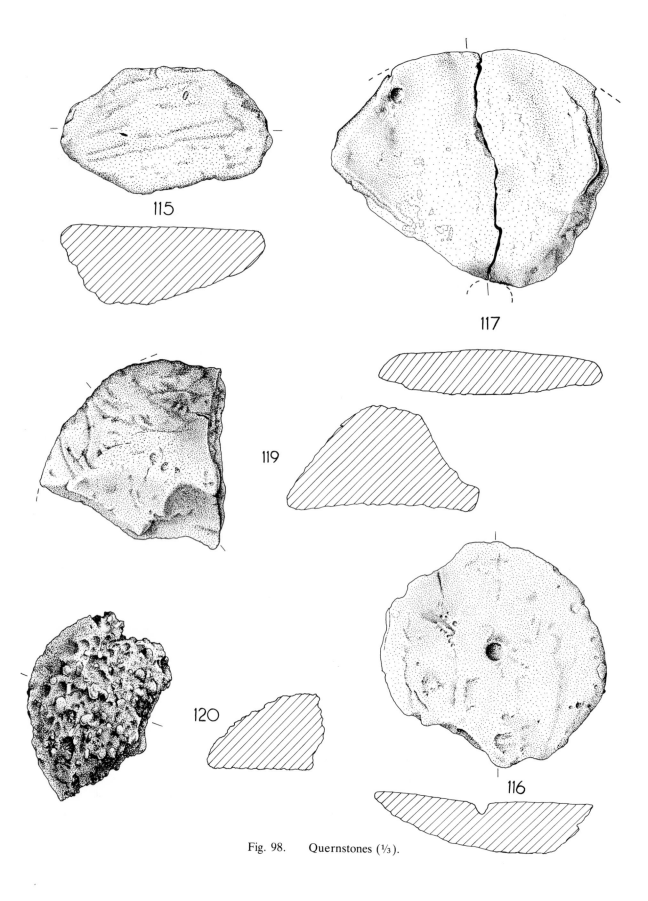

115

117

119

120

116

Fig. 98. Quernstones (⅓).

H. OBJECTS OF WOOD

(Fig. 97)

113 RLP (101 S, 126)

Miss Joan Liversidge writes:
Fragments of wood found in a water-logged condition in a well. The most interesting piece (Fig. 97) was broken in two with a dowel-hole at the point of the break and traces of another one at the end on the right. Also at this end, the end of a nail protrudes through the wood on the upper side. On the underside another nail keeps a scrap of wood in position. The upper surface of these pieces is recessed as if to accommodate a mattress and also retains faint traces of red paint.

It is possible that this is part of the seat of a couch with high back and sides, a type familiar from Romano-British tomb-stones. (J. Liversidge, *Furniture in Roman Britian* (1955) pl. 1, 8-9.) There is not enough evidence to explain the nails and dowel-holes; the possibility of a veneer of more decorative wood should not be forgotten. A second piece, also broken, may come from the same article of furniture. The other fragments are too fragmentary to be explicable and may not all be of the same wood.

I. QUERNSTONES

(Fig: 98)

115. RLP (59) Fragment of sandstone.

116. RLP (118) Incomplete lower quernstone with central hole: sandstone fabric.

117. RLP (127) Upper circular quernstone with two small depressions for a side fitting. Sandstone fabric.

118. RLP (167B) Lower circular quernstone fragment, grey coarse limestone fabric. (Not illustrated).

119. RLP (184) Fragment of an upper circular quernstone with part of a circular hole at the centre. Grey coarse limestone fabric.

120. RLP (243) Fragment of Hertfordshire Puddingstone quernstone.

121. RLP (276) Fragment of lower circular quernstone, very worn. Grey, coarse lime-stone fabric. (Not illustrated).

Fragments of quernstones were also found in the following layers: RLP (121), (167), (208A), (220), (249), (251), (272), (281), and Gas Lane (16). These are still being studied; the results will be included in a subsequent report.

J. THE SWORDS AND PIECES OF EQUIPMENT FROM THE GRAVE

Description Graham Webster

The two swords and fragments of belt-fitting were found lying side by side with the upper burial as if the two baldrics had been thrown in after the two bodies had been tipped into their hasty graves. One blade is 65.5 cm. long and its maximum width is 5.9 cm., with a tang 21.5 cm. long (Fig. 99). The other blade, complete, although found in pieces, is 69 cm. long, with a well-formed point; it tapers very slightly from 5.6 to 5 cm., and the tang is 22.5 cm. long (Fig. 99). They are examples of the long sword known as the *spatha*, which was normally carried in the early Roman Imperial

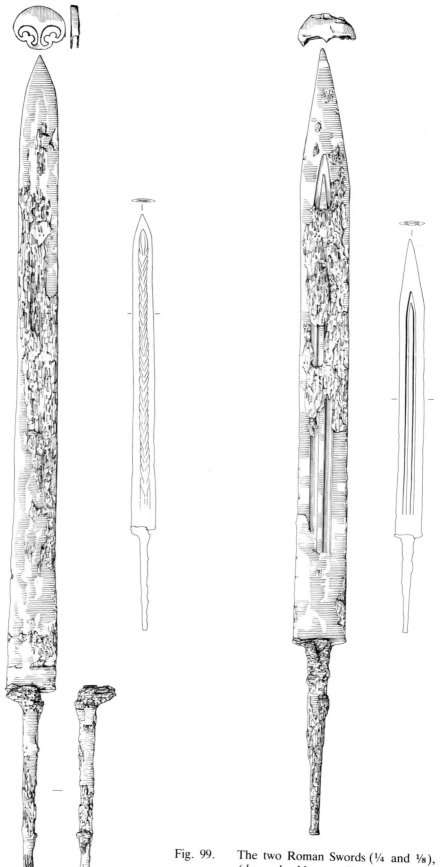

Fig. 99.   The two Roman Swords (¼ and ⅛),
(drawn by Margaret Tremayne).

period by auxiliary cavalry,[1] but had replaced the legionary short sword (*gladius*) by about the end of the second century A.D.

The longer blade (Fig. 99) has been assembled by what might be termed 'proto-pattern-welding' (see below). A most unusual feature on the shorter blade (Fig. 99) is the double groove or fuller, following the outline of the blade itself. It is not possible to say, from the present evidence, whether this is present on one side or on both, but the X-radiograph suggests that the former is more likely; this is also normal. Fullers are a feature of Celtic swords and may have originated in the linear engraved decoration on bronze swords and daggers,[2] especially those made in Hungary.[3] Later, it was a feature to be developed in the elegant ribs on the Hallstatt swords.[4] When black-smiths began to produce copies in iron, they evidently tried to emulate these features of bronze casting, but the different technique led to the development of delicate fullering instead.[5] The tradition clearly survived into the Roman period to impart to these weapons an unmistakeable ethnic quality, which is not surprising when one considers that the auxiliaries were recruited from frontier zones and equipped in the manner of their original formation.

The only fittings belonging to the swords are a bronze scabbard chape (Fig. 99), identical to one from Newstead[6] found on the site of the bath-house, which indicates a probable Antonine date, *c.* A.D. 120-200,[7] and part of what appears to be the iron chape of the shorter sword (Fig. 99), but too little survives for positive identification. There are several other pieces of equipment of bronze and iron (Fig. 100), of which the two bronzes offer the most convincing evidence. One is a cloak-fastener (Fig. 100B), with a circular head and central boss, a good example of Wild Class Va,[8] which has been usually associated with the early second century A.D. The other bronze is a baldric or belt-mount, with open fretted decoration (Fig. 100A), a type commonly found on the Antonine forts of the Rhine-Danube *limes*.[9] The iron objects are more difficult to identify. There are fragments of what may be a belt-ring (Fig. 100D) of the type which came into use in the late second century A.D.,[10] and a 3.5 cm. diam. button on a strip with two rivets for attachment to leather (Fig. 100C). An odd, almost brooch-shaped piece of iron (Fig. 100E) was attached to the iron chape (Fig. 99). This may have been an iron scabbard ring, only part of which has survived, or there may have been a small ring terminal at the end of the scabbard, a feature often found on

1. *SHA Hadrianus* 10; P. Couissin, *Les Armes romaines*, 1926, 489-92; the two fine examples from Newstead are somewhat shorter than these Canterbury specimens, the blade of the larger one being only 65 cm. (J. Curle, *A Roman Frontier Post and its People*, 1911, Pl. XXXIV, nos. 6 and 7.)

2. J.D. Cowen, 'The Origins of the flange-hilted Sword in Continental Europe', *PPS* 32 (1966), 262-312.

3. Harold Peake, *The Bronze Age and Celtic World*, 1922, Pls. VII-XI.

4. J.D. Cowen, 'The Hallstatt Sword of Bronze: on the Continent and in Britain', *PPS*, 33 (1967), Pl. LXVI, 3-6.

5. *BM Guide to early Iron Antiquities*, 1925, Fig. 28. The channels are cut out with a gouge. (I am grateful to Claude Blair for help on the technical details.)

6. Curle, *op. cit.*, Pl. XXV, no. 13.

7. Prysg Field Part II, The Finds, *Archaeol. Cambrensis*, 86 (1932), Fig. 34.

8. *Britannia*, 1 (1970), Fig. 1.

9. cf. *Obergermanische-Raetische Limes*, no. 33, Kastell Stockstadt, Taf. VII, no. 40; no. 73, Kastell Pfünz, Taf. XIII.

10. It is well illustrated on the tombstone of the centurion M. Aurelius Nepos and his wife at Chester; I.A. Richmond and R.P. Wright, *Catalogue of the inscribed and sculptured Stones in the Grosvenor Museum, Chester*, 1955, Pl. XIII, no. 37; *RIB*, 491; the name, the knee *fibula* and the wife's hair-style, all indicate a late-second to early-third century date.

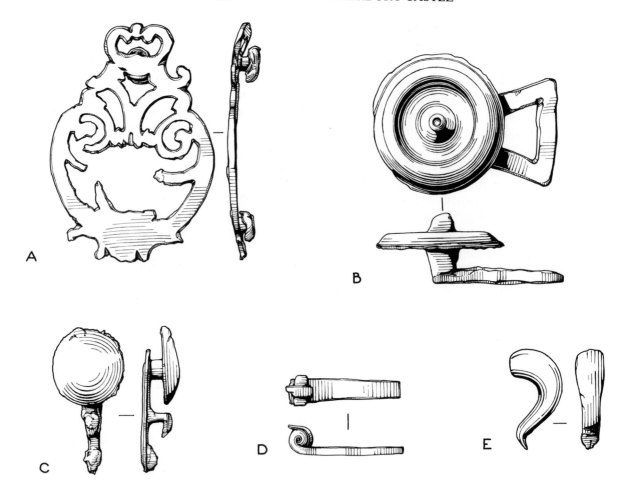

Fig. 100.   Roman Bronze and Iron Fittings from the Sword Burial (1:1).

first-century A.D. dagger scabbards.[11] It is rare to find this on the larger *spatha* scabbards, and it appears to be a type introduced from the Baltic.[12]

Scientific and technological examination.[13]

Jacqui Watson, John Anstee and Leo Biek.

The various fragments were found covered in unusual concretions of unexpected colours, possibly due to the contamination of the burial by effluent from the town gasworks. Although initial corrosion products would not be expected to have been much affected by this, it was felt that little would be gained in the absence of detailed information on site conditions by an investigation of surface deposits on the metal objects. Careful mechanical removal of these deposits revealed

11.   E.B. Thomas, *Helme, Schilde, Dolche*, 1971, Taf. LXIX-LXXX.
12.   *Saalburg Jahrb.*, 13 (1954), 67, Abb. 5; Couissin thought it was a late third-century type and illustrates an example from a late Roman cemetery at Cologne (*op. cit.*, Fig. 183, ed. 490-91).
13.   The full data are deposited as AMLab Report No. 3085 with the National Monuments Record.

extensive areas of ferrified organic material on both swords. Most of this had clearly been wood and showed detail of different grain directions from which scabbard remains and the construction of the hilts could be inferred (Figs. 99 and 100). The microstructure of the remains suggested, in the case of the shorter sword (Fig. 99), that the wood of the scabbard and the grip had been *Populus* sp. (Poplar) or *Salix* sp. (Willow), that of the cross-piece *Acer* sp. (Maple). Tentative identifications of Maple are given for all corresponding portions of the longer sword (Fig. 100). Some of the material on both swords indicated possible leather, overlying the scabbard wood, but this could not be definitely identified; there was no trace of any fibrous residues from a fleece lining.

Among the other odd fragments also received in the Laboratory, X-radiography indicated and mechanical cleaning revealed, as far as possible, the completely mineralised remains of the iron chape, scabbard and belt fittings described above, as well as the tip of one sword (Fig. 99), a large buckle-pin and other fragments. The 'bronze' fittings had sound metal cores, but were covered with tarnished redeposited copper. After cleaning, the very friable mineralised organic residues were consolidated with Paraloid B 72, the swords repaired and gap-filled with Araldite AY 100, and finally supported on polyester resin mounts covered with specially prepared hessian.

Detailed examination of the X-radiographs — and particularly the stereo-radiographs taken by John Price — suggests that, ultimately, the shorter sword (Fig. 99) was made up from at least four strips of metal. There is a central bar, possibly twisted, and this is flanked by two straight fibrous strips of which one is folded over the other, and over the core, at the pointed end, so that this assembly in effect constitutes a kind of inner sword shape. Each of these three components would itself have been normally put together by hammer-welding several strips — containing a certain variable amount of carbon, piled up and thinned out several times by reforging — so that (for the given composition and treatment) the maximum hardness and strength was achieved. The piled strips had been laid 'in section' and had corroded differentially, so that they were clearly distinguishable in the X-radiograph.

Around this assemblage, it would appear that a complete envelope of relatively homogeneous and, by contrast, plain-structured metal was then forged. Part of it was subsequently ground away on one face to reveal some of the straight-grained pattern and produce the fuller described above (Fig. 99).

By comparison, the structure of the larger sword (Fig. 99) is more easily recognised in the X-radiographs. Its core consists of a single piled bar of the kind used in the shorter sword, but here a very slow twist is noticeable (*c.* one complete turn per 25 mm.). Unusually, this bar has been taken *down* the blade length, through a plain U-turn at the tip, and up again beside the 'down' portion, to be welded to itself in a point shape at the *top* of the blade just below the crosspiece. The core has been backed by a relatively plain metal strip in the shape of the full sword, providing the cutting edge in the usual way. This kind of 'proto-pattern-welding' was copied in Anstee's 'First Experiment'[14] and appears in some of the early Roman period swords illustrated by Rosenqvist.[15]

14. J.W. Anstee and L. Biek, 'A Study in Pattern-welding', *Med. Arch.*, 5 (1961), 71-93.
15. A.M. Rosenqvist, *Universitetets Oldsaksamlings Arbok*, (1971) 167-8, 143-200.

The length of the hilt is considerable on both swords. This would react on the balance of the weapon, not only in the weight of the pommel, but also particularly in the hand. Despite the apparent disadvantages to a horseman, it would seem that these were both intended for use as two-handed swords. This may reflect an 'ethnically' superior free-hand control of the horse by what were, after all, hardly-Romanised barbarian borderers.

K. THE ROMAN COINS Richard Reece

The numbers in brackets are the small find number, followed by the layer number.

122.	(177.286)	CALIGULA	(A.D. 37-41)	RIC 32	*As*
123.	(2.1/10)	CLAUDIUS I	(A.D. 43-54)	RIC 66	regular coin
124.	(68. 211)	CLAUDIUS I	(A.D. 43-64)	copy, RIC 66	
125.	(37a.103)	DOMITIAN	(A.D. 81-96)		*As.* Rev. Illegible
126.	(84.300)	Bronze coin	(1st-2nd century)		Very corroded, Illegible.
127.	(62.159)	PHILIP I	(A.D. 244-7)	RIC 53	Rev. Heavily corroded.
128.	(32a.100)	BARBAROUS RADIATE	(A.D. 270-90)		Rev. VIRTVS ?
129.	(33a.100)	BARBAROUS RADIATE	(A.D. 270-90)		Rev. Illegible.
130.	(33b.100)	CARAUSIUS	(A.D. 286-93)	RIC 878	Rev. PAX.
131.	(37.103)	CRISPUS	(A.D. 323-4)	RIC 7	Trier 431.
132.	(32b.100)	CONSTANTINE II	(A.D. 323-4)	RIC 7	Lon. 292.
133.	(32c.100)	HOUSE OF CONSTANTINE	(A.D. 330-45)	copy as HK 181	

Gas Lane

134.	(3a.16)	CLAUDIUS II	(A.D. 268-70)	RIC 90	
135.	(17.16)	CLAUDIUS II	(A.D. 268-70)	as RIC 53	
136.	(3b.16)	TETRICUS I	(A.D. 270-3)	as RIC 75	
137.	(1.2)	CONSTANTINE II	(A.D. 320-22)	RIC 7	Trier 410
138.	(16a.16)	CONSTANTINOPOLIS	(A.D. 330-5)	HK 59	
139.	(16b.16)	URBS ROMA	(A.D. 330-5)	HK 546	
140.	(11.16)	URBS ROMA	(A.D. 330-45)	copy as HK 190	
141.	(3c.16)	URBS ROMA	(A.D. 330-45)		
142.	(3d.16)	CONSTANTIUS II	(A.D. 335-40)	as HK 100	
143.	(4.16)	CONSTANTINE II	(A.D. 337-40)	HK 779	
144.	(3e.16)	HOUSE OF CONSTANTINE	(A.D. 345-50)	copy as HK 137	
145.	(2.10)	HOUSE OF CONSTANTINE	(A.D. 350-60)	copy as CK 25	

PART IV

SPECIALIST REPORTS

A. THE CREMATED BONES T.P. O'Connor

Layer 156:   Pot B.
Mass of bone fragments = 802.5 gms.
The remains are those of a minimum of one adult, the lack of any fused sutural fragments indicating an age in the range 20-40 years. In the absence of any well-preserved pelvic fragments, the sex must be considered as uncertain, although the robust nature of the long bones suggests the deceased to be male. Fragments of several molars were present, but these were so distorted as to yield no useful information about age. All parts of the skeleton are represented.

Layer 257:   Pot F.
Mass of bone fragments = 266 gms.
A minimum of two individuals is represented, both being of indeterminate sex. One is a child, the degree of development of an unerupted maxillary p3 indicating an age of 4-5 years. The other individual is adult, but not elderly. A fragment of the root of the maxillary molar is fully developed, but at least one cranial fragment indicates that the lamboidal suture was not fully fused at death. Analysis of the bone fragments present indicate that both bodies were entire at the time of cremation.

B. THE BONES FROM THE DOUBLE ROMAN INHUMATION
P.H. Garrard

Layer 102:   Upper Burial.
Only a fraction of the skull survived the cutting of the later pit. The skeleton was well preserved and soaked in a tar-like residue. The heavy build of the bones and the narrow sciatic notch of the pelvis indicates a male. The degree of lipping on the anterior edges of the bodies of the lumbar vertebrae suggests an age of about 30. There were no teeth and only a few fragments of skull.
Stature was calculated from the long bones and is 1.73 m., or 5 ft. 9 in., using the formula of Trotter and Gleaser in Brothwell, 1972.
There were clean fractures on the left humerus, left radius and left ulna and left femur. There was an exostosis at the lower end of the right femur, which may have interfered with the proper functioning of the knee joint. There was an old fracture with callous formation of the right fibula.
The multiple rib and other fractures were probably caused by severe modern disturbance to the ground surface.
There was no indication of the cause of death.

Layer 120:   The lower skeleton in the same grave. This skeleton was better preserved and less damaged and more or less complete. The heavy structure of the bones and the narrow sciatic notch indicates a muscular and heavy male. The age, about 20, indicated by the union of all the epiphysis and the lack of lipping on the lumbar vertebrae and the good condition of all sixteen teeth of the mandible which show very little wear. There is a straight clean-cut injury at the lower end of the tibia, postero-medically, suggesting a downward and outward blow with a sharp-edged instrument on the ankle bone, during excavation.

The fragmentation of the ribs and other bones were probably caused by modern disturbances to the overlying ground surface. The height, based on the measurement of long bones, is 1.815 m., or 5 ft. 11½ in. (Brothwell, 1972).

There was no indication of the cause of death.

C. THE OTHER HUMAN BONES P.H. Garrard

Area I (Ditch)

Most of the bones were stained with a tarry material.

Layer 77:   A piece of one of the bones of the vault of the skull. Thin, possibly female. Probably temporal bone.

Layer 75/76:   Five pieces of bone from the vault of the skull. Thick, adult male. Also a fragment of a vertebra and a fragment of the scapula including part of the glenoid cavity.

Layer 33:   A piece 5 ins. long from the middle part of the tibia. Pieces of the mandible including the front of the jaw.

8 7 6 5 4 3 2 1   1 2 3 4 5 6 7 8
8 7 6 5 4 3 2 1   1 2 3 4 5 6 7 8

Teeth unworn. Male 20-25.

Layer 57C: Broken ribs, eleven vertebrae, right tibia, both humeri, parts of radius. Skull with part of maxilla. There is a well-defined groove 3mm. deep inflicted with a sharp instrument above the right fronto-zygomatic suture.

Dentition:

8 7 6 5 4 3 2 1   1 2 3 4 5 6 7 8
8 7 6 5 4 3 2 1   1 2 3 4 5 6 7 8

Male, age 35; 1.70 m. tall (5 ft. 8 in.).

Layer 82:   Manubrium sternu, rib fragments, right humerus covered by a tarry substance, a thoracic vertebra. Male, age 20-30.

Layer 10:   Upper part, left femur. Male; age 25-35.

Layer 57D: A piece of a bone of the vault of the skull. Male. Adult.

Layer 4:   Upper 4 in. left radius. Adult.

Area I (Topsoil Deposit).

Layer 41:   Three complete and one incomplete lumbar vertebrae. A piece of radius 100

mm. long. Young adult male.

Comment: There are parts of three and possibly five separate skeletons in the ditch, judged by skull bones. The vertebrae in Layer 41 mentioned above are from a different skeleton to those in Layer 57C.

Layer 39:   Right tibia. Young adult male.

Area II (Ditch).

Layer 263B: Skull and 8 in. section from the middle of one humerus. The vault is intact on the left but cleanly broken and fragmented on the right. This suggests injury rather than deterioration. The facial bones are impregnated with a tar-like material. Depression on right frontal bone suggesting old injury.

Dentition:

8 7 6 5 4 3 2 1   1 2 3 4 5 6 7 8
8 7 6 5 4 3 2 1   1 2 3 4 5 6 7 8

Molar attrition I. Teeth in good condition. Male, age 35. Height 1.70 m. (5 ft. 8 in.).

Other Layers:

Layer 176:   Part of the detached upper epiphysis of a tibia age 16-20. Sex not determined.

Layer 259:   Permanent first or second incisor tooth with no wear or injury.

Layer 201:   Left femur, lower end missing. Medium heaviness with rather a small head. Adult, probably female.

Comment on Areas I and II:

Many of the bones described above have been very cleanly broken at or about the time of death, particularly the humeri in Layer 57C and the femur in Layer 10. Also the skull in Layer 263B. These fractures are consistent with injury or rough handling.

Key to Dentition:

X   loss A.M.
U   Unerupted.
A   Abscess.
E   Pulp exposure.
C   Caries.
/   loss P.M.
O   Erupting.

Area missing.

D. HUMAN INFANT BONES Rosemary Powers

Layer 173: Late-2nd century pit.
Right tibia, present length 70 mm., but distal end damaged. Mid-shaft breadth 7.7 mm. Same colour and age as below, and may be regarded as scatter from it, if the archaeological circumstances permit.

Layer 242: Mid-1st century pit.
Homo Sapiens, Infant.
Left arm bones complete:
Humerus, length 68 mm., breadth at midshaft 6 mm.
Ulna, length 63 mm., breadth at midshaft 5.4 mm.
Radius, length 56 mm., breadth at midshaft 4.8 mm.
Also proximal third of a right (?) femur, proximal half of right humerus, and a rib. All the above bones are stained dark brown, presumably from tar residue in the soil. They represent an individual slightly older than newborn (as compared to the specimens of recorded age in St. Bride's colombarium and the Royal College of Surgeons).

One small anomaly is present, an exostosis on the humerus. This is the supracondylar process, a structure similar to one found in animals which occasionally occurs in humans as a variant, but this is a remarkably young age for it to be apparent.

Layer 277: Later-1st century pit.
Homo Sapiens. Neonate.
Right radius; length 49 mm., midshaft breadth 3.5. mm. (Lighter in colour than the others). Age about newborn.

Layer 278: Mid to late-2nd century pit.
Right ilium, distal portion damaged. Maximum breadth of bone 34 mm. Age about newborn.

Layer 304: Late-1st century pit.
Right scapula, two ribs and legs as follows:
Right femur, length 76 mm., midshaft breadth 7 mm.
Left femur, length 75 mm., midshaft breadth 7 mm.
Right tibia, length 68 mm., midshaft breadth 7.3 mm.
Left tibia, length 67 mm., midshaft breadth 7.5 mm.
Fibula (end damaged) now 61 mm. long, 4.5 mm. broad.
All are very dark stained and belong to one body. The age is about birth, the tibia being long relative to the femur as compared to the controls. This is similar to the proportions in the younger specimen from the 11th century level (Layer 159).

Layer 159: 11th century well.
Homo Sapiens. Foetus.
Bones of right leg and ulnae of foetus (about 7 months in utero).
Right femur, length 58.5 mm., breadth at midshaft 5.3 mm.
Right tibia, length 53.5 mm., breadth at midshaft 5 mm.
Left ulna, length 49.5 mm., breadth at midshaft 3.3 mm.
Right ulna lacks distal end.
Stained dark brown, with blackish patches on the legs perhaps from contact with some object.

Comparison with measurements of an R.C.S. foetus recorded as 342 mm. crown-rump length before maceration, estimated at 7 months I.U., makes the femur length similar, but the tibia and ulna lengths are greater in the present case. The difference probably reflects a stockier build in the R.C.S. baby (presumably of 19th century London stock).

E. THE ANIMAL BONES Anthony King

This section is concerned with the animal bones found on the site during the excavations of 1975-6. A small number of bones had been kept from the 1949 excavations, but they are too few to allow for quantitative analysis and are not included here. Points raised by these earlier finds, however, are included in the discussion.

Methods

7,179 bones were examined, of which 4,048 were identified to species and the remainder divided into groups corresponding to those on Table 1. BN on that table (bone numbers) is the absolute maximum number of fragments attributed to each species, disregarding any modern breaks. MN (minimum numbers of individuals) was obtained by finding the most frequently occurring paired or unpaired elements of the skeleton. No account was taken of size, age or sex for this calculation, nor, in view of the large size of the sample and the limited working space available, was it possible to find actual pairs in the case of paired elements (Chaplin 1971, for method). This has led to a lower estimate for MN than would otherwise have been the case, but in practice this makes little or no difference to the proportions between species and phases. Also, the method adopted precludes estimation of the actual number of animals or carcases on the site (Casteel 1977), but the time-span of each phase and the large number of variables affecting the supply of animals to the site render it neither desirable nor necessary to obtain such an estimation.

Other studies carried out on the material include an examination of ages at death, animal sizes and pathology. The last two aspects will be dealt with elsewhere, when more data are available from other recent excavations in Canterbury. Butchery marks have not been studied systematically but comments on them are made in the discussion.

The Data

Summaries of the data are in the tables and diagrams that follow. The original identifications are filed with the author and with the Canterbury Archaeological Trust. Of the bones themselves, none except zoologically interesting specimens have been kept, due to problems of museum storage.

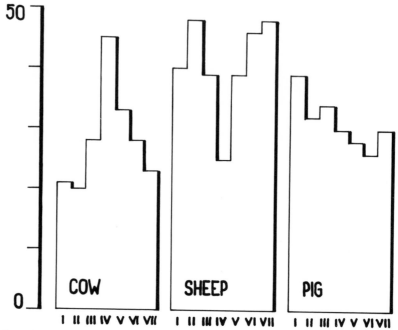

Fig. 101.   The Percentage of Bones of Cow, Sheep and Pig in each Phase.

Table 1. Species represented and Breakdown of unattributable Fragments.

Phase		I	II	III	IV	V	VI	VII
Dating		A.D. 60-90	70-90	50-150	150-400	1000-1080	1080-1250	1250-1600
Cow	BN	219	195	195	196	78	23	16
	MN	8	9	6	10	4	2	1
Sheep	BN	412	479	273	107	91	38	34
	MN	20	26	13	6	6	4	2
Goat	BN	3	5	—	—	—	—	—
	MN	1	1	—	—	1	—	—
Pig	BN	398	324	239	128	65	21	21
	MN	20	19	12	7	3	1	2
Horse/ Donkey	BN	108	8	7	5	22	2	1
	MN	3	1	1	1	2	1	1
Dog	BN	8	16	35	8	6	1	–
	MN	1	3	2	2	1	1	—
Cat	BN	—	—	—	15	—	3	—
	MN	—	—	—	1	—	1	—
Red Deer	BN	1	3	—	1	—	—	—
	MN	1	1	—	1	—	—	—
Roe Deer	BN	—	—	4	1	—	—	—
	MN	—	—	1	1	—	—	—
Hare	BN	1	—	1	—	—	3	—
	MN	1	—	1	—	—	1	—
Bird/Fish/ Amphibian vertebrae	BN	51	56	58	34	13	14	1
	l	27	34	20	21	10	5	6
	s	35	43	9	9	9	1	2
ribs	l	182	141	97	76	49	13	11
	s	320	372	126	97	63	17	10
long bone frags	l	66	97	89	95	40	9	9
	s	170	197	113	113	37	14	6
other frags	l	40	23	43	25	13	—	1
	s	28	53	27	10	7	—	1

BN = bone numbers MN = minimum numbers of individuals
l = cow size s = pig size or smaller

Table 2. Tooth to Bone Ratio.

		I	II	III	IV	V	VI	VII	I-VII	Mean
Cow	T	41	27	24	20	9	3	6	130	1863
	B	178	168	171	176	69	20	10	792	7759
	T/Bx100	23%	16%	14%	11%	13%	15%	60%	16.4%	24.0%
Sheep	T	182	143	70	23	33	6	9	463	1860
	B	230	336	203	84	58	32	25	968	3554
	T/Bx100	79%	43%	34%	27%	57%	19%	36%	47.8%	52.3%
Pig	T	204	145	120	50	20	14	10	563	1874
	B	194	179	119	78	45	7	11	633	2273
	T/Bx100	105%	81%	101%	64%	44%	200%	91%	88.9%	82.4%
Horse	T	49	4	3	—	3	—	—	59	n.a.
	B	59	4	4	—	19	—	—	86	
	T/Bx100	83%	100%	75%	—	16%	—	—	68.6%	

Table 3. Bones and Fragments per minimum Animal.

		I	II	III	IV
Cow	a	141	131	148	116
	b	87	75	96	64
	c	8	9	6	10
	a/c	17.6	14.6	24.7	11.6
	b/c	10.9	8.3	16.0	6.4
	a/b	1.62	1.74	1.81	1.54
Sheep	a	215	318	201	82
	b	158	230	149	63
	c	20	26	13	6
	a/c	10.8	12.2	15.5	13.7
	b/c	7.9	8.8	11.5	10.5
	a/b	1.36	1.38	1.34	1.30
Pig	a	183	164	109	77
	b	128	119	88	59
	c	20	19	12	7
	a/c	9.2	8.6	9.1	11.0
	b/c	6.4	6.3	7.3	8.4
	a/b	1.43	1.38	1.24	1.31

'a' is the number of fragments compiled from the following parts of the body:- cranium/ maxilla, mandible/ramus, scapula, humerus, radius, ulna, metacarpal, pelvis, femur, tibia, metatarsal. Note that teeth, digits and vertebrae are not included.

'b' is the minimum number of bones, compiled from the same groups as 'a'.

'c' is the minimum number of animals.

'a/c' is the number of fragments per animal, 'b/c' is the number of bones per animal and 'a/b' is the number of fragments per bone.

Table 4. Bones represented. The figures are the minimum number of occurences for each part of the body, and do not represent the actual number of fragments found.

	Cow					Sheep					Pig			
	I	II	III	IV	V	I	II	III	IV	V	I	II	III	IV
core	7	3	3	6	3	5	7	2	0	2	—	—	—	—
cranium	3	4	4	2	1	3	5	2	1	1	4	3	3	1
maxilla	2	1	4	3	0	9	8	0	0	0	18	9	8	7
mandible	11	11	7	10	3	38	34	20	6	6	38	33	20	13
atlas	3	2	2	2	2	4	3	1	0	0	1	5	2	1
axis	4	3	0	1	1	1	2	0	0	1	0	0	0	0
scapula	10	12	5	10	3	12	9	9	1	5	9	12	7	6
humerus p	2	0	2	1	2	1	4	4	2	1	0	0	0	0
humerus s	4	4	4	12	3	14	26	15	7	2	3	3	3	4
humerus d	8	5	5	7	3	6	13	13	5	1	2	3	1	2
radius p	3	4	3	9	5	4	10	5	1	3	8	3	1	4
radius s	2	2	6	4	5	16	25	14	8	6	4	6	5	5
radius d	1	4	2	5	1	5	8	3	1	2	3	0	1	1
ulna	5	5	3	9	3	10	5	7	2	1	10	13	8	2
metac. p	7	13	8	11	3	8	9	12	7	3				
metac. s	6	5	6	4	3	11	11	16	8	4	11	4	5	4
metac. d	4	11	7	6	5	2	3	4	2	4				
pelvis	15	9	5	12	4	6	14	5	5	4	13	10	10	1
femur p	6	3	4	1	1	2	7	3	1	1	3	0	0	0
femur s	1	2	4	0	3	12	11	13	3	0	10	5	9	5
femur d	1	1	1	0	0	3	6	1	0	1	4	3	0	1
tibia p	2	1	1	1	1	3	4	2	1	1	1	1	0	0
tibia s	2	0	1	5	0	21	52	26	11	9	11	14	13	12
tibia d	3	1	1	4	2	8	17	11	3	3	10	10	12	6
calcaneum	6	3	8	3	3	2	6	0	2	0	3	7	3	0
astragalus	4	4	4	2	1	1	1	0	0	0	2	2	3	0
metat. p	8	4	5	9	2	6	10	8	3	3				
metat. s	11	5	8	4	3	8	29	20	11	4	5	13	1	3
metat. d	8	4	6	9	2	5	5	2	0	0				
phalanx 1	8	9	18	9	0	3	2	2	1	0	1	0	2	0
phalanx 2	2	4	9	3	1	0	0	0	0	0	0	0	0	0
phalanx 3	2	1	5	4	0	0	0	0	0	0	0	0	0	0

N.B. The groupings represented by the brackets on the left side of the table are those used in the compilation of Fig. 102.

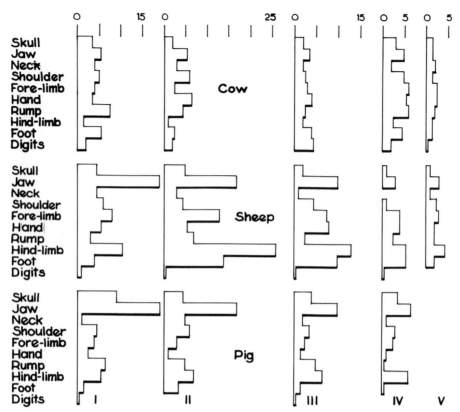

Fig. 102. Parts of the Body in Cow, Sheep and Pig. (Scores have been standardized from Table 4 to conform to one-half of a longitudinally bisected carcase. The values for pig phase V are too low to be of use.)

Table 5. Ages at Death from Fusion of the Epiphyses. The left-hand figure is the number unfused for that bone, and the right-hand figure is the number fused. The age of fusion in months is given after each bone.

Cow		I	II	III	IV	Sheep		I	II	III	IV
scapula	10	0-10	0-12	0-5	0-10	scapula	8	0-12	0-9	1-8	0-0
pelvis	10	0-13	0-7	0-5	0-12	pelvis	10	0-6	1-7	1-4	1-3
humerus d.	18	2-6	1-4	1-4	0-7	humerus d.	10	5-1	4-9	8-5	4-1
radius p.	18	0-3	0-4	0-3	0-7	radius p.	10	0-4	1-9	0-5	0-1
tibia d.	30	1-2	0-1	0-1	0-4	tibia d.	24	1-7	2-15	4-7	1-2
metac. d.	30	1-3	3-8	1-6	2-4	metac. d.	24	0-2	1-2	2-2	2-0
metat. d.	36	2-6	1-3	1-5	2-7	metat. d.	30	2-3	1-4	1-1	0-0
calcaneum	42	2-4	1-2	1-6	0-3	calcaneum	36	1-1	2-3	0-0	0-2
femur p.	42	4-2	0-3	2-2	1-0	radius d.	36	2-3	3-5	2-1	0-1
femur d.	48	0-1	0-1	0-1	0-0	femur p.	36	0-2	3-4	2-1	0-1
tibia p.	48	1-1	1-0	0-1	1-0	femur d.	42	1-2	3-3	1-0	0-0
humerus p.	48	0-2	0-0	0-1	0-0	tibia p.	42	1-2	3-1	1-1	1-0
radius d.	48	0-1	1-2	1-0	1-4	humerus p.	42	1-0	3-1	3-0	1-0

Pig		I	II	III	IV
scapula	12	0-9	0-10	0-6	0-5
pelvis	12	0-13	0-10	0-10	0-1
humerus d.	12	0-2	1-2	0-1	1-1
radius p.	12	1-7	0-3	1-0	0-4
tibia d.	24	7-4	5-5	6-6	3-3
metac. d.	24	6-3	3-0	2-1	1-1
metat. d.	27	3-1	6-2	1-0	2-0
calcaneum	30	3-0	7-0	1-2	0-0
humerus p.	42	0-0	0-0	0-0	0-0
radius d.	42	3-0	0-0	1-0	1-0
femur p.	42	2-1	0-0	0-0	0-0
femur d.	42	4-0	3-0	0-0	1-0
tibia p.	42	1-0	1-0	0-0	0-0

Table 6. Percentages of Bones fused.

Cow	I	II	III	IV	Sheep	I	II	III	IV
scap./pelvis	100	100	100	100	scapula	100	100	89	—
hum.p./rad.p.	82	89	88	100	pelv./hum.d./	69	81	61	50
tib.d./mc.d.	71	75	88	75	rad.p.				
mt.d.	75	75	83	78	tib.d./mc.d.	90	85	60	40
calc./fem.p.	50	83	73	75	mt.d.	67	25	50	—
fem.d./tib.p./	83	60	75	67	calc./rad.d/	67	60	33	100
hum.p./rad.d.					fem.p.				
					fem.d./tib.p./	57	36	20	0
					hum.p.				

Pig	I	II	III	IV
scap./pelvis/	97	96	94	92
hum.d./rad.p.				
tib.d./mc.d.	35	38	47	50
mt.d./calc.	14	13	50	0
hum.p./rad.d./	9	0	0	0
fem.p.&d./tib.p.				

Table 7. Ages at Death from Tooth Wear Stages of Sheep.

	months	0-2	2-6	6-12	12-24	24-48	48-72	72-108
	stage	A	B	C	D	E-F	G	H-I
I-II	a	4	5	9	15	7	9	4
	b	8	9	17	28	13	17	8
	c	24	18	18	15	3.5	4.5	1.3
I-IV	a	4	9	10	19	10	12	5
	b	6	13	14	28	14	17	7
	c	24	27	20	19	5	6	1.7
I-VII	a	4	9	12	22	11	12	8
	b	5	12	15	28	14	15	10
	c	24	27	24	22	5.5	6	2.7

a = the number of mandibles for each stage.
b = the percentage for each stage.
c = the equivalent deaths *per annum*.

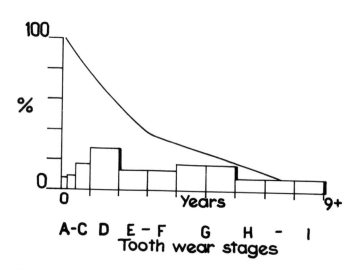

Fig. 103.   Tooth Wear Stages in Sheep Mandibles, Phases I — II. (The
histogram represents the percentage of jaws in each stage and the
line represents the percentage of animals still alive, using the data
from Table 7).

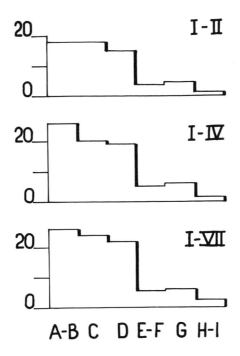

Fig. 104. Equivalent Deaths *per annum* from the Tooth-wear Data for Sheep.

Conclusions

The species present. From the point of view of zoological studies there is nothing remarkable about the assemblage. The range of animals is no greater than is to be expected from a series of urban refuse dumps. All of the material studied has been redeposited to a greater or lesser extent and, as a result, inferences from the species list about the environmental conditions on the site cannot be made. In this respect information from the small mammal and amphibian bones, which will be the subject of a separate report, may be of more use in determining the local environmental conditions than the larger animals, for the bones are less likely to have been moved from their original burial places.

The cow bones from Roman levels appear to have come from the 'Celtic shorthorn' or *Bos taurus longifrons*. No other types have been detected, although the possibility exists of some interbreeding during the Roman period with a larger breed, for there are some larger long bones from the late-Roman levels (Phase IV) but no change in skull shape. Medieval cattle from the site were of *Bos taurus* type. There was a higher incidence of large bones in phases V-VII, which may indicate an increase in the number of castrates present.

The sheep from phases I-IV also conform to the type commonly found on Iron Age and Roman sites in Britain, that is with a shape and stature approximating to the semi-wild Soay breed of St. Kilda. In the later levels, however, a larger type is dominant, although its size and hence its meat weight is not as great as any modern breed.

Pigs from all levels have many primitive characteristics, particularly a long straight snout and large male teeth. It could be that many of these animals lived in a feral state, being left free to forage in woodland and only coming into contact with man when being hunted or rounded up for food (cf. *Strabo* 4, 4, 3). As a result, no development of breeds seems to have taken place.

The horses from Canterbury Castle are all of pony size. Due to the similarity between horse and donkey bones, it cannot be ruled out that some of the animals may, in fact, have been donkeys or, of course, mules.

Sizes of the dog bones found were very variable, but the sample is too small to detect trends through time. Little need be said about the other animals present in terms of their appearance except to note that the antler fragments of red deer indicate fairly old animals, although precise ages at death or ages of shedding cannot be calculated because of the incomplete nature of the finds.

Proportions of animals present. The interpretation of the quantitative data from the assemblage is affected by a number of factors, which must be accounted for in any estimation of the relative proportions of animals that were used on the site. The most important of these factors is the differential preservation of the bones from different parts of the body and from different species due to disposal practices and soil conditions. Thus, in an acidic subsoil the assemblage can be biased in favour of large dense bones, and conversely where preservation is good but the degree of fragmentation high, fewer successful identifications will be made of the bones from larger animals.

The acidity of the soil can be assessed directly by measuring the pH, but also a relative measure can be obtained by comparing the ratio of teeth to bones with a mean for that ratio compiled from other sites in Britain. The mean used in Table 2 comes from that for nineteen Roman sites published in King 1978, Table 2. Where survival is poor there will be a greater proportion of teeth since they are more resistant to attack than other bones. In the case of the Canterbury Castle site soil acidity seems to have had little effect on the bone proportions, for the ratio compares favourably with the mean. This suggestion is corroborated by the pH measurements which indicate neutral or slightly acidic soil conditions (6.75-7.0 for three samples from Layer 8a). Thus, erosion of the bones by post-depositional soil action is not at a level high enough to affect seriously the findings. It should be noticed, however, that pig bones, and to a lesser extent sheep bones, are not so well represented as those of cattle. This is a phenomenon widely noted elsewhere and is reflected in the mean given in Table 2. The consequences of this can be seen in Table 3 where the number of fragments per animal (a/c) and the number of bones per animal (b/c) tend to decrease in the order cow, sheep, pig. In other words, the proportion of the carcase surviving in the bone assemblage is highest for cow, and followed by sheep and pig, respectively. This is possibly due to soil processes or to varying butchery and disposal practices, for it does not appear that the degree of fragmentation (a/b), which is roughly the same for all three animals, is the sole cause.

It is now possible to assess the proportions of the domestic animals present, bearing in mind the influence of the various factors outlined above. By referring to Table 1 and Fig. 1 it can be seen that sheep is the dominant animal, both in terms of BN and MN, during phases I to III. Pig follows closely, then cattle and at a much lower level, horse and goat. Such proportions are fairly typical of the late Iron Age and the early Roman period in Lowland England (King 1978), although pig numbers are unusually high, possibly due to the existence of areas of woodland nearby. Alternatively, this may be a cultural preference of the Belgic peoples (as noted in Strabo; see White 1970, 320). In later periods pig proportions decline, which may reflect a smaller amount of available woodland due to clearing or some other agency.

The proportions in the early phases indicate that local farmers were, in terms of animal husbandry, concerned mainly with sheep farming. Phase IV, however, marks a major change. Sheep proportions diminish to just over a half of their former level, and cow proportions show a corresponding rise. It appears that some stimulus in the late-second or third centuries brought about a major change in animal husbandry. This change has been noted at other sites in East Anglia and the Home Counties and possible causes are discussed in King 1978. In terms of its effect on the appearance of the landscape, a decline in sheep farming means a diminished need for open grazing, and it may be that land was allowed to revert to scrub and wood, or more likely (in view of the gradual decline of the woodland-preferring pig noted above) that the arable area was increased. These observations are, at present, only based on the trends observable in the bone data; they have yet to be corroborated by palaeobotanical research.

The medieval levels show the trend of increasing sheep numbers that has been widely noted elsewhere and is associated with the developing wool trade of the Middle Ages (Ryder 1964, 6). However, the sheep proportions are not as high here, or in other urban deposits, as those from rural sites (Fleck-Abbey and King 1975). This may be due to a low price for mutton because of the large flocks being kept, which would make it the preferred choice of the poorer rural population. The more affluent urban society would have been able to enjoy more variety in its diet.

Horse bones were present on the site in rather variable proportions. The high numbers in Period I are due to the presence of a skeleton in one of the Belgic ditches which is tentatively associated with the events that resulted in the human bones being deposited in the ditches (see p. 30). The high proportion in Period V may be fortuitous, but if the pattern here is repeated elsewhere in Canterbury, it may be that the late Saxons used horses to a greater degree than in other periods. The proportions of horse bones found probably reflects the availability of the animal in the town, for it is doubtful whether horse was anything more than a casual addition to the diet, only being eaten when the animals died or were useless for other purposes.

Venison and hare, like horse-meat, were also very minor constituents of the diet in all periods. The small number of bones found may indicate that very little wild game was available in the surrounding area, but an alternative explanation is that the remains on the site are not those of a section of society able to afford such meats in large quantities. In the case of hare, it is likely that many of the bones were destroyed during cooking since all those found (ulna, distal tibia, skull and mandibles) could be interpreted as uncooked waste.

Dog bones are common in Periods I to III, but decline in the late-Roman period IV in favour of cat bones. There is no clear explanation of this trend, and the numbers are too low to make confident conclusions. No complete skeletons were found, although there were some articulated limbs and vertebrae. This probably indicates that the material from which these bones came was surface rubbish for some time before the deposit was buried, allowing scavengers to scatter the skeletons.

Parts of the body and butchery. Only from the Roman and late-Saxon levels are there sufficient bones to be able to make meaningful histograms of the different parts of the body of the common domesticates on the site (Table 4 and Fig. 102). It can be seen that the general shape of the histograms indicates that sheep and pig are represented on the site in much the same way in Periods I to III, but that the sheep proportions in Period IV are more like those of cattle than in the previous periods. It seems that the size of the animals and, consequently, the butchery method have determined the differential representation of parts of the body in the three species. Butchery marks are much more common on cow bones than on those of the other species (the pattern following that at Ashville, Oxon.: Wilson 1978, 119-23), and it seems that the bones were broken up to a slightly greater degree (Table 3 a/b). It is also likely that beef joints were de-boned more often than those of mutton or pork and as a result more of the bone has survived as waste. It is possible that many of the bones left in mutton or pork joints were destroyed in the process of cooking or eating.

This aspect of osteological studies is one where detailed comments are not possible without comparative information from other sites and from experiments. At present, unfortunately, there are not enough such comparanda to do so (but see Grant 1975 and Jourdan 1977).

Ages at death. The fusion of epiphyses has been used to calculate the ages at death of cow, sheep and pig in Periods I to IV (Tables 5 and 6). From Table 6 it can be seen that the majority of cattle were still alive after 48 months, although a greater proportion of juveniles were killed in Period IV. This change is probably connected with the sharp increase in the relative numbers of cattle in this period noted above. Sheep were killed when they were juvenile, for only half, on average, survived into their third year. For pig, the pattern of juvenile slaughter is even more distinct with few animals surviving beyond their second year.

An alternative method of establishing ages at death has also been used for sheep, where enough mandibles survived to make tables and diagrams of tooth wear stages (Table 7, Figs. 103 and 104; method from Payne 1973). This method has advantage over that using fusion of the epiphyses, for the teeth wear at a uniform rate and thus the data are continuous, rather than specific to certain times in the animal's life, which is the case with bone fusion. It can be seen that the tooth wear method corroborates the conclusion noted above that less than half the animals survived into their third year. It is also possible to be more specific and to note that a large number of animals were killed in their second year, at a time when they were virtually fully grown, but without a great percentage of fatty material (Hammond 1971, 123, Table 6.4, with allowance for earlier development of the modern breed in that table). The calculation of equivalent deaths *per annum* in Fig. 104 also shows clearly that the rate of slaughter was high for the first two years and then drops to a much lower level thereafter. This pattern would seem to indicate that sheep were being kept primarily for meat rather than wool and milk, for if the latter was the case a much lower rate of slaughter for the juveniles and consequent survival of a greater proportion of the flocks into old age would be expected. Of course, the pattern may have been badly affected by the buying preferences of the town's population and as a result the conclusions given above need to be tested against the data from other bone assemblages from the surrounding countryside. It is unfortunate in this respect that too few mandibles were found from Periods V to VII to make a separate analysis and comparison, for in the medieval period a wool economy is well attested from documentary sources.

Summary

The study of the animal bones from Canterbury Castle is part of a larger project concerned with assemblages from many other parts of the city and its hinterland. The results presented above should be studied with the proviso that future data may alter or amplify them.

The Roman assemblage indicates a mutton-dominated food supply until the third century when beef becomes relatively much more common. In general the mutton was from young animals and the beef from adults. Pork was also a major constituent of the meat diet, with nearly all the meat coming from juveniles. Pork becomes relatively less common throughout the time-span of the site, the trend continuing into medieval times. In this later period, although the low absolute total of bones places less confidence in the results, it can be seen that proportions have reverted to, and even equalled, their early Roman levels and is probably a phenomenon associated with the developing wool trade. The very low proportion of wild animals indicates that the surrounding area was intensively exploited by man in both the Roman and medieval periods.

F. SHELLS Mrs. P. Garrard

The common European oyster (*Ostrea edulis* Linné) occurred over most of the site and in large quantities in the Belgic ditch complex — 1703 valves. The range in size (lower valve measurement) was from 9 cm. to 5 cm. long.

Other shellfish found were whelk, buckie (*Buccinum undatum* Linné) in the Belgic ditch and ne in Layer 266 (Post-medieval pit).

The common mussel (*Mytilus edulis* Linné): from Layer 101s, the lowest level of the Roman well, one valve; from the Norman ditch, Layer 18, one valve; from Layer 300, one valve.

A limpet (*Patella vulgata* Linné), from Layer 101s.

All these shellfish are distributed around the coast of south-east Kent in some abundance.

G. TREE-RING ANALYSIS OF A ROMAN TIMBER-LINED WELL, (LAYER 101 S) Jennifer Hillam.

In 1977, excavation at the Rosemary Lane Car Park site uncovered the remains of a timber-lined Roman well. Sections were removed from four of the stout oak boards and sent to Sheffield for tree-ring analysis. The work was funded by the Department of the Environment.

Dendrochronology can be a very precise method of dating, which makes use of the annual rings of a tree. A new ring is produced each year and its width is controlled by such factors as climate and soil type. Thus, trees growing simultaneously, under the same ecological conditions, will show similar patterns of wide and narrow rings. A tree-ring chronology is constructed by over-lapping series of matching ring patterns from the present day back in time so that each ring is equivalent to a calendar year. Alternatively, if the sequence is not linked to the present, it is known as a floating chronology. Although it is not absolutely dated, this can be useful in providing relative dating for a site.

In the British Isles, oak is generally used for tree-ring dating. Apart from being the timber found most frequently in medieval buildings or waterlogged archaeological sites, its wood has well-defined rings which are relatively easy to measure under a low power binocular microscope. There are none of the problems associated with double or missing rings which often occur in some other species e.g. some conifers or alder. Furthermore, there are now available many reference chronologies for oak from different parts of the country. Several floating sequences exist for the Roman period. Once these have been cross-matched with the absolutely dated German curve for the area west of the Rhine (e.g. Hollstein 1974), then it will be possible to date timber of this age very accurately.

Results

The samples were sawn into sections of 5-10 cm. thickness for easier handling. They were deep-frozen to harden the soft waterlogged timber. The cross-sections were cleaned with a plane to give a smooth surface on which each annual ring was easily visible. Sample A[1] had only 32 rings and was not included for measurement. Timber with less than 50 rings is generally rejected as it cannot be dated with confidence; ideally at least 80 rings is preferred.

The rings were measured on a travelling stage which was connected, via a linear transducer, to a digital voltmeter. The width was flashed up on the screen of the voltmeter after each ring had been traversed, so that it could be recorded. The ring widths, in 0.10 mm., were plotted against time, in years, on transparent semi-logarithmic recorder paper. Each board consisted of two or three sections, all of which were measured. Mean curves A, B C and D were made by averaging the data of the individual samples for the four boards (Table 1). When the graphs of Means A, B, C and D were compared by sliding one graph over another, they were all found to match; their relative positions are given in Figure 105. The level of correlation was so high that it was not felt necessary to check the matches by use of the computer. The boards may have derived from the one tree and reference to the sketches in Table 1 indicates that

Table 1

Sample no.	No. of rings	Sapwood	Average width(mm)	Sketch	Dimensions (cms)
A	67	—	2.47		5-6 x 44
A[1]	32	—	4.52		2-5 x 18
B upper	54	—	3.87		4 x 23
B lower	70	—	2.67		5-6 x 18-19
B[1]	51	—	2.81		3-6 x 18
C upper	85	—	2.40		4 x 20
C lower	48	—	2.75		4.5-6 x 22
D upper	52	—	3.93		5.5 x 21
D lower	85	—	2.46		6 x 22
D[1]	69	—	2.66		1-3.5 x 21
A mean	67	—	2.47		one radius
B mean	72	—	2.89		three radii
C mean	81	—	2.83		two radii
D mean	88	—	2.89		three radii
Site mean	92	—	2.75		4 timbers (1 tree?)

Details of all timbers examined, showing the number of rings and their average widths. A rough sketch is given to indicate the way in which the wood was cut.

numerous timbers could be obtained from a single tree. A site master with 92 rings was constructed by averaging the widths of Means A, B, C and D; the resulting ring widths are given in Table 2. The first part of the site mean was rather complacent, showing little variation in width, whilst the second part tended to be narrow-ringed and sensitive, with marked changes in width from year to year (Fig. 106).

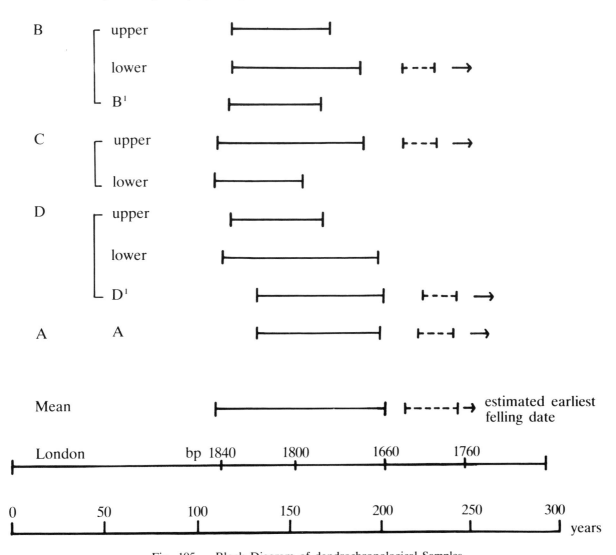

Fig. 105.   Block Diagram of dendrochronological Samples.

Block diagram showing the relative positions of all the measured samples. The calculated felling date is represented by the dashed lines; the number of sapwood rings is taken as 32-9. Arrows signify that the felling date could be later. The relationship between the Canterbury and London mean curves is illustrated; also given are the Harwell C-14 dates for London — each date has a 1 S.D. error of ±60. The overall time scale is arbitrary, since both curves are floating.

Table 2   Canterbury Roman Mean Curve

years	0	1	2	3	4	5	6	7	8	9
0		20	20	13	21	28	22	30	24	21
10	26	28	32	25	22	39	32	34	35	38
20	32	33	31	35	37	36	31	36	33	40
30	31	35	28	31	37	37	39	36	34	31
40	27	35	26	36	28	29	23	35	28	37
50	34	26	22	17	26	31	21	13	32	26
60	30	18	23	27	25	24	15	22	20	29
70	26	23	21	20	16	25	17	28	17	29
80	29	32	30	26	16	22	22	27	21	34
90	26	28	21							

The floating chronology is constructed using data from four oak planks. The mean ring widths are in 0.1 mm.

The master was compared with many of the Roman tree-ring chronologies, making use of the Belfast cross-dating computer program (Baillie and Pilcher 1973). This calculates the value of Student's 't' for each position of overlap between two sets of data. A value of greater than 3.5 is statistically significant, although not always acceptable. A cross-match which gave a t-value of e.g. 7.5 would, however, be a very good match. All computer matches are checked by visual comparison for confirmation. The only Roman chronology to give a high t-value with Canterbury was that from the London Waterfront (Morgan and Schofield 1978). The t-value was 4.79 and the visual match, shown in Fig. 106, was found to be acceptable. It will be noticed that the earlier complacent rings do not correlate as well as the later ones, as would be expected. The London curve is dated by four radiocarbon results (HAR-1864, HAR-1865, HAR-1867, HAR-1868) to *c*. A.D. 1-300 (Fig. 105). This gives a date for the last measured ring of approximately A.D. 220.

None of the samples had their sapwood preserved. This is the outer portion of wood, softer and lighter in colour than the inner heartwood, which performs the living functions of an oak tree; the heartwood serves solely as a strengthening agent. The presence of sapwood is valuable in estimating a fairly accurate felling date since the number of its rings is relatively constant. The total number has been calculated as 32±9 years for a mature oak, where ±9 represents one S.D. from the mean (Baillie 1973). Even if only the heartwood-sapwood transition remains, an estimation of the date of felling can be obtained. However, its softer texture makes it subject to decay and it is frequently absent from waterlogged samples. In such a case, the earliest possible felling date must be calculated, i.e. assuming that no heartwood was removed during the working of the timber. Fig. 105 shows the position of the estimated felling dates for each of the four timbers. It will be seen that they are roughly contemporary, sugg-

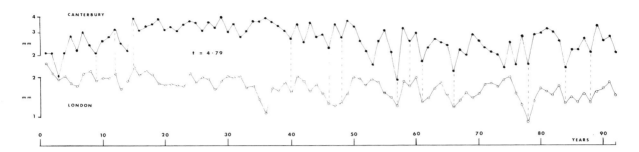

Fig. 106. Match between Canterbury and the London Waterfront Chronology (Morgan and Schofield, 1978).

esting that little heartwood was lost in trimming the wood. This gives a felling date of *c.* A.D. 250. As it is unlikely that the timber was seasoned for of any length of time (Hollstein 1965), this can be taken as the construction date of the well. However, this date is based on radiocarbon dating and so must be regarded as approximate. Only when the London curve is firmly dated by the German chronology will it be possible to give a more exact date for the well.

Additional Note (July 1981). The timbers have now been dated absolutely by cross-matching with Germany. The Canterbury mean curve spans the period A.D. 38-129, and the timbers were felled some time after A.D. 152, a date more acceptable from the archaeological point of view than the one indicated by the C^{14} results.

PLATES

PLATE I

Area I : General View of the Excavation.

PLATE II

Area I : The early Roman Ditches.

PLATE III

Area II : The early Roman Ditches.

PLATE IV

Area I : The disarticulated human Skeleton from the Sump of the PII Ditch.

PLATE V

Area II : The articulated Carcass of a Horse from the Sump of the PI Ditch.

PLATE VI

Area II : Human Skull from the Sump of the PII Ditch.

PLATE VII

Area II : The primary Roman Street.

PLATE VIII

Area I : Amphora Base *in situ*.

PLATE IX

Area II : The Roman Pit Complex in the south-east Extension.

PLATE X

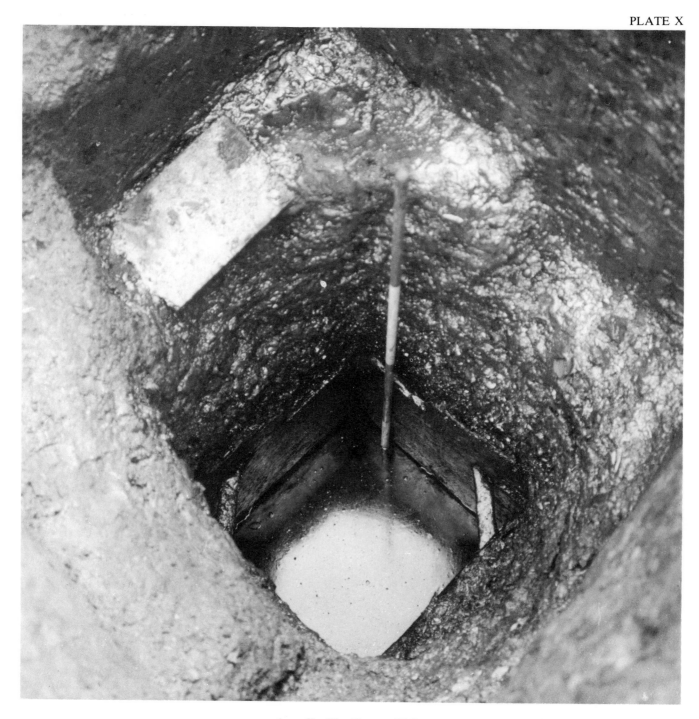

Area II : The Roman Well.

PLATE XI

Area II : Excavated Features to the East of the Roman Streets.

PLATE XII

Area II : The double Sword Burial.

PLATE XIII

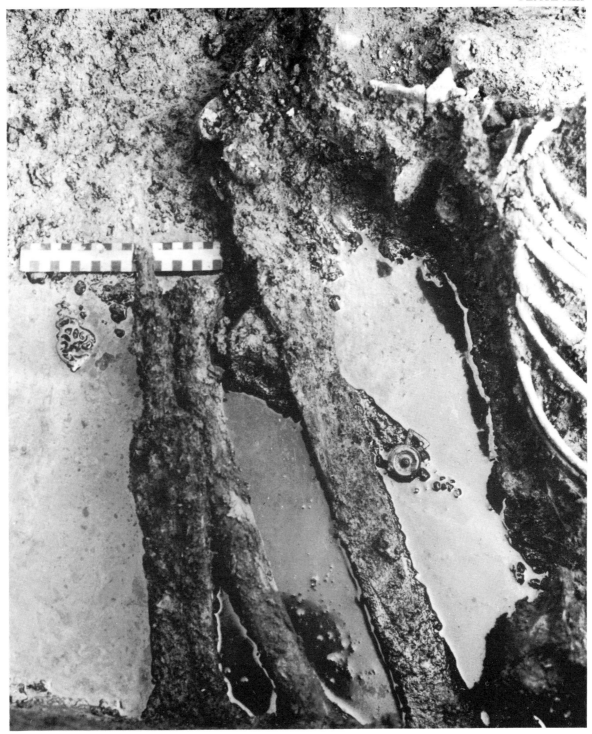

Area II : Detail of the Roman Swords and Belt Fittings.

PLATE XIV

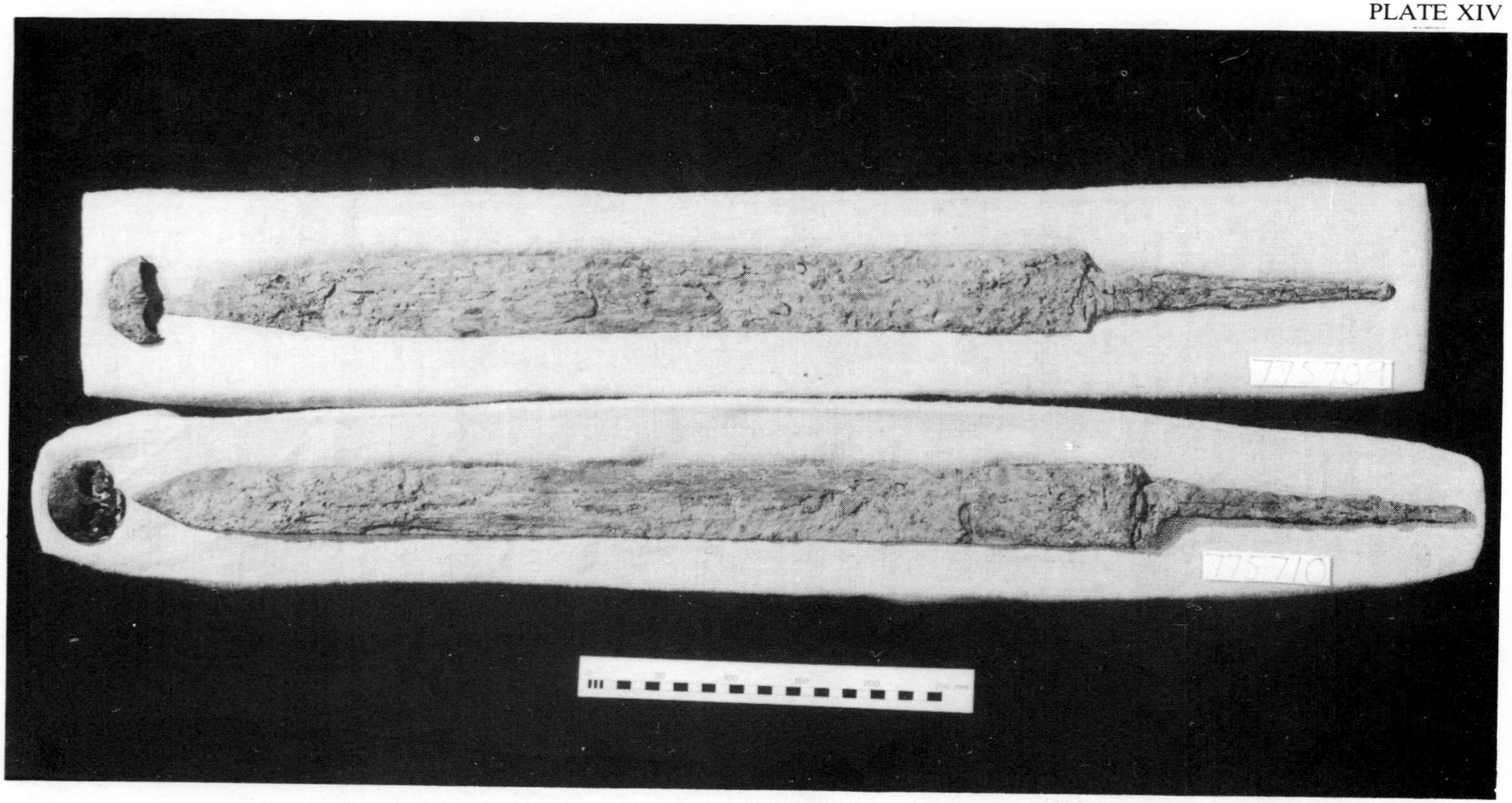

The Roman Swords.

PLATE XV

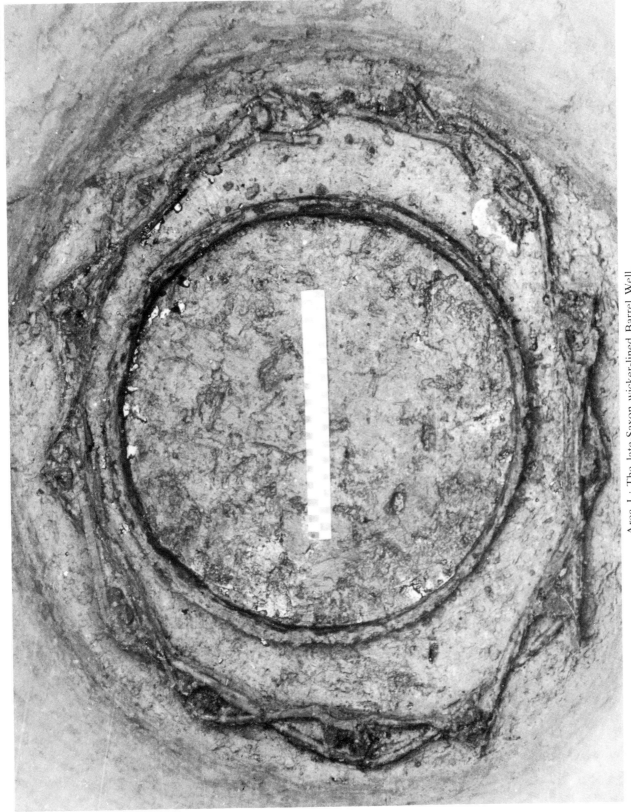

Area I : The late-Saxon wicker-lined Barrel Well.

PLATE XVI

Area II : The wicker-lined Well.

INDEX

GENERAL INDEX